THE
LOIRE VALLEY

THE HELM FRENCH REGIONAL GUIDES

Series Editor: Arthur Eperon

Auvergne and the Massif Central
Rex Grizell

The Dordogne and Lot
Arthur and Barbara Eperon

Languedoc and Roussillon
Andrew Sanger

Provence and the Côte d'Azur
Roger Macdonald

THE LOIRE VALLEY

Arthur & Barbara Eperon

Photographs by Joe Cornish

CHRISTOPHER HELM
London

© 1989 Arthur and Barbara Eperon

Photographs by Joe Cornish
Line illustrations by David Saunders
Maps by Oxford Cartographers

Christopher Helm (Publishers) Ltd,
Imperial House, 21-25 North Street,
Bromley, Kent BR1 1SD

ISBN 0-7470-0802-7

Title illustration: Porte de Guérande: there is
still no breach in the 15th-century walls of the
old town

Typeset by Leaper and Gard, Bristol
Printed and bound in Italy

Contents

THE
LOIRE VALLEY

1
Introduction

If the Seine is the bride of Paris, then the Loire is the mistress. Voluptuous and soft-moving, it can at times be moody, capricious and perverse. In spring, when the snow melts in the Massif Central and water pours down the tributaries, and in the rains of October, it can be dangerously bad-tempered. And its power through the centuries has been far greater than any other river in France, for it virtually cuts the country in half. From the Visigoths striking northwards in the 6th century to both the Germans and the French armies in World War II, tribes, peoples, armies and conquerors who could not cross the Loire were often doomed.

Through history, people from all corners of Europe have coveted the beautiful Loire valley for its lush lands and kindly climate and for its strategic importance as a defence barrier. For centuries the valley has been the playground of Parisians, and their market garden, too. Its well-watered meadows, splendid wine slopes, and its network of beautiful if moody rivers, all running into the majestic Loire, lured the kings and courtiers of France for centuries. From 1453, when the English were finally thrown out, until Louis XIV commanded them to stay in the crowded discomfort of his beloved Versailles, the French courtiers

besported themselves here for months every year and France was ruled from the Loire valley much of the time.

With short warmish winters, spring arriving as early as March, hot summers, and autumn days made delicious as early morning mist gives way to sun, it is a land which invites you to relax.

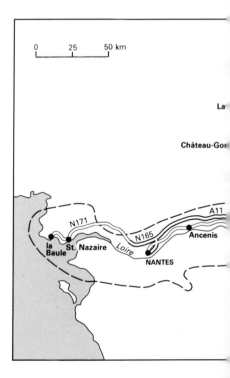

The arrival of the motor car turned the whole Loire area into a rural retreat for the people of Paris, luring them for weekends. And now that the A10 motorway runs from Paris to Orléans and along the Loire valley to Blois and Tours, Parisians drive to the Loire for a day's outing to see an historic château, for a bathe from one of the riverside beaches and a picnic. Orléans is only 130km from Paris and Tours only 230km. So traffic can be formidable during the French school holidays of July and August, especially now that the N10 is double-tracked nearly all of the way to Bayonne and the Spanish frontier. More and more people go that way on holiday, and stop off in the Loire valley for an overnight and to look around.

It can be very hot in the Loire in July and August; May and early June are more pleasant, with fresh greenery and many wild flowers, when the Loire and its tributaries are higher and flow faster. In midsummer the gentle rivers are sometimes down to a narrow trickle, which barely washes the pillars of medieval bridges. Then they reveal a lazy landscape of riverside trees, beaches where children play, sand-banks and green islands. But all these rivers — Loire and Indre, Cher, Loir, Vienne, Allier and Maine — can play unpleasant tricks around these islands, with awkward and perverse currents. So do take local advice before bathing. And in spring and in autumn rains, the water can flood down in such torrents that fields are flooded, trees carried

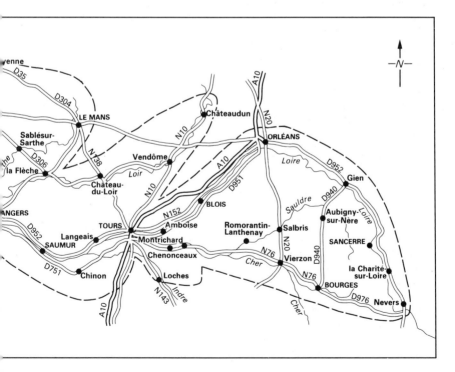

3

away, and islands so inundated that only the tops of their trees show above the raging water. Men have been defending themselves against these floods since the Middle Ages. But spring comes very early to the Loire valley, bringing warm balmy weather and superb early vegetables.

Of course, the Loire basin in the West, near the sea, has Atlantic winds which blow quite hard in winter and give a refreshing breeze in summer. Touraine and Anjou usually have hot summers tempered by sea breezes, mild autumns and benign winters, and you will see many Mediterranean-type plants and trees — magnolias, camelias, hydrangeas, cedars, eucalyptus, even palms and fig trees. It can blow very cold around Orléans in winter but upstream you are beyond the Atlantic winds and winters can be harsh, summers hot.

If the châteaux of the Loire as we know them today were made for love, leisure and hunting, they were not always so. Many of the earlier castles, like those of the Dordogne, were built originally for war and converted or replaced later to fit them for comfortable living. The future of France was decided in fighting around here in the Hundred Years' War and the Wars of Religion.

Every guide book reminds you that the Loire is the longest river in France, measuring 1,020km from a volcanic knoll, Mont Gerbier-de-Jonc, from which it rises in the south-east Massif Central to the estuary west of Nantes, where it flows into the Atlantic. So it passes through many regions of France. But for this book we have followed it from Tours, the pivot of the Loire valley, as far as the border of Burgundy in the east, just crossing over

in a few places, south into the Sologne and Cher and into part of Indre, north towards Île-de-France, into Sarthe and Mayenne. Westward we have gone to the estuary, although we think of La Baule, officially in the Loire–Atlantique, as part of Brittany, which it was for centuries, as was Nantes. Chartres, though in Eure-et-Loire, is really an Île-de-France city, an extension of Paris. Indre below Valençay seems to us to belong with the Vendée, Vienne, Deux Sèvres and Charentes.

This Loire valley which we have followed is by no means one region. The infertile Sologne is a world apart from the richly fertile Petite Beauce between Orléans and Beauce, a land for farmers rather than tourists. Touraine boasts lush pastures, flower gardens, vineyards, magnificent castles and manors, and a few choice industries. Anjou, rich in history, has its horticultural valley along the Authion, strawberries near Saumur, soft fruit and artichokes near Angers, and hillsides of soft stone south of the river where vines are grown and wine is stored in caves.

Orléans itself has been very much attached to Paris since it was the property of each king's second son. Now it supplies Paris with flowers, lettuce, cucumbers and tomatoes.

In the 1950s many small farmers, market gardeners and farm workers left the land for the Paris factories. New factories in places like Tours have stemmed the rural exodus, but the population is ageing somewhat as Parisians avail themselves of its pleasant scenery and milder climate on retirement or buy themselves second homes here. The A10 motorway has brought it all nearer to Paris but blessedly keeps most of the hurrying

4

through-traffic away from the pleasanter small roads and villages.

The old lands of Berry, Indre and Cher are still little known and, apart from the historic city of Bourges and a few market towns, are given over to farmers. Unlike the cosmopolitan people of the Loire valley, who are used to tourists, these are retiring people, in no hurry, and you do not get to know them in a hurry, either. But the land has some charm and much variety — forests, wheat prairies, rich pastures and grassy hillsides watered by thousands of small streams. Beyond Loches and Vierzon, where most tourists abandon them, the valleys of the Indre and Cher rivers are equally unfamiliar.

It is a calm, secretive, sometimes mysterious land which has appealed more to imaginative storytellers, from George Sand to Alain-Fournier, rather than writers of guide books. But it played a vital role in French history when Joan of Arc's beloved Dauphin hid there and was scathingly called 'King of Bourges' until she persuaded him to be crowned at Reims. And it was a Bourges banker, Jacques Coeur, who paid for the upkeep of the entire campaign against the English.

The Loire-Atlantique is a very different world. This is the land of Muscadet wine-producers and fishermen. Not only did this region, with Mayenne to the north-east, miss the tourist revolution which came with the family car but all except a few cities missed the industrial revolution, as well.

Unlike the Loire, which has 'existed to look beautiful' since the arrival of railways, the river Sarthe from Le Mans to Angers was a fairly important waterway until World War II and is still navigable by hire cruisers. In places it has parallel canals. It flows slowly across rich countryside of woodlands and meadows, with some light arable soils growing cereals, potatoes and cabbages.

The Mayenne valley from Laval to Angers is far more spectacular. It winds and twists through deep-sided valleys and is particularly attractive between Ecluse and Ménil. It was canalised in the 19th century, and has 39 locks between Laval and Angers. In some places the river flows between very steep slopes where chestnut and broom grow, and the villages and houses are perched on green hills with farmland and woods. The river keeps away from most main roads and towns, passing watermills, some still working, and secretive reaches, shaded by trees. By keeping to small roads and lanes and crossing the river several times, you can drive through delightful scenery nearly all the way from Laval to Angers. Better still, you can hire pleasure boats at several places. Work is in hand to repair canals for pleasure boating north of Laval, too.

The Loire has many tributaries and they are almost as important as the Loire itself. Certainly, they have determined the geography and in many ways have changed the history of the Loire. They have, for instance, brought vast quantities of silt into the main river, putting an end to navigation to most of the Loire. And their spring and winter floods have caused the flooding of the Loire valley. They, too, have their own tributaries, and it is a brave person who could claim to remember the names of all the little rivers and streams.

The Allier, running 345km from the Cévennes, drives into the Loire at Bec d'Allier, west of Nevers, with such force that the Loire is driven into a loop. Most of the salmon left in the Loire tend to join the fast running Allier at this point. And the meeting of the waters when the rivers are running high gives birth to most of the Loire floods which can come suddenly and cause havoc.

From here to around Tours, only smaller rivers such as the Cosson and Beuvron run into the Loire. Then the Cisse comes in from the north-east and, just below Tours, the Cher arrives from the south-east after a 352km journey from the north-west foothills of the Massif Central, not far from the tapestry town of Aubusson. It reaches the plains at Montluçon, ambles through the Berry and the city of Bourges, meanders along the edge of the Sologne and is still flowing calmly as it joins the Loire.

The Indre river rises in the same foothills of the Massif Central as the Cher, but north of Aubusson. Like the Cher, it is a peaceful river, in no great hurry to complete its journey of 265km. In fact, 16km before it reaches the Loire, it turns west as if reluctant to be swallowed by the bigger, faster river, and that is a fine thing, for it is very attractive and it washes the lawns and the very piles on which part of the superb château of Azay-le-Rideau is built. Then it brushes meadows, orchards and woods until, while flowing into the Loire near Léman, it has much of its water stolen by a nuclear energy station.

The Vienne, which enters the Loire a mere 8km from the station, evades that indignity. Like the Cher and Indre, the Vienne rises in the Massif Central, but south of Aubusson, on the plateau des Milles Vaches. On its 370km journey to the Loire it drinks liberally from the waters of the Creuse, which has already flowed for 255km, swallowing the waters of the Gartemps (181km long) on the way. The Vienne is a faster flowing river, very attractive, with sandbanks and shoals like the Loire. Yet in mid-summer it can be so narrow that it does not wash the piles of Chinon bridge.

The most confusing river is the Loir (Le Loir, La Loire). Rising in the hills of Normandy it flows for 312km, first going south-east almost to Chartres, then through Vendôme where it veers west until it seems to be making for the Atlantic, only to wind southward at Durtal in great loops towards Angers. But about 14km before it gets there, it runs into the Sarthe, which itself runs into the Maine before it reaches Angers. So does the Mayenne. And the Maine is only 10km long. It is really the mouth of the Mayenne, running into the Loire. There's a particularly attractive stretch of the Loir between Troo and Château du Loir.

Both the Mayenne and the Sarthe also rise in the hills just south of Normandy and are in no hurry. But little rivers and streams drain into them in the Maine and the Beauce, and when all these rivers are in full flow or flood there is a great deal of water pouring into the Loire at Angers, creating the islands and sandbanks which abound eastward. Some of the best Loire river scenery is from here along the south bank to the very edge of Nantes.

Many of the most beautiful and interesting châteaux were built beside these tributaries. And certainly some of the best Loire Valley scenery is here, especially on the local lanes. You will find the true tranquillity of the Loire Valley along these minor roads, particularly beside the minor streams and rivers. Those who explore only the cities, the famous châteaux, and drive the well-worn, sometimes crowded roads along the Loire banks from Angers to Orléans without diverting on the minor roads, will surely never understand why knowledgeable travellers seek the Loire valley for beauty, peace and relaxation.

FESTIVALS

Of course, the Loire has its joyous celebrations. From its great châteaux days of royal courts, the Loire has inherited festivals, and they are legion. Oldest is the Festival of Joan of Arc in Orléans on 7th–8th May, celebrated for five centuries. Saumur has its traditional Tattoo of the Black Squadron, once for cavalry, now for tanks as well, in late July. Touraine's classical music festivals are in June and July, Anjou has a great summer festival of music, dancing and art, Cheverny has a concert of horn music and hunting horns on Saturdays in July and August, and Doué-la-Fontaine's medieval arena is the site, in mid-July, of one of the world's biggest rose shows, with 100,000 blooms of 500 species.

Son et Lumière started at Chambord castle and nowadays in summer eleven Loire châteaux put on shows, with the biggest at Le Lude.

The largest fête in central France, however, is still held at Le Mans in mid-June — the 24-hour motor race.

GLOSSARY

A good simple guide to styles of church and secular architecture, with drawings, appears in the green Michelin guide *Châteaux of the Loire*. Here are explanations of some words which appear often in guides to churches, châteaux and manor houses.

Ambulatory — continuation of church aisles around the choir.
Apse — large recess behind chancel or choir, often semi-circular and containing the altar.
Arabesque — carved decorative foliage.
Aubusson — town on the Creuse, famous since 15th century for its carpet and tapestry works, where carpets and tapestries are woven on hand mills.
Baluster — shaped or short squat column.
Baroque — architectural style around 1600–1750.
Base — foot of column or pillar.
Campanile — belltower, usually free-standing.
Capital — top of a column.
Cenotaph — memorial to dead buried somewhere else.
Chapterhouse — rooms where monks, nuns or church officials hold business meetings.
Choir — where church services are sung.
Classical — revival of Greek or Roman architectural features.
Cloister — four-sided covered walk, with arcades, around a central courtyard.
Corinthian — style with richly decorated capitals.

Cornice — projecting upper piece of wall.
Crypt — burial place under church.
Curtain wall — outer defensive wall of castle.
Doric — style of columns without base and with flat capitals.
Empire style — French classical style of early 19th century.
Faïence — glazed pottery named after Italian town of Faenza.
Filigree — intricately perforated carvings or stucco (originally applied to work in gold or silver wire).
Flying buttress — arches to strengthen outer walls.
Frieze — decorated strips for edges of walls.
Gable — triangular upper part of a wall.
Gobelin — tapestry woven in Gobelin's factory in Paris.
Ionic — style with columns on a base of two or more tiers.
Keep — tower of castle used as refuge in case of siege or attack.
Lantern — small turret with window on top of roof or dome or tower.
Mansard — angled roof with lower slope steeper than upper.
Mullion — window divided vertically.
Nave — central parts of church for congregation.
Orangery — buildings in castles or parks for housing orange trees and exotic plants, often used for meeting places or parties.
Oratory — private chapel.
Oriel — protruding window on upper floor.
Peristyle — continuous colonnade surrounding a temple or courtyard.
Portico — porch supported by columns.
Refectory — monastery dining hall.
Relief — carved or moulded work, the design standing proud of the background.
Renaissance — Italian architecture and art from the early 15th to mid-16th centuries.
Rococo — elegant, dainty Baroque style.
Romanesque — architecture of the years 1000–1300.
Rose-window — round window with rich design — usually coloured.
Sanctuary — area behind church altar.
Sarcophagus — stone coffin.
Stucco — plasterwork of gypsum, lime, sand and water.
Terracotta — fired but unglazed clay vessels.
Tracery — geometric stone decoration.
Transept — part of church at right angles to nave, usually joining it to the chancel or choir.
Tympanum — panel in the lintel and arch of a doorway, often half-circle.

Conversion Tables

km	miles	km	miles	km	miles
1	0.62	8	4.97	40	24.86
2	1.24	9	5.59	50	31.07
3	1.86	10	6.21	60	37.28
4	2.48	15	9.32	70	43.50
5	3.11	20	12.43	80	49.71
6	3.73	25	15.53	90	55.93
7	4.35	30	18.64	100	62.14

m	ft	m	ft	m	ft
100	328	600	1,968	1,500	4,921
200	656	700	2,296	2,000	6,562
300	984	800	2,625	2,500	8,202
400	1,313	900	2,953	3,000	9,842
500	1,640	1,000	3,281	3,500	11,483

ha	acres	ha	acres	ha	acres
1	2.5	10	25	100	247
2	5	25	62	150	370
5	12	50	124	200	494

kg	lbs	kg	lbs
1	2.2	6	13.2
2	4.4	7	15.4
3	6.6	8	17.6
4	8.8	9	19.8
5	11.0		

°C	°F	°C	°F	°C	°F
0	32	12	54	24	75
2	36	14	57	26	79
4	39	16	61	28	82
6	43	18	64	30	86
8	46	20	68	32	90
10	50	22	72	34	93

2
A Little History

More of the history of France, even of Europe, has been decided in the Loire than in Paris. Long before Henry IV announced that 'Paris is worth a mass' and entered it in 1586, before Joan of Arc freed beleaguered Orléans from the English in 1429 and effectively ended English rule of much of what is now France, before that rule of the English started with the wedding of Henry Plantagenet and Eleanor of Aquitaine in 1152, even before Charles Martel beat and turned back the invading Arabs in Chinon forest in 732 and changed the story of the world, the Loire valley was playing a major role in world history.

You can see the reason at the tiny market town of le Grand-Pressigny, 48km south of Tours, at the meeting of two small Loire tributaries, the Claise and Aigronne. In the castle, an elegant 16th-century house behind a fortress-like, 14th-century perimeter wall, is a Museum of Prehistory, with a superb collection of flint tools, daggers, arrowheads and hand axes.

In the New Stone Age (20,000–2000BC) there was a factory of flint tools and weapons here. The flint, mined in yellow clods, was easily split into sharp blades which were carved and polished, then exported all over Europe and North Africa.

The people of the Loire had earlier been huntsmen and fishermen, using deer antlers as harpoons. With the so-called 'Neolithic Revolution', settlers from the Danube basin introduced stock raising — cattle, sheep, pigs, goats — via Provence.

In the Bronze Age, which lasted until around 600BC, long-distance trade grew. The Phoenicians sailed up the Loire to trade, copper was mined near Bourges and Azay-le-Rideau, craftsmen from the Loire spread around Europe. Meanwhile the Celts had arrived — tall, blond and strong — headstrong, too, it seems. Their major tribe, the Carnutes, were the aristocrats of the valley, bearing highly decorated shields, throwing insults at the Roman legions of Caesar's armies moving north to conquer Gaul. They were reverent only to their elders and Druids who met each year at St. Benoît, between Orléans and Gien.

Oddly, they did not at first put up much resistance to the Romans. Perhaps they had seen the advantages already gained by a neighbouring tribe, the Aedui, who were recognised as official allies of Rome. But unrest spread among the Loire valley tribes. Genabum (Orléans) was attacked and Roman citizens killed, and Caesar had to return to put down rebellions.

In fact the valley prospered under Roman rule, especially agriculture and transport. The most important highway was between Lutetia (Paris) and Orléans — and it still is. But the river remained the main highway for transporting goods and the towns grew up along it, with bridges over it. Augustus Caesar made the Loire the boundary between Lugdunensis in the north and Aquitania in the south, and so it stayed for 300 years.

Christianity came in the 3rd century with St. Maurice and St. Gatien but did not spread outside the towns. However, it did make one important convert — Martin, a Roman soldier born in what is now Yugoslavia. The well-known story about him is how he split his military coat in two to give half to a beggar. He himself was living a simple life in the chalk caves of Marmoutier, 8km from Tours, when he was elected Bishop of Tours. He founded Marmoutier Abbey in 372 and became so popular in Tours that when he died the city became a major centre for pilgrims and a whole suburb, Martinopolis, was built to house the tourists. While building their monastery, the monks lived in the chalk caves. The Norsemen destroyed the monastery in 853, killing 100 monks, but it was revived by Benedictines from Cluny and became so prosperous that by the 17th century it controlled 200 priories and domaines in France and England. It survived wars with the English, all the religious wars, then it was sold in 1818 as national property and an asset stripper demolished it. There are a few medieval remains, including a 12th-century Prior's house, a 13th-century main gateway, the belltower where Pope Urban III called for the first crusade, and the hermit caves cut in chalk, of St.

Brice, St. Gatien and St. Patrick. St. Patrick's has the remains of a medieval stained-glass window showing the shamrock — symbol of the Trinity to the French, symbol of more still to a true Irishman.

Once the Romans had gone, the Asian and Germanic tribes coveted this lush and fertile valley with its flow of rivers for transport. Attila was beaten by Bishop St. Aignan in 451 when the Huns tried to take Orléans but the Franks, who had crossed the Rhine as mercenaries of the Romans, turned on their Gallo–Roman allies and became rulers of the land. Most powerful were the Salian Franks under their leader Merovius. His grandson, Clovis, a courageous young man who became leader at 15, beat the Gallo–Romans at Soissons in 486 and made Orléans his capital. He became a Christian to please his strong-willed wife and, more important, to get the backing of the growing church.

Clovis halted his armies on the north bank of the Loire at Amboise because the other side had been taken by other invading conquerors, the Visigoths under Alaric. One or other of these invaders was going to rule. They met in the centre of the Loire on Île St. Jean (Île d'Or), which you can see under the bridge — now one of the Loire swimming beaches. They feasted and swore eternal friendship and set up donges (earth mounds) to mark the frontier. But Clovis was ruthless. He attacked the Visigoths at Vouille, near Poitiers, in 507, killed his 'friend' Alaric with his own hand, and drove the Visigoths almost to the Pyrenees.

He ruled from Orléans a land almost as big as modern France and has been called the founder of France. But when he died in 511 the land was divided among his sons. Local lords took power in the Loire valley. One was Charles Martel, who checked the Arab invasion, then drove it back. His son, Pépin le Bref (the short), deposed the last Merovingian king in 752 and founded a new dynasty.

Pépin's sons was Charlemagne (742–814), who spread his rule over France, Germany and Italy and was crowned Emperor of the West. Like many conquerors, he was a great admirer of learning and arts. Literature and learning flourished in the Loire, churches and abbeys were built. And much was due to the influence of an Englishman, Alcuin, sometimes called Albinus, headmaster of the cloister school of York cathedral. Alcuin was sent to Rome in 781 to fetch the pallium of the new Archbishop of York. In Parma in Italy he met Charlemagne who was so impressed by his scholarship that he asked him to be teacher to the Imperial family — children and adults, even the Emperor himself. Sons of nobles came to him and visitors from afar.

Not surprisingly, Alcuin tired a bit and dreamed of retiring to an abbey. Charlemagne made him abbot of the Benedictine monastery and school at Cormery, near Tours, and when he died in 804 it was the most influential house of learning in the whole empire, spreading culture and civilisation which lasted for another hundred years. He is remembered now for his scriptorium, teaching monks to copy books, particularly, of course, of the bible.

By custom, Charlemagne's empire was divided among his sons after his death and France soon became a series of feudal lordships ruled by ambitious counts (a title given by Charlemagne to his representatives).

Then the Normans came sailing up the Loire to loot, kill and destroy. They ravaged the land from Nantes to Orléans, looting the treasure of St. Martin from Marmoutier, virtually destroying the abbey of St. Benoît where St. Benedictine's bones lay, occupying Angers for six years. The real resistance to them came from the warlike local counts, especially the Counts of Blois and Tours, who halted them. Surprisingly perhaps the Normans did not settle in this fertile, sunny valley to carve out a dukedom as they did from Rouen in Normandy.

As the feudal lords warred for power, the Loire sprouted castles and strongholds on every vantage point. The great rivalry in the 10th and 11th centuries was between the Counts of Blois and Anjou, and their stories became interwoven almost completely with the history of England.

A violent, greedy but brilliant young man Foulques Nerra (Foulques the Black — 987–1040) became Count of Anjou at 17 and spent his life fighting the Counts of Blois. The Blois lands separated the Anjou lands and Foulques was expected to pay tolls or fight his way across. He chose fighting (his particular enemy was Thibault le Tricheur (the Trickster) of Blois). He built an incredible number of fortresses and donjons, but he also built abbeys and took a rest from fighting to make three pilgrimages to Jerusalem. In moments of repentance he would make gifts to churches. Inevitably, Eudes, Count of Blois, ravaged his lands while he was in Jerusalem and Foulques' penitence soon turned to blind rage. These Counts had some descriptive names — 'the Good', 'the Red', 'Greyfish', 'the Hammer', 'the Surly'.

A revolution began in the Loire in the 11th century which had a bigger effect on its future than did these feudal fights. The forests were being cleared, heathland ploughed, agriculture improved. It went on apace for three centuries, turning the Loire into the garden which has supplied Paris with so much of its produce ever since. And the land was able to support many more people. The landowners became wealthier and more important.

Geoffroy V, Count of Anjou, married in 1128 Matilda of England, daughter of Henry I of England. He conquered most of Normandy. He carried a sprig of broom (*plante de genêt*) in his hat and was known as 'le bel Plantagenêt'. He was the founder of England's Plantagenet Royal line. Meanwhile, a daughter of William the Conqueror, sister of Henry I of England, married the rival Count of Blois. Their son was Stephen.

When Henry I died in 1135, Stephen and Matilda both bid for the English throne. The English lords backed Stephen. So the Counts of Blois now ruled Blois, Champagne and England.

But the Plantagenets were on the march. Louis VII of France had married Eleanor of Aquitaine, a brilliant, formidable and attractive woman who accompanied him to the Second Crusade and, he believed, was unfaithful to him in Antioch. He was almost certainly right. Just before he died, Geoffrey Plantagenet went to Paris to make a treaty with Louis. He took his 18-year-old son Henry. Eleanor, now 29, took great interest in him. Louis' jealousy rose alarmingly. He pulled down fortresses in her Aquitaine, recalled his soldiers, then called an ecclesiastical council at Beaugency on the Loire to dissolve the marriage on the grounds that he and Eleanor were too closely related.

Eleanor slipped back to Aquitaine by night, to avoid suitors desiring her lands. Henry's 16-year-old brother even tried to kidnap her. Then the son of the Count of Champagne tried the same at Tours. Partly because he was Louis' great rival, she married Henry Plantagenet, a passionate lover who desired her and her lands.

Henry now ruled from the English Channel to the Pyrenees. He went to England and forced Stephen of Blois to make him heir to the kingdom which his own grandfather had ruled. Stephen died next year. As Henry II, Henry Plantagenet ruled from the Scottish Borders to the Pyrenees.

He was a difficult, impetuous man. His fight for civil power against the church in Rome nearly brought him down. His chance remark 'Who will rid me of this turbulent priest?' caused the murder of Thomas à Becket at Canterbury by over-zealous knights and put the power of the church against him. And in 1180 Paris had a new young, clever king, Philippe-Auguste. But Henry was brought down by a quarrel with Eleanor. He had a Welsh girl friend in England; she was playing around with a page in France. He imprisoned her. Their passionate love turned to vindictive hate. She turned their sons against him. First Richard Coeur de Lion, the man of whom Philippe of France was afraid, turned against his father, allied himself with Philippe, and forced a humiliating treaty on Henry at Chinon in 1189. Here Henry gave up and died.

Richard was killed in 1199 by a stray arrow while besieging a minor castle. The new Plantagenet King, John, was no match for Philippe-Auguste, and he gradually lost his lands in Normandy and the Loire, though the English remained in Aquitaine.

Through most of the Hundred Years' War, started when Edward III of England claimed the throne of France, the fighting made little difference to the Loire. It was in the north (Crécy and Agincourt), in Gascony and the Dordogne that the fighting took place, though the Black Prince did win a great English victory at Poitiers in 1356. But after Agincourt, the victorious Henry V of England married the King of France's daughter in Paris and was declared, soon, King of France. The Dauphin, eldest son of the French King, weak and indecisive, scuttled around the Loire châteaux and, on the death of his father, when he should have been King, he refused to be crowned and was known scathingly as 'King of Bourges' while Henry V's son, Henry VI of England, claimed the French throne.

In 1428, the fighting moved well and truly to the Loire, with the English army besieging Orléans, albeit with a force far too small to blockade it completely.

It was then that the Burgundian peasant girl Joan of Arc went to Chinon, persuaded the Dauphin to give her an army, entered the city with a food convoy, roused the depressed spirits of the French garrison and led them to victory.

She almost *forced* the Dauphin to be crowned Charles VII. He did nothing to prevent her disgraceful death. The English were finally driven out by her friend Dunois, called the Bastard of Orléans because he was the illegitimate son of the Duke of Orléans. But the new King continued to spend

most of his time on the Loire, not in Paris, setting up sumptuous courts at Chinon and Loches. His new-found wealth came from a shrewd reorganising of taxation by a Bourges merchant, Jacques Coeur, who restored the prosperity of France.

Under these Valois kings the Loire became a playground for the rich and powerful. Hunting lodges and châteaux were built by the court and by the new powerful class of successful merchants, the bourgeoisie who became financial experts to the kings.

Charles VIII lost his military campaign in Italy but gained a love of Renaissance art and architecture and brought back Italian designers and craftsmen to transform his château at Amboise. It was the beginning of the French love-affair with Renaissance art and building, brought to fruition by the flamboyant lover of show and pageantry, Francis I, at Amboise and Chambord. He was the king who met England's Henry VIII at Guines in northern France at what must have been the greatest picnic in history — The Field of the Cloth of Gold. He even brought Leonardo da Vinci to Amboise. And here on the Loire he practised his two favourite sports, hunting game and women. Amboise became a centre of sumptuous court junketings, with magnificent festive balls, masquerades, tournaments and fights between wild animals.

Many of the châteaux started as hunting lodges. Others were built for prestige. But the shadow of the Religious Wars fell on the Loire from 1562, with murder, abduction and atrocities on both Catholic and Protestant sides, and members of the Royal family and noblemen using the religious fanatics to gain power for themselves.

The atrocities reached their climax when Henry II's vacillating widow Catherine de Médicis brought her boy-king son, Francis II, and his girl-wife Mary, later Queen of Scots, to Amboise in fear of Protestant risings. In 1560 foolish Protestants planning a badly organised coup were betrayed to the odious, all-powerful Duke of Guise. They were tortured, broken on the wheel and strung out from Amboise castle balconies. Royals and court would come out after dinner to watch their agony. The Duchess of Guise warned Catherine: 'What vengeance is here being stored for the future!' And the Royal family paid. The boy-king died within months. His brother Charles IX died in terror and remorse after a blood-stained reign. The Duke of Guise was finally murdered. Mary was finally beheaded.

Meanwhile Henry III came to the throne in 1574, the Duke of Guise formed the Catholic League, more of a terror organisation than a religious one. Their arch enemy was the Protestant Henry of Navarre. Henry III fell foul of the League. He allied himself with Henry of Navarre. He had the Duke of Guise and his brother, the Cardinal of Lorraine, murdered at the château at Blois. Eight months later a monk who was a League member murdered Henry.

But Henry of Navarre had won his battles. All he needed was Paris. To gain it, he became a Catholic — at least theoretically. 'Paris is worth a mass,' he explained. His plan was to unite France. After he was crowned Henry IV he chose Nantes, which had supported the League against him, to issue his Edict making Protestantism legal.

The Loire valley's age of glory and parties was over for a while. Not that this Henry disliked enjoyment. He was famed for his love of wine and women and was called Le Vert Galant. But his incentive to visit the area went when his handsome and intelligent mistress Gabrielle d'Estrées, who came from Touraine, died.

Young Louis XIV was hidden at Blois during the Fronde uprising in 1651 and for a while he revived the tradition of the Loire valley as the playground of the Court, with visits to the Château of Chambord where Molière created plays to be performed for him. But Louis was determined to kill the power of the feudal lords who held separate courts in their châteaux. He appointed his own bureaucrats, royal intendants who had the power of the king behind them. The country was divided into areas (généralités) and these men ruled them down to the finest details. The monarchy was absolute: 'L'Etat c'est moi' — 'I am the State'. He built Versailles as the glittering centre of his Court and the aristocrats fought for the slightest favours there. If you had no abode there, however humble, you were nothing. To be rusticated at the King's whim to your country château was the ultimate disgrace.

The Loire valley was all but forgotten until the railways came. Then it became a place for Parisians to spend weekends and holidays. Its new role as one of Europe's leading tourist centres had begun, although the Loire river had ceased to be a transport highway.

The valley did become a refuge for French Governments in times of war defeats.

In 1870 during the Franco-Prussian War when Napoléon III has capitulated, Gambetta escaped from Paris by balloon and set up a republican French Provisional Government in Tours. A

THE LOIRE VALLEY

tiny army of the Loire inflicted the first
two defeats on the advancing Prussians, at Orléans and Coulmiers, but
they were outnumbered and the
Government fled to Bordeaux.

In the First World War, the Americans had their headquarters at Tours.
They were called 'Les Sammies'. On
10th June 1940, with the Germans
advancing on Paris, the French
Government fled to Tours, and dis-
cussed surrender. The Germans bombarded Orléans and Tours and French
military resistance was crushed. But the
cadets of Saumur military school
ignored orders to retreat and for 24
hours held three Loire bridges against
Nazi tanks until their ammunition ran
out.

In a railway carriage near the railway station at Montoire on the Loire,
tactically placed beside a tunnel, in
case the RAF attacked, Adolf Hitler and
the aged 1914–1918 war hero, Marshal Pétain, head of the Vichy Government, signed the full French surrender
on 24th October 1940. The Loire
was the main boundary between
Occupied and unoccupied France.

Now motorways join Orléans and
Tours to Paris and both cities have
become part of the modern French
industrial revival. But agriculture still
thrives. The Loire valley is still the
larder of Paris and the fresh-air haunt of
Parisians. The significant change is that
they can drive there and back in a day
on motorways.

3
Food and Wine

FOOD

For centuries the Loire valley, Berry and Touraine were the larder of Paris. Even in these days when modern transport means that the green beans on offer in the vast new Paris market are as likely to have been flown in from Kenya as brought by lorry up the motorway from Orléans, and the salmon much more likely to have been brought in from Vancouver than from the Loire river, where salmon is very scarce now, the Loire still supplies a lot of fresh food for the capital.

In medieval times few vegetables were eaten in France. When starving peasants were said to be reduced to eating grass, it was often green vegetables. And little fish was on the tables of the rich or important people. Fish was for fast days such as Friday when men thought they were being abstemious by refusing meat. The Loire was known for its game, poultry and fruit.

Fish appeared more often in the time of Francis I, but it was mostly freshwater fish from the local rivers, for the court was centred on châteaux in the central Loire and with such appalling roads fish from the sea would not have been in very good condition by the time it reached table. Rivers were still rich in salmon, pike, carp, sandre,

crayfish and little eels (*anguilles*) and these were usually grilled, then stewed in wine — called *chaudemer*, ancestor of *matelote*.

Francis' daughter-in-law Catherine de Médicis brought from Italy not only new recipes and cooking techniques but new vegetables and ways of using those already grown. Coming from the courts of Florence, she thought little of the medieval French cookery or of French cooks, and brought to France her own chefs, recipes and new vegetables, including the artichoke and what we now call French beans. It was in the Loire that most of these vegetables were grown, for it was a lush, fairly warm valley and here the court spent most of its time.

Catherine brought too the famous Italian pastrycooks, and the superb French gâteaux were born. Blois still produces pastries which are works of art. When the court settled in Paris, the products of the Loire simply had farther to travel.

Market gardens of the Loire still produce some of Europe's best vegetables and it seems perverse to use modern recipes with matchsticks of carrots, six French beans and slivers of kiwi fruit as décor when there are such

17

glorious *haricots verts* (green string beans), artichokes, broad beans (*fèves*), which the French either cook very young or when older remove the tough skins before cooking, which makes them into a different vegetable. They are superb when cooked, then dressed with butter and cream (*mogettes*). Leeks of Touraine are often made into a simple leek sauce by stewing in butter then adding Béchamel sauce. It is served often with the chicken of la Flèche. Bourges is a great poultry area, and Nantes is known for duck. Poulet Lochoise is delightful — chicken with onion, brandy and double cream sauce. Loire cabbage, tossed in a lot of butter, can be delicious (called *chouée*). *Cardon*, tall relative of the artichoke, is cultivated for its root and its stem (like a coarse celery — usually boiled, served in white sauce).

Market gardens of the Loire produce excellent lettuce and other salad produce. Superb asparagus, thick, white varieties, is grown especially in Loir-et-Cher, second biggest producer to the Gard. But the little town of Candes, where the Vienne meets the Loire, north of Fontevraud Abbey, is considered to produce the best asparagus in France, and we would not argue. Champignons de Paris, button mushrooms grown in Paris outskirts in the last century, emigrated to the Loire long ago as Paris suburbs spread over the caves. They are grown mostly in caves unsuitable for wine storage or, as at Chênehutte-les-Tuffeaux, west of Saumur, in quarries dug out for tufa stone.

The pride of the valley has always been its fruit, and despite EEC's disorganising regulations, production has been kept up fairly well.

Le Mans Reinette apples have survived the French national marketing campaign for Golden Delicious. Raspberries, strawberries and blackberries are prolific in season, with Saumur as the main centre. Orléans produces quince (*coing*) and you can buy lovely quince jelly (*gelée de coing*), quince marmalade (*marmelade de coing*) and raspberry jelly (*gelée de framboise*). These are not usually spread on bread or toast but eaten with a spoon with sweet biscuits, cream or put in flans and tarts. A paste of quince and apple is called *cotignac*. Incidentally, bread spread with jam is usually called *tartine*. The jellies are especially delightful with *crémets* of Angers or Saumur (cream cheese mixed with white of eggs and served with cream).

Tours is best known for plums and prunes and dishes made from them. Damson prunes (*gros damas de Tours*) are claimed to be the best in the world. Before nouvelle or moderne cuisines became fashionable and fruit was served with many meat dishes, French chefs despised the mixture of meat and fruit, with one exception — *porc aux pruneaux*. *Prunes fourrées* are plums stuffed with almond paste. You can buy the paste (*pâté d'amandes*).

Tours also produces walnuts and they are used in salads and made into walnut oil to put on salads. A mixed dressing of walnut oil and red wine vinegar is delicious. Wine vinegar, white and red, is a speciality of Orléans. Pithiviers is the centre for almonds and they make a cake called *pithiviers* of puff pastry with almonds and rum, traditionally bought after mass on Sunday as a lunch dessert. Another local dessert which you can buy ready-made at a pâtisserie is *savarin* made in a ring of baba dough

The Prince of Gastronomes

In the 1920s and 1930s a man called Curnonsky started to teach the French about simple local and regional dishes. He was called the Prince of Gastronomes and he preached the joys of cuisine bourgeoise and cuisine régionale, until then despised by the gourmet lovers of grande cuisine, with its magnificent but complicated sauces and huge meals.

Curnonsky was particularly impressed by Loire cooking. He wrote: 'In the Loiret, the cuisine is imbued with a concern for gentle living that is found also in the Loire. It is a cuisine of chefs and its preparation requires time, patience and a little genius. Nothing replaces butter and things are in their natural state.'

Of Anjou, he said: 'The cooking is forthright, reasonable, good-natured and does not strive for effects. Anjou is the paradise of easy digestions.'

Perhaps he was a *little* prejudiced. His real name was Maurice Edmond Sailland, and he was born in 1872 ... in Angers.

(like rum-baba), soaked in a rum syrup which includes cinnamon, coriander, aniseed and mace. The inside of the ring is often filled with fruit and cream — or it is served with crystallised fruit.

A more modern dessert which swept France and has survived even the most modern cooking fashions was invented by two sisters in a little inn in Lamotte–Beuvron in the Sologne, which Michelin has never recognised. Tarte Tatin is an upside-down caramelised apple tart, made with firm eating apples, delicious when well made, horrible when mushy or heated up.

For centuries the Sologne's game-rich marshes and rather sad-looking forests have supplied the top tables of France. It is still recognised to have the best winged game in France, with deer and wild boar to compare with most others. Two of its old specialities are still loved — *faisan en barbouille* (pheasant casserole) and *côtelettes de chevreuil poivrade* (venison cutlets with a vinegar marinade and pepper sauce) which you won't meet often because it takes at least five hours to prepare and cook properly. Wild duck, hare, partridge and quail abound in season and appear both fresh and in pâtés. The old lark and thrush pâtés regarded as such delicacies are now illegal and we hope never to run into them again, but the French, almost as much as the Italians, find it very difficult not to catch and eat almost anything that flies. Rabbit pâté is a speciality of Anjou, hare pâté of the Sologne.

Rillettes are made all over France but the best are from Le Mans and Tours. They are usually made of pork, but Le Mans adds goose and you can get rabbit. The meat is shredded, seasoned heavily, cooked, pounded and potted in its own fat. Some people love *rillettes*, others find it bland and stringy. We are divided within our family. If you buy it, go to a charcuterie which makes its own. Some of the factory-produced versions in supermarkets are an insult. Serve it on toast using its own fat and no butter. Luxury versions are *rille d'oie* made entirely with goose, and *rillettes de lapin de la Garenne* made from wild rabbit. *Rillons* and *rillauds* are quite different. They are pieces of pork cooked in seasoned lard and preserved in jars, or simply pieces of pork cooked until their own fat is rendered and they are crisp and crunchy. They also come in open tarts (*quiche Tourangelle*).

Fish is still the mainstay of Loire and Lower Loire tables. Though local salmon has gone, *anguilles* and *anguillettes* (eels) still come from the estuary, shellfish comes from the neighbouring Poitou coast, freshwater pike, perch, sandre (a more delicate fish, but a sort of pike-perch), gudgeon (*goujon*), tench (*tanche*) and shad (*alose*) still come from all the rivers and from the lakes and streams of the Sologne. *Friture* — a fry of mixed freshwater fish — is a basic Loire dish, usually of gudgeon, perch and tench. Pike in mousse and in quenelles (tiny, lightly poached mousse) are so tasty that we marvel that so many thousands of this fish are tossed back into lakes, rivers and reservoirs by fishermen all over Britain. Another modern English prejudice is against eels, although Britons consumed them in huge quantities until recently. Most eels taste more like delicate, juicy meat than like fish, and in the Loire you will find them in pâté, braised, casseroled and baked and served with prunes. Do try Bouilliture, a *matelote* of eels in red wine with prunes, onions and mushrooms.

Beurre Blanc, the sauce of butter, shallot and wine, came from Nantes and is used in the Loire valley mostly with freshwater fish, but with plaice, turbot or seabass in the Loire–Atlantique. It is popular all over France and a great standby of 'modern' cooks (see recipe on p.22).

Nantes produces Lard Nantais, made of pork rinds, liver, lungs and pieces of pork, chopped in small pieces, fried and served with pork chops. Amboise produces outstanding ham. Le Mans is known for *boudin blanc*, the soft sausage of eggs, onions, pork fat, herbs and spices, usually grilled. Le Mans is a good area for eating. It produces fine veal and excellent chickens — *poulet gris*, fed on wheat and milk. And splendid nuts are grown locally — hazelnuts called *culroux*, a chestnut called *nouzillard*, and *franquette* walnuts. Le Mans is also famed for its pastries, cakes and confectionery, as is Blois. But Blois is famous for chocolate and chocolate cake (*gâteau chocolat de Blois*) in which the thin chocolate decorations are twisted into almost-miraculous shapes.

CHEESES

Within the arms of the Loire valley are made many excellent goat cheeses, mild and strong and strong-smelling. But a number of excellent cow's milk cheeses are made, too. The best are made around Olivet, near Orléans.

Bondaroy au foin (or Pithiviers au foin) — tangy cow's cheese cured in hay-filled bins.

Caillebotte — soft with mild creamy taste; cow's milk; made on farms in spring and summer.

Chabichou fermier — firm with sharp taste; goat's milk; truncated cone shape; farm-made.

Chavignol-Sancerre — small disc of mild goat's cheese which becomes *crottin* when old and dark-coloured.

Couhé-Vérac — another farm-made goat's cheese; square, covered with chestnut leaves. Nutty taste.

Crémet — fresh, mild, creamy cow's milk cheese, used in Anjou for making a dessert (see recipe on p.25) served with fruit and cream.

Crézancy-Sancerre — similar to Chavignol, from Southern Loire area.

Crottin de Chavignol — made by farmers of Sancerre area since the 16th century, now, like the local wine, protected by an official AOC (appellation contrôlée) to make sure it isn't copied. Made from full-cream goat's milk, small and white at first, but with age goes dry with a dark-brown, almost black rind when it is regarded as a gourmet's delight, with a slightly-rancid taste and a powerful smell (*crottin* means goat's dung!). When younger it is excellent grilled or fried — a fashionable starter or savoury dish at present.

Entrammes — unpasteurised, washed rind cow's milk cheese of the St. Paulin type made in the monastery of Entrammes in Maine where the monks first made Port Salut. They sold the Port Salut formula and it is now made in a factory.

Frinault — from Orléans; small disc of strong cow's milk cheese, sometimes matured in woodash (*cendré*). Best in summer and autumn.

Gien — delightful but difficult to get; made only on farms in Gien area. Lovely nutty taste. Can be drum-shaped or truncated cone, and sometimes cured in ashes.

Graçay — goat cheese in shape of big truncated cone, dusted with powdered charcoal, making it dark-blue.

Laval — a cow's milk cheese made by Trappist monks at Laval monastery in Maine, it has an interesting sharp flavour. The discs weigh about 2kg.

Ligueil and Loches — factory-made goat's milk, rather like Ste. Maure.

Montoire — nice fruity goat's milk in cone shape.

Olivet bleu — blue cheese with lovely mouth-filling flavour, made from cow's milk, matured in Olivet chalk caves.

Olivet cendré — firm, supple cow's milk cheese with interesting flavour, cured and coated with ashes. Fairly low fat. Made in farms and small dairies. Very pleasant.

St. Benoist — from St. Benoît-sur-Loire; farm-made from skimmed cow's milk. Nice fruity flavour.

Ste. Maure — two versions: Fermier, made on farms, has a goaty smell, strong beautiful flavour, has straw running through it and is a gourmet's delight. It is cylindrical. Laitier is the factory-produced version with no straw. Not so good but pleasant.

Selles — made at Selles-sur-Cher, it is a gourmet's goat's cheese, mild but attractively flavoured, and protected by an AOC rating. It is made from unbroken curds, salted, coated with ash and left to mature for about three weeks. It is also called Romorantin.

Valençay — Fermier version is mild, made from goat's milk on farms around quite an area of the Loire; truncated pyramid shape, dusted with charcoal. Laitier, the commercial version, sometimes called *pyramide*, is much stronger, with a powerful smell and rancidy sharp taste. Levroux is a similar cheese.

Recipes

All recipes serve 4, except where otherwise indicated.

Beurre blanc (butter sauce)

INGREDIENTS

100g unsalted butter	6 tablespoons dry white wine
3 shallots	(or 3 tablespoons wine,
few drops lemon juice	3 tablespoons wine vinegar)
salt, pepper	

METHOD

Served usually with pike or shad — brochet or alose — but also with any fish likely to be dry.

Chop shallots finely, boil them in a small saucepan in the wine until reduced to 2 tablespoons of liquid. Take off heat. Cut butter into little knobs, whisk two knobs into liquid until creamy, put on very low heat and whisk in the butter knob by knob. Season. Add lemon juice.

Pâté de saumon et mousse de cresson (salmon pâté with watercress mousse)

INGREDIENTS

¼ litre (almost) milk	salt, pepper
75g butter	
100g flour	For mousse:
2 small eggs	150ml stiff mayonnaise
350g skinned fish	150ml whipped cream
½ tablespoon fresh cream	bunch watercress, chopped roughly
½kg salmon	pinch paprika

METHOD

The white fish can be pike, whiting or plaice. It must be skinned and boned — as must be the salmon.

Make a smooth sauce with heated milk, 60 g butter and 100 g of flour. Bring to boil and cook for a few minutes, stirring. Remove from heat, add lightly beaten eggs, one at a time. Mince white fish very finely and add to mixture with the cream, remaining butter and seasoning. Line a terrine dish with the fish mixture and arrange salmon in the centre. Cover with rest of mixture. Cook for about 1¼ hours in a covered bain-marie (180°C, 350°F. Mark 4). Leave to cool. Make the mousse by mixing all ingredients in a bowl with seasoning. Serve with the pâté.

Mousse chaude de brochet au coulis d'écrevisses (hot pike mousse with crayfish purée)

INGREDIENTS

600g boned pike	1 litre fish stock made with
4 egg whites	pike bones and head
1 litre cream	100ml Cognac
salt, pepper	100ml cream
	1 tablespoon butter
For purée:	1 tablespoon flour
1kg crayfish (or prawns)	

METHOD

Salmon trout can be used as an alternative to pike, which we prefer, and prawns for crayfish, which we don't.

Pound fish or put through electric blender with salt and pepper. Add egg whites. Mix well. Stir in cream. Butter a mould (preferably a ring mould), fill with mousse, put in bain-marie and cook for 45 minutes in oven (180°C, 350°F, Mark 4).

To make purée: scald crayfish or prawns if uncooked (take out little black intestine); peel crayfish tails or prawns; crush shells and fry in butter; add Cognac; reduce by half; add fish stock, cook for a few minutes over low heat. Strain. Season. Thicken a little with flour and butter. Add cream. Unmould mousse, arrange crayfish tails in centre or around it, pour sauce over.

Bouilleture d'anguilles (stewed eels)

INGREDIENTS

1kg eels	For garnish:
1 bottle of red wine	200g small onions
1 glass of marc (spirit)	200g little mushrooms
2 tablespoons butter	6 slices bread, all fried
1 tablespoon flour	in butter
thyme, parsley, bay leaf	
salt, pepper	

METHOD

This recipe will serve between 4 and 6 people.

Our advice: buy the eels (preferably small Poitevin eels) ready skinned and cleaned. Wash, cut into sections, put into stewing pot and cover with red wine. Season, add herbs. Bring to boil, add glass of marc, flambé. Cook for 15 minutes. Remove pieces of eel. Thicken cooking liquor with butter and flour, stirring in well. Strain sauce over eels. Serve with garnish (above).

Noisettes de porc aux pruneaux
(nut of meat from pork chump chops with prunes)

INGREDIENTS

4 big pork chops	40g butter
(or one per person)	flour for dusting
16 large or 20 smaller prunes	1 tablespoon redcurrant (or
1 finely chopped onion	cranberry) jelly
200ml white wine (Vouvray) or red wine	salt, pepper
200ml double cream	few drops vinegar

METHOD

This is a simple recipe. Alternatively use the chop on the bone trimmed of fat. We prefer white wine.

Soak prunes overnight in the wine. Dust chops with salt, pepper and flour. Melt butter in largish pan with lid, brown chops on both sides. Tip in prunes and their wine liquid, onion and wine vinegar, cover the pan and simmer for about 50 to 60 minutes. Remove chops to hot dish, surround with prunes. Reduce pan juices, stirring in redcurrant jelly until it dissolves, add cream slowly, let it bubble but stir briskly until smooth. Pour over chops.

Côtelettes de chevreuil poivrade
(venison cutlets with poivrade sauce)

Serves 6

INGREDIENTS

6 venison cutlets	6 black peppercorns, parsley
4 carrots	game trimmings (bits removed before
3 shallots	cooking — bones if possible, if
2 medium onions	not, beef bones)
1 leek (white part)	500ml dry white wine
6 tablespoons oil	1¼ tablespoons flour
100g butter	150ml wine vinegar
salt, pepper	1 tablespoon redcurrant jelly
thyme, bay leaf	

METHOD

Make a marinade with chopped vegetables, wine, vinegar, peppercorns, thyme, bay leaf and parsley. Put cutlets in it for at least two hours. Fry vegetables from marinade in oil until brown. Add flour, stirring well. Add marinade liquid and herbs, simmer for about two hours, reducing. Strain. Sauté cutlets quickly in half the butter. Take out and keep warm. Add the sauce liquid to the pan, add salt and pepper, stir, reducing further if necessary. Strain. Melt in reducurrant jelly and butter. Pour over cutlets and serve.

Gibelotte de lapin solognote
(rabbit in red wine à la Solognote)

For 6 people

INGREDIENTS

1 rabbit, about 2kg	Garnish:
½ litre red Touraine wine	250g prunes
(preferably Gamay)	½ litre red Gamay wine
1 bouquet garni	50g sultanas, 50g currants
150g thinly sliced onions	50g cubes of bacon
1 dessertspoon flour	100g button mushrooms
150g thinly sliced carrot	200g small onions
1 clove garlic	3 slices bread for fried croûtons
salt, pepper	3 pears

METHOD

Cut the rabbit into pieces and marinade for 24 or 36 hours in ½ litre red wine with bouquet garni and thinly sliced onions and carrots. Drain the pieces and fry them until they are well browned. Sprinkle with flour. Gradually add the marinade with the carrots, onions, bouquet garni, the clove of garlic, salt and pepper. Bring to the boil and simmer gently. When the rabbit is completely cooked, remove the pieces and keep warm. Continue to cook the sauce until it has completely lost its acidity, about 3 hours, adding water if necessary. Pour the sauce through a strainer over the rabbit.

Garnish: Poach the sultanas and currants in water. Poach the cubes of bacon in water. Glaze the little onions and button mushrooms, add them to the sauce before reheating to serve.

Cut the pears into four and cook in red wine. Cook the prunes in red wine. Cut the bread into heart-shaped croûtons and fry in butter. To serve, arrange them attractively over the pieces of rabbit.

Crémets d'Angers ou de Saumur
(cottage cheese mixed with fresh cream and egg whites)

INGREDIENTS

250g crémets (like cottage cheese)	pinch of salt
60g fine sugar	100ml thick cream
whites of 3 eggs	

METHOD

Served with fruit and cream as dessert or for breakfast.

Drain cheese in a sieve (if necessary). Put in mixing bowl; whisk in cream until smooth and thick; beat in sugar. Whip egg whites with salt until stiff, fold into mixture. Tip on to square of muslin, pull corners together, tie and hang in refrigerator with bowl to catch drips. Leave for 24 hours. Serve with cream and fruit.

Pithiviers (almond cake)

INGREDIENTS

500g puff pastry	2 whole eggs, plus 1 yolk
100g ground almonds	1 tablespoon flour
125g fine sugar	3-4 tablespoons rum
50g butter	

METHOD

Roll out pastry and cut into two, one piece thicker than the other. Beat almonds, sugar, butter, flour, whole eggs and rum together for 5 to 6 minutes. Spread this filling on the thinner piece of pastry and cover with the other piece. Score top of tart with knife, brush with egg yolk and bake in hot oven for 30 minutes. Preferably serve hot, but it is pleasant cold.

Tarte Tatin (upside-down apple tart)

INGREDIENTS

500g firm apples, sliced	150g sugar
short pastry	serve with cream
125g butter	

METHOD

Butter a 27cm tart pan with 2 tablespoons butter, sprinkle with half the sugar. Arrange apple slices in pan, sprinkle with rest of sugar. Dot with rest of butter in small pieces. Put pan over hot heat on top of cooker for about 3 minutes to caramelise the sugar. Cover with pastry. Bake 30 minutes (180°C, 350°F, Mark 4). Turn on to plate with caramelised apples on top.

WINE

Both the white and red wines of the Loire have gained in popularity in France over the past 15-20 years and some have become fashionable in Paris, pushing up their price. But the lesser-known wines are gaining popularity, especially reds. The reds of Bourgueil and of Chinon in particular have not only improved but have become popular on good hotel wine lists. The owner of a Michelin-starred hotel on the Seine told us recently: 'I am buying Chinon. Let the Americans have the Burgundy and the British their Bordeaux — too dear!' And Touraine Sauvignon white wines are being sought by the knowledgeable to replace dearer Sancerre. Not long ago, the Sauvignon grape was used for white wines in the Eastern Loire —

Sancerre/Pouilly-sur-Loire — area, the Muscadet grape in the Western Loire. Muscadet originated in Burgundy where it was also called Melon de Bourgogne, but is no longer grown there. In the main central area nearly all white wine is made with Chenin Blanc, known here as Pineau. But the Sauvignon has strayed very successfully to Touraine.

Muscadet, once drunk almost entirely with shellfish, has become so popular as an apéritif and for general drinking that it has become a problem wine. At its best a delightfully refreshing drink, it has suffered from over-popularity. There are hundreds of small growers and some are producing some rough wines, which suggest that the Appellation Contrôlée (AC) rules are being stretched. AC should mean that the grapes come from a designated area, are of permitted varieties only and the wine is made by a laid-down process. Vins Délimités de Qualité (VDQS) rules allow more elasticity in yields and areas of production. Vins de Pays must come from a region. Vins de Table need only come from grapes grown in France.

Muscadet should be light, fresh, bone dry and drunk young. Now, trying to get rid of honest acidity to please people used to less-aggressive tastes, some makers are producing bland, dull wine ('collapsed'). 65 million bottles are produced every year. Only Beaujolais beats that.

It is worth paying a bit more for a good Muscadet. The best comes from around Vallet, Clisson and Le Ballet in Sèvre-et-Maine. Muscadet des Coteaux de la Loire is often heavier and uninteresting. Good domaines are Château Galissonnière and its neighbours Châteaux Jannière and Maisdonnière Domaine des Quatre—Routes, and the Drouet wines. The Sauvion family have owned the historic Château du Cléray since Grandpa bought it in 1935. Now son Ernest, helped by his three sons, produce excellent wine — vital, lively, flowery and reliable. They are also négociants (wine merchants) and each year pick ten Découvertes (Discoveries) of outstanding Muscadet. A jury picks the top wine, called Cardinal Richard after a previous owner of the Château, which has perfect wine-keeping caves. The château once belonged to the Malestroit family. Comte de Malestroit lives the other side of Vallet in the elegant Palladian-style Château Noë de Bel Air, built in 1836 to replace one burned down in the Revolution. The family have made good wine here since 1741.

Muscadet-sur-lie means that it has been bottled straight off its lees (pips, skins, etc.) after fermentation and not racked. This gives it more flavour, especially of fruit. Indeed, in the 1930s Muscadet was used to 'stretch' Chablis!

In the Muscadet area (vaguely south, west and east of Nantes just past Vallet), Gros Plant is produced from a grape of the same name. In good years when the grapes ripen well, it is light, dry and fruity and some Frenchmen prefer it to Muscadet with shellfish. In many years it is tart and acidic.

Wine from Pineau (Chenin Blanc) grapes suffers the same problem of acidity in years when the grapes do not ripen or when drunk too young, but becomes much gentler and rounder when kept for a couple of years. It has suffered from the current French fashion of drinking wines too young — a fashion not discouraged by some producers, who thus save the cost of storage and keep the cash flowing faster.

Anjou vineyards fan out from Angers along the Loire towards Muscadet and eastward along the south bank beyond Saumur, where some of the best white wines are made. Another good area is along the Layon river south of Angers. Look also for Savennières white, which improves after three or four years. Sweet wines from here are called Coteaux du Layon.

In 1811 an Alsatian named Ackerman taught the people of Saumur to put the sparkle in white wine by the Champagne method. For long it was the next best sparkling wine to Champagne but now that could be disputed. It is still very pleasant. Still white is produced, mostly demi-sec (semi-dry) and the best has a honey bouquet and crisp fruity flavour, rather like Vouvray but not so good.

Vouvray wines can be delightful. Most years they have a delicacy and finesse far above most Chenin Blanc wines, and can be drunk young or kept four to five years. Some demi-sec will keep and improve up to ten years or more. Sweet wines from the best years can be kept thirty or forty years and are as luscious as Sauternes — superb with strawberries or raspberries. Sparkling Vouvray is pleasant. All Vouvray should be chilled but not iced as much as Muscadet. (See box, p. 39.)

Montlouis from across the Loire, once passed off as Vouvray, has less taste or character and should be drunk young.

Touraine Sauvignon wines do vary but the best are a fair cheap substitute for Sancerre. Jasnière along the Loir river produces good sweet white but little of it.

Unlike Pouilly-Fuissé of Mâcon, made with the Chardonnay grape, Pouilly-Fumé of the Loire is made from Sauvignon. No one has ever given me a satisfactory explanation for its smoky, flinty taste. I found this taste very strong at one time but now I have to search for it a bit, so I am convinced that the wines are made differently now. But Barbara says that the smokiness is as strong as ever. Perhaps it is because I gave up smoking cigars. Anyway, the wines have a super, unusual taste and keep their freshness for at least four or five years whilst growing softer. We admire the growers — they put up with all sorts of problems like unpredictable late spring frosts and hail.

They make also a dry, light fruity wine from the Chasselas grape, mixed with Sauvignon, for lapping in litres — just called Pouilly-sur-Loire. Drink it very young.

Sancerre, across the river, makes twice as much wine as Pouilly and most of it is white. Sancerre and Pouilly are ardent rivals and will not admit that their wines are similar. In fact, we find Sancerre usually fruitier but not so interesting.

The hail storms seem to miss Sancerre. They say locally that there are three types of soil, producing three different wines. Wines from around Bué are fruity and for drinking young. Chavignol's steep chalky slopes produce a distinguished wine to be kept three years or more. Ménétréol area wines are softer and less fruity.

Where Sauvignon grapes will not grow well in Sancerre, Pinot Noir has been grown to make rosé, and, in good years, red wine. In the unfathomable way of one-upmanship in Paris this rare red has become fashionable suddenly and they drink it young and cold. To us,

In caves cut into the hillside, Daniel Jarry produces superb Vouvray wines

it tastes raw. Pinot Noir does not make wines for drinking very young. Ask them in Beaune.

Quincy, west of Bourges, produces dry white wines from Sauvignon grapes with less individuality than Sancerre and Pouilly-Fumé. They are softer, but very aromatic and fruity and when drunk young make a good cheaper substitute. So does white Reuilly, which is not quite so smooth, but very aromatic. A spicy, light red Reuilly is made, too, but very little of it. Next fashion in Paris?

St. Pourçain-sur-Sioule is just off the N9 south of Moulins. Although in the Allier département, its wines are technically 'Loire', though are much like Burgundy. The light, refreshing and slightly cidery white wines are made from several grapes, including the local Tressalier. Red wines made from Gamay are more like a Beaujolais than Touraine and the Pinot Noir reds quite like Burgundy. All are good value.

The Gamay grape, Cabernet Sauvignon and Cabernet Franc (sometimes called 'Le Melon') are main grapes used for nearly all red wines in the Loire, with Cabernet gaining in popularity. Touraine Gamay reds are not up to most Beaujolais standards — more acidic, less fruity. But they are mostly cheap and have become more popular with 'modern light' cuisine, drunk young and cold. Mesland is one of the villages allowed to add its name to the appellation Touraine and is the producer of one of the better Gamay reds and a Gamay-based rosé. It is fruitier with more acid than Touraine–Amboise. Touraine Cabernets are best kept for three years. The French drink them too young, then criticise them!

The best reds come from Chinon and Bourgueil. At Champigny also a good red is made from Cabernet Franc. Bourgueil red is made mostly from Cabernet Franc, though some is made from Cabernet Sauvignon on which most of the best Bordeaux wines are based. On different soils, two types of wine are produced — one is light and fruity, with a pleasant smell of raspberries, and the other is heavier and needs time to mature. Often the two are blended, producing a wine which when kept up to ten years produces a most satisfying drink with a clean, no-tannin taste but enough acidity to keep it from collapsing. The kinship to Médoc allowed these wines to be blended into Bordeaux many years back. For years we drank Bourgueil as we drank Cahors, well pleased with our secret bargain. However, a Paris fashion for the wines a few years back pushed the price up a bit. It is still good value, though. St. Nicolas-de-Bourgueil wines are said to keep best. Some Chinon and Bourgueil producers have cashed in on the Beaujolais Nouveau fashion, selling new 'Primeur' wine in November to get instant cash. Don't fall for it. The Cabernet grape is unsuitable. You will get little but indigestion.

The improvement in Chinon reds has been very noticeable. They have deserved their growing popularity. The Gamay is fashionable in Paris, drunk young and cold but wines from Cabernet Franc are better. Clean and fruity they have the flowery smell which the trade calls *violets* and should have a beautiful ruby colour. Smoother than most other Loire reds, a little dearer, they are pleasant drunk young at cellar temperature to taste the fruit, but can be a revelation in good years when kept five years or so and drunk at room temperature.

Anjou became known for rosé wines after World War II when rosé was popular with people just starting to drink wine — outside France. It was then semi-sweet. Now palates have matured and a drier wine is offered called Rosé de la Loire.

Rosé can be made with Gamay, Groslot and Cabernet Franc grapes but the best are from Cabernet only.

Part One:
From Tours to Orléans

4
Tours and Environs

Tours remains the pivotal centre of the Loire valley for transport and industry, as it has been for centuries. Roads radiate in all directions. But since the terrible destruction of World War II, when 9,000 citizens were killed, rebuilding has changed it almost totally from a proud, beautiful but crumbling old provincial capital to a vital, lively part of modern France — one of the new technological industrial cities of which the French are so proud, with all their welcome prosperity and less welcome ugly expansion. The march of industry, traffic jams, ugly concrete expressways to clear the traffic and concrete suburbs to house industry and people have hit Tours to an extent which other towns of the Loire valley have managed to avoid — even Orléans.

Old Tours filled just a narrow strip of land between the Loire and the Cher. The new city spreads for 7km along the Loire, north to the industrial zone of St. Symphorien, and south of the Cher to residential suburbs.

From silk, food and wine, industries have spread to metallurgy, plastics, electronics, chemicals, textiles, pharmaceuticals, motor-tyres and printing. It is still growing, aided by the A10 motorway which runs to Orléans, Paris,

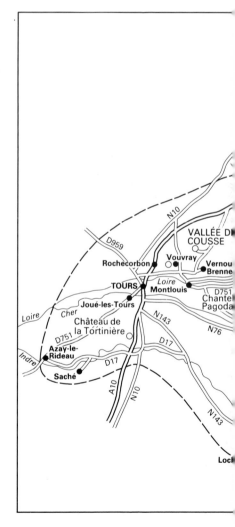

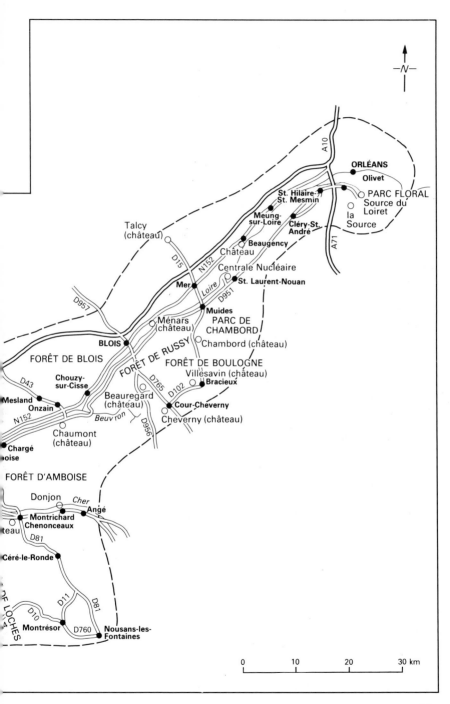

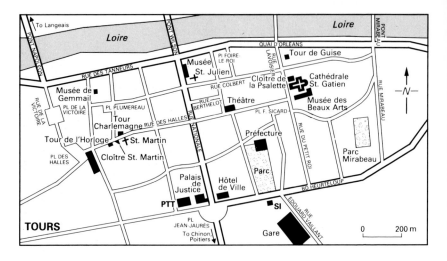

Lille and Belgium to the north, Bordeaux, Toulouse, Narbonne and Spain to the south. It is a busy, cheerful city of 250,000 people, kept young by the 12,000 students of its very modern university, set up in 1970.

But the heart of Tours still beats in its delightful old quarter, attractively and expensively renovated after war damage — some say *over*-renovated, like a film set. To reach it from the north bank of the Loire cross the 18th-century pont Wilson which the locals still call Pont de Pierre — a lovely bridge with 15 arches, 420m long. You are on rue Nationale, once rue Royale, then rue Napoléon. Almost all of the old part of the city lies within 300m either side of it. So you can walk all of it, which is wise because of crowding traffic and because there are a number of interesting smaller attractions rather than one big tourist trap. Come if you can in spring or autumn, to avoid not only summer crowds but damp heat from its site in a bowl between two rivers.

The city grew around the tomb of St. Martin, who died in AD 397. As his body reached Tours, trees grew green, plants flowered, birds sang. Hence a 'St. Martin's Summer'. The Normans destroyed the original sanctuary, a new basilica of St. Martin's was built during the 11th-13th centuries, but it fell into disrepair in the Revolution and was pulled down to make way for rue des Halles in 1802. Two Romanesque towers, Tour Charlemagne, much restored, and Tour de l'Horloge (11th-13th century) are all that is left. The crypt containing the saint's tomb was rediscovered in 1860 and lies below the choir of a new Basilica built between 1887 and 1924 by a local architect. It's a strange building, very pretentious. He must have seen St. Paul's in London, judging by the dome. The nave columns are of Vosges granite. The crypt has been described as 'like an oversized Victorian waiting room'.

These buildings are on the west side of rue Nationale. Towards the Loire from St. Martin's is place Plumereau, the old hat market, with fine old gabled houses, restored after war damage, and a vaulted passage leading to a delightful tiny square called place St. Pierre-le-Puelier, with pleasant gardens and excavations of a medieval cemetery and early church. It leads to rue Briconnet, another charming street with houses of a variety of styles from the 12th century to Romanesque houses of the 18th century. This is a delicious area, well worth exploring. It looks even better on a fine night.

On the east side of rue Nationale, beside the Loire, are two 12th-century towers which were part of the old city gates and castle built by Henry II of England. One is called Tour de Guise. After the murder of the Duke of Guise by Henry III of France, his 15-year-old son was imprisoned on the top floor. To prevent his escaping to revive the sinister Holy League, the new King Henry IV ordered strict guarding. He came down from the tower only for Mass in the chapel, and was then heavily guarded. After nearly three years, a laundress smuggled a rope to him. Coming out of chapel, he challenged the guards to a race up the spiral stairs hopping on one leg. Being young, he got well ahead, then ran to the top on both legs and bolted himself in his room. While the guards banged on the door, he let himself down to the ground outside on the rope, ran down the quay chased by shouting crowds, stole a baker's horse and rode away.

A hundred metres down rue Jules Simon is the Cathedral of St. Gatien. It took a very long time to build, the tufa limestone is crumbling a little, giving it a slightly neglected look, but it is graceful and beautiful — a harmonious composition of Gothic styles and almost a museum of superb stained-glass windows.

It began with a Romanesque church, which burned and partly collapsed.

Place Plumereau in Tours old town is surrounded by 15th-century timber-framed houses

Reconstruction started round about 1239 with the apse (eastern end) which is pure 13th century. The façade, with its rich Flamboyant decoration and adorned gables over the doorway, was made between 1427 and 1484. The north tower, crowned with an early Renaissance dome, with lantern (little turret with windows), was finished in 1507 and represents the Father. The south tower, from around 1550, representing the Son, is deliberately 2m shorter.

The interior is simple, but when the sun shines through, the colours from the early stained-glass windows are gorgeous. The glass panels of the chancel, showing the Passion and legends of saints, were put there 700 years ago and survived even the wartime bombing. The great rose-windows

35

are even more stunning. You can imagine the awe which such colour and beauty brought to the hearts of simpler citizens of the Middle Ages.

Outside the north door of the cathedral is a delightful cloister, with a pretty 16th-century open staircase. It is Cloître de la Psalette — close of the choir school. In Balzac's *Curé of Tours*, Mlle Gamard lived here, while the curé lived in 8 rue de la Psalette.

Balzac, who loved Tours, was born on rue Nationale (when it was rue Napoléon) on 20th May 1799. He called it 'the Queen of Streets'.

Just south of the cathedral is the old Archbishop's Palace, dating from 17th-18th centuries but with remains of the 12th-century building, including the Ecclesiastical Tribunal, which now houses the Musée des Beaux Arts (Fine Arts Museum). In the Tribunal in 1498 a charade was held which was a disgrace to human dignity but profitable to the French nation.

Louis XI had married his daughter Jeanne de France to the heir-apparent Louis of Orléans to keep the throne in direct line. Louis was 14 years old, handsome and fit. Poor 12-year-old Jeanne had a hunched back, diseased hip and 'a veritably simian appearance'. She did all she could to please him and once got him freed from prison, but she repelled him. When Charles VIII died in 1498, and Louis became King Louis XII, he set about getting rid of her. Charles had been married to the Duchess Anne of Brittany and her marriage contract said that if he died she must marry the heir to the throne. France wanted to hold on to

Brittany. Anne was quite prepared to go back there and sever ties with France.

So Louis had a double-incentive to get rid of Jeanne. He asked the Pope for the right to bring a case before an Ecclesiastical Court claiming a forbidden blood relationship and non consummation. The interrogation of Jeanne by the church judges in the Tribunal at Tours was vicious, with constant references to her deformities. To clinch his case, Louis knelt at the altar in the church in Amboise, in the presence of holy relics, with his hand on the Testament, and perjured himself, swearing that he had never slept with Jeanne and that all she said was untrue. He added coarse gratuitous insults. When the judges had found for him, the crowd outside gave *them* a few insults, too. Jeanne was popular. Later she founded the religious Order of the Annunciation and was canonised as Sainte Jeanne de Valois in 1952 — a pleasant twist of history.

The Fine Arts Museum is rather dull, though the panelling and silks from the time of Louis XIII to Louis XVI are a delight. Louis XI introduced the manufacture of silk and cloth of gold to Tours, moving it from Lyons whose people he thought to be too lazy: 20,000 artisans were employed at 2,000 looms in the 16th century. There is also Rembrandt's 'Flight Into Egypt', painted on wood, pictures by Rubens, Dégas, and local 15th-century artist Fouquet. Of more general interest is the Musée du Compagnonnage (Crafts Guild Museum) in a 16th-century monks' dormitory of the former Abbey of St. Julien at 8 rue Nationale. On show are extinct crafts of the medieval journeymen-craftsmen, who formed secret groups and consorted with

St. Gatien, Tours — a harmony of different styles making a magnificent cathedral

rogues and vagabonds, but knew their trades. In the old abbey cellar is a fine museum devoted to wine and its whole process of growing and production.

Rue Nationale has the big shops. The interesting small shops are in rue Colbert, running from Nationale towards the Cathedral, a delightful street of old buildings, some, alas, stuccoed over. The gabled building, No. 41, has a metal sign outside of Joan of Arc in armour and the words 'A la Pucelle Arméé (To the Armed Maiden). To an earlier house here Joan came to be fitted with her armour while a Scot living in Tours, Hamish Power, painted her standard.

Place Foire-le-Roi off Colbert has some fine 15th-century gabled houses and at No. 8 a Renaissance mansion of 1520 which belonged to the Babou family. Philibert Babou, who built the house, was Francis I's Treasurer and his wife Marie (la Belle Babou) liked to sleep with the king or anyone else important, such as the Emperor Charles, on his visit to France. Her granddaughter was none other than Gabrielle d'Estrée, the elegant mistress of Henry IV. In this square, medieval food fairs were held and trestle tables raised for performances of Mystery plays. Now it has pleasant gardens.

The hub of Tours, where locals still arrange to meet, is place Jean-Jaurès, at the south end of Nationale. To the west is what is left of the Château of Plessis-lès-Tours, one wing of brick and stone of the three wings in a U-shape built by Louis XI in 1463. The following year his daughter Jeanne was born here. He died here in 1483. If Walter Scott in *Quentin Durward* and most historians are to be believed, it was a gloomy court. Louis was a pious, serious, frightened man. He had a stroke towards the

The simple brick building is all that is left of Château de Plessis-lès-Tours, where the ill-famed Louis XI died

end of his life and retired behind the walls of Plessis for fear of his enemies. He had many. He was cruel, ruthless and had a foul temper. At Loches he used iron cages for imprisoning people who upset him (see p.56). They were like bird cages, not big enough for the victim to stand, and suspended from the cell ceiling so that they rocked and tilted every time the prisoner moved. At Plessis he had a trellis of iron bars put round the whole château, spikes on the walls, and crossbowmen were ordered to shoot anyone approaching suspiciously. Armoured mobile sentry boxes were made with slits for firing through.

He had hunted in the forest using a leopard to chase the game. Now he dared not leave the castle, he had boar, rabbits and foxes brought in for the leopard to chase round the courtyard. The Calabrian hermit, Francis of Paola, founder of the severe Minim Order, gave him his last rites — but refused to pray for his recovery.

The Wines of Vouvray

The Vouvray wine producer Daniel Jarry's 1985 dry and demi-sec white wines were superb in their fruity smell and flowery taste. He knew right away that this was a great vintage which would keep for five, ten or more years. But he had a space problem as so many of his recent wines were worthy of keeping. So he simply dug deeper into the chalk hillside, making his caves bigger.

Daniel is one of the great wine makers of Vouvray whose families have thrived here for centuries. His wines are drunk all over the Western world. To grow, make, bottle and care for his wines, he has just the family and two employees.

The Jarry caves are on route Vallée Coquette, a little road left from the N152, just 6km from Tours, nearer to the industrial centre of St. Symphorien and in a different world from either. It is wine country, pure and simple, this stretch north of the Loire between Tours and Amboise. Motorists and lorries pound the N152 but the villages like Vouvray and Vernou-sur-Brenne go very quietly about the wine-making business and cannot be hurried. No great wine 'factories' here — just little family caves using the old methods so effectively that the sweet white (moelleux) Vouvray wines from a good year can be kept 30 years and are not really ready until 10 years old. The best are a wonderful contrast of nectar and fruit. They can be luscious as Sauternes. The still wines are much more popular than the sparkling now. Past the villages, the roads become tracks, but lead to more caves and producers. The village Vouvray has a statue to a truly illustrious local hero — Balzac's fictional travelling salesman the 'Illustrious Gaudissant'. Balzac wanted to live here but couldn't afford a house. He was always broke.

On the south bank, along D751 towards Amboise, is another wine village, Montlouis. Here you can see the caves along the main road, cut in the cliffside, and many offer you tastings (dégustations) to lure you in to buy. The Producers' Co-operative has a modern tasting room outside its old caves.

Montlouis, like Vouvray, produces white wines and like Vouvray it is made only from the Pineau grape, called Chenin elsewhere. Montlouis wines were sold as Vouvray until 1938, but can be acidic when young and do not become so luscious with age.

A few metres off this road, 2km past Amboise but high above the road and looking straight to the river, is an enchanting little château called de Pray. It has been turned into a pleasant, family run hotel with charm, shady, quiet gardens and no pretentions. It is well worth visiting to see how the lesser-lights of the Loire high-society lived, without the pomp and ostentation of those in power. It was built in the 13th century and the two round towers with pointed roofs still survive from this feudal fortress, one with a bigger circumference than the other. They are joined by a 16th-century Renaissance house with a charming terrace and steps to lawns. Here you can taste some good regional old-style Loire dishes and local Touraine cheeses like Ste. Maure, a creamy goat's milk cheese, and Pithiviers cow's milk cheese from near Orléans.

Later Plessis was the scene of a meeting between Henry III and Henry of Navarre, later Henry IV, to arrange their successful alliance against Guise and his Holy Leaguers.

The N10 south from Tours is still a dreary and fairly crowded road, though the A10 motorway has taken much of its traffic, and Montbazon is an unexciting little town. But just before you reach it, at Gués de Veigné, is **Château de la Tortinière**, a Second-Empire turreted château on a hill in 40 hectares of woodland, meadows and flower beds and lawns running down to the Indre river. The owner has turned her home into a delightful hotel, far from traffic and people, yet handy for the sights of the Loire. The terrace with shrubs and lawns is a pretty, peaceful spot for an apéritif before dinner. There is a swimming pool and boating and fishing on the river.

It is not cheap, of course. Nor is **Château d'Artigny**, a magnificent hotel in a sumptuous château reached along D17 west from Montbazon. Built in 1912 for the perfume magnate René Coty in 18th-century style, its enormous rooms are most expensively furnished, its dining room circular, its cooking superb, its very smell opulent.

For a lovely country drive, take D17 over the river Indre, then stay on that side of D84 to Azay-le-Rideau. Or you could continue to the 16th-17th century château at **Saché**, then cross over. Here is a Balzac museum. Honoré de Balzac hid here, often for months at a time, evading his creditors and creating great works like *Le Lys dans la Vallée*,

Chateau at Azay-le-Rideau — a beautiful home posing as a fortress

set in this area. His room is furnished as it was in 1850. Alexander Calder (1898–1976), the American artist who invented *mobiles* (sculptures relying on moving parts) and *stabiles* (static sculptures), lived in Saché village. Some of his work is shown outdoors at le Carroi.

We have included **Azay-le-Rideau** with Tours rather than Chinon because almost everyone staying around the city visits its magnificent and beautiful castle — one of the six loveliest and most interesting in France.

The château was a beautiful home rather than a fortress. The turrets, moats and cobbled sentry walk are token defences, to show the importance of the owner. It is graceful Gothic, peeping through trees on the riverside beside a lake made by diverting the Indre. Like Chenonceau, that other beautiful house, its building in 1518–1529 was directed by a woman, Philippa Lesbahy, while her husband, the powerful financier Gilles Berthelot, was away making money. But she never lived in it.

A medieval fortress had stood on the site. In 1418 Joan of Arc's Dauphin, a frightened man but petulant and ruthless when he had power, said that he had been insulted by the château's Burgundian guard. He sacked the castle, burned it down and put 350 Burgundian prisoners to the sword. For long the town was called Azay-le-Brûlé — Azay-the-Burnt.

Philippa Lesbahy inherited the ruin about 100 years later. Her husband Gilles Berthelot was Treasurer-General of the Finances of France and Mayor of Tours. They built the new château. But all the powerful financiers were intermarried and Philippa was cousin to the de Semblançay family of whom the 82-year-old Jacques was King Francis I's treasurer. Francis ordered Jacques in 1522 to send a large sum of money to Marshal Lautrec in the Milanese. When he lost the Milanese, Lautrec said that he had not received the money, but Semblançay proved that he had sent it. They both accused the King's mother, Louise of Savoy, of embezzling it — which was almost certainly true. But the high-spending King took umbrage, At 82 Jacques de Semblançay, who had a reputation for integrity, was found guilty of corruption and sentenced to death. Gilles Berthelot took fright and fled to Italy. The king took this as a sign of guilt, his books were examined and he was pronounced guilty of corruption, too. The king took his property but seemed not to know what to do with Azay-le-Rideau. He gave it to the captain of his guard — a gift any old soldier would appreciate.

The château now houses an irrelevant but excellent Renaissance museum, with fine furniture and 17th-century tapestries, and has a splendid vaulted kitchen. Among the portraits is a glorious painting of Gabrielle d'Estrées, looking elegant and dignified in her beauty whilst showing the world one beautiful and completely bare breast. Why was it that so many Royal mistresses of France seemed so much more regal than her queens?

The summer Son et Lumière performance has a Renaissance theme.

Azay-le-Rideau has narrow streets and gets crowded in summer but has pleasant river views nearby. The old inn, the Grand Monarque, in the same family since 1900, is a true scene from old France, yielding nothing to the world of pre-portioning, plastic and micro-wave; faded, perhaps, but friendly, cosy and offering superb traditional cooking.

5
Amboise, Chenonceau, Montrichard

Amboise is the most charming and evocative of the big Loire cities. Despite the traffic build-up at some times of day to cross its important bridge, its narrow streets and old houses give it the atmosphere of a small old town, and the traffic jams which plagued it have been eased by liberal car parking and pedestrian precincts. It is wise to take to your feet as soon as possible in nearly all these Loire towns.

Most of the town is on the south bank of the Loire and you see it at its most attractive from the north bank or from the bridge. The big island in midstream is the Île d'Or where in AD 503 Clovis, King of the Franks, and Alaric, King of the Visigoths, feasted to swear eternal friendship as mentioned on p.11. The bridge rests on island rock, But it is the great castle perched on the opposite hill which dominates Amboise and the whole stretch of the Loire. Most of it was demolished after the Revolution, yet what remains is as impressive as other whole, undisturbed castles. And it evokes still the scenes of its history. The French Renaissance began here. One of the bloodiest dramas in French history was enacted in its gardens.

With its island and approaches, Amboise was destined to be important.

Crassus, one of Julius Caesar's commanders, set up camp here for his attack on Tours. Two medieval castles stood there, but not until Charles VII stole it from the counts of Amboise in 1434, and gave it to his wife Charlotte of Savoy as a residence, did it have much importance. Charles claimed that Louis of Amboise had conspired against him. It was possibly a spurious charge: to have an attractive castle or site was dangerous in those days.

Charles VIII, who was born there, started to rebuild it in 1492 after he married Anne of Brittany. Then he went off to conquer Italy. Powerful enemies were ranged against him — the Pope, the Emperor, Spain, Venice, Milan — and he lost the campaign. But he gained a passionate enthusiasm for Italian Renaissance architecture, furniture, textiles and works of art. He came back laden with booty and brought back the craftsmen and artists to teach the French.

He put his men to work on Amboise with enormous energy. Work went on by torchflame at night and fires in winter kept the stone warm enough to work. But Charles did not see it finished. Inspecting work at the château, he hit his head on a low lintel. He said that he was all right but then he collapsed and died at midnight. The

43

gossips were soon at work. There was no bruise or mark from the blow. A little earlier he had eaten an orange brought by one of his court — a Neapolitan. His heir and cousin, Louis, was very ambitious to be king, he was probably in love with Anne, and the rumour was around that Charles was going to have him arrested for plotting a rebellion.

Louis continued work on the château, but was more interested in Blois and it was Francis I who brought it to its true Renaissance glory. He was only six when brought here, where he grew up and was educated. He made it his court when he was crowned. He was an extraordinary man — almost uncouth in his love of hunting and ostentation, yet a true lover of the arts, and he made his court the centre of cultural life. He was, of course, a contemporary of Henry VIII of England. All they had in common, though, was their love of women and showmanship.

He kept lions, tigers, leopards and bears in a dry part of the moat, and sometimes one of the animals would sleep on his bed. Leopards were trained for hare-coursing in the nearby country, which must have surprised a few locals somewhat. He pitted a bear against a lion so that the Court could watch the nasty bloody spectacle. Then at a wedding feast he brought in a wild boar which stampeded the guests. He had to kill it with his own sword. He even had a wooden town built in the fields and had it bombarded, causing injuries and death. But it was he who in 1515 brought Leonardo da Vinci to

Amboise — view from the north bank of the Loire

Amboise and lodged him in the little 15th-century manor house, Château Clos-Lucé (then called Cloux), where he died in 1519.

Clos-Lucé is a charming place to visit. Charles VIII gave it to Anne of Brittany as her hideaway and you can see the private chapel he built for her. There are some delightful rare furnishings in the house.

Leonardo was over 60 and had given up painting because of an arthritic right hand when he arrived at Amboise. A sketch he made of Amboise from his bedroom window is in the Royal collection at Windsor. And he did design costumes for Francis' splendrous fêtes and continued his engineering and scientific schemes. One was a plan to drain the Sologne by building a canal to drain into the Loire. He did of course anticipate many later discoveries, making designs for a submarine, swing bridge, air conditioning plant, parachute, armoured car and helicopter. None was built, but you can see models from his designs in the basement at Clos-Lucé. Alas, none of his pictures is here.

Leonardo brought some of his masterpieces with him, including 'Virgin of the Rocks' and 'Mona Lisa', which is surprising considering he travelled over the Alps on the back of a mule. Francis bought them after his death.

In less than fifty years Amboise château disappeared into obscurity. The cause was that appalling blood bath by the Duke of Guise in 1560, as mentioned on p.14. The corpses of the tortured, broken Protestants, strung from the castle walls, the trees on the terraces and every balcony of the King's lodgings, stank so appallingly that the court left and no one wanted to

The Chapel of St. Hubert at Amboise is a fine example of Flamboyant Gothic architecture

live in the château for a long time. It became a prison. In 1816 it was given to the Duchess of Orléans and it passed to Louis-Philippe, the 'citizen king' friend of Queen Victoria, who did it up and stayed there sometimes. You can see his bedroom, with portraits of the Orléans family by Winterhalter. It was a sad end to such a magnificent building.

You enter the fragment of the castle which survives up a ramp on to a terrace overlooking the river, with superb views of the river valley and the old pointed roofs of the town. In Charles' day this terrace was a courtyard surrounded by buildings, and used for festivals. The main part of the château which escaped demolition is Logis du Roi (the King's apartments), its façade lavishly decorated with pinnacles and dormers. Charles' Gothic wing overlooks the river. The Renaissance wing was built by Louis, but Francis added two storeys in full Renaissance style.

A large room in the Gothic wing with pointed arch vaultings supported by columns was Salle des États (Hall of States). This was where the Protestant plotters were sentenced to death. And it was a prison for the Algerian leader Emir Abd-el-Kader from 1842 to 1852. Elected to resist the French annexation of his country, he fought for twelve years before losing. He became a lover of French culture and supported local charities when a prisoner and, by releasing him, the newly crowned Emperor Napoleon III made a good friend for France. He went to live in Damascus and, in 1860, when Christians in Syria were being massacred, he saved thousands.

Charles' Tour de Minimes has a broad spiral ramp for horsemen and for horse-drawn carts and sledges to bring supplies straight off the river boats. The river was the main highway until well into the 19th century, the most useful and comfortable way to travel. Roads were awful, coaches sprung only with leather straps and horses pulling carts could manage only about 5 to 8 kilometres a day.

But the jewel of Amboise is now the delightful Flamboyant Gothic St. Hubert's chapel, which bestrides the wall of the castle, projecting over the ramparts supported by a buttress. It was finished in 1493 and has almost-miraculously survived nearly 500 years of dangers in this precarious position, even a 1940 shell exploding on a main cross-beam and the 1944 bombardment. It is named after the patron saint of hunting who was converted by a miracle. A fun-loving Frank nobleman, he was hunting one day in the forest of the Ardennes when a stag turned at bay to reveal a cross shining between its antlers. Furthermore, it warned Hubert that unless he mended his ways he would soon go to hell. Hubert was so impressed that he got down on his knees and swore to devote his life to Christian service. He entered the deep forests of Flanders and converted the pagan people, and was rewarded by being made Bishop of Liège.

You can see the legend in stone on the right of the lintel over the chapel door. On the left is St. Christopher carrying the infant Jesus, who unfortunately received some head injuries from a wartime shell. Above the lintel on the tympanum is a more modern carving of the Virgin with figures of Charles VIII and Anne of Brittany.

Charles built the chapel for Anne. Though it is only small, it was heated by corner fireplaces. Royal worshippers obviously rated more comfort than peasants in draughty cathedrals. A flagstone in the floor claims to cover the bones of Leonardo da Vinci but this is doubtful. The Flamboyant lacelike carvings of the frieze are sheer delight.

The Son et Lumière at Amboise castle depicts Francis I's merrymaking, not the Guise's blood bath.

On the quai at Amboise, just past an odd fountain given to the town by the sculptor Max Ernst, is the Romanesque basilica of St. Denis (12th–16th century). A bay of the nave has capitals with strange people with animal heads. For a marble sculpture of a drowned woman the model was 'La belle Babou' herself, the mistress of Francis I who was so generous with her charms to the high and mighty.

Pagode de Chanteloup

An avenue right off D31, the Chenonceaux roud south of Amboise, leads to the strange Pagode de Chanteloup, a folly with balconies at every second level giving wonderful views of Amboise, a pond below and the forest around. It was commissioned in 1775 by the Duke de Choiseul from his architect Louise le Camus. The Duke wanted a copy of the pagoda built at Kew Gardens in 1762, but something much bigger — 38m high, with six storeys. Each circular room diminishes in size as you climb the inner stair-case, and the classical colonnade and four wrought-iron balconies do not evoke Eastern mysteries.

It was built as a gesture of gratitude for the kindness of his friends who had risked royal wrath to visit him in his exile.

Choiseul was the trusted Minister of Louis XV — counterpart to England's Pitt. He had been given the job through the influence of Madame de Pompadour. He extricated France somewhat from the mess she was in after losing her American Empire in the Seven Years' War by concluding with Britain in 1763 the Treaty of Paris, modernised the French forces, planning for a revenge war against England, and arranged the marriage of Marie-Antoinette to the Dauphin to seal an alliance with the Habsburg Empire.

He fell foul of Pompadour's successor as offical mistress to the King, du Barry, and it was believed that she got rid of him and had him rusticated to the Loire. In fact, he fell because he wanted to declare war on England over the Falkland Islands when the French royal finances were bankrupt. Louis had had enough of wars.

In 1761 he bought the Domaine of Chanteloup, with a massive château. In the Loire he set out to make *his* court far more attractive than hers at Versailles. The wits, the cultured people, even the fashionable, suddenly preferred country air on the Loire. He spent his fortune rebuilding the château, on lavish entertainment and expensive hunts in the forest. And he started experiments in farming, so that Arthur Young, the English agricul-turalist who saw it in 1787 after the Duke's death, though disapproving of the emphasis on hunting, wrote of a 'noble cowhouse and the best sheep-house in France'.

One of Napoléon's ministers gained the property, an industrial chemist named Jean-Antoine Chaptal. He had helped Napoléon out of his diffi-culties, caused by the English blockage of the West Indies, by inventing the process at Chanteloup of extracting sugar from beet. Alas, he also intro-duced chaptalisation, the process of adding sugar to wine-must before fermentation to strengthen it. An asset stripper (or perhaps a wine-lover?) pulled the château down last century.

The little roads of Amboise forest southwards bring rewards to wander-ers. Take D81 to the Cher river, turn left at Civray-de-Touraine and you find what we believe to be the most beauti-ful house in the world. The Château of **Chenonceau** was made by three women. Catherine Briçonnet, wife of

the financier Thomas Bohier, designed it, and it was a revolutionary design for comfort and convenience. Then the attractive, intelligent mistress of Henry II, Diane de Poitiers, added a gorgeous formal garden and hired Philibert

Chanteloup Pagoda — the Duke of Choiseul's attractive folly

49

Delorme, one of the architects of Fontainebleau, to build a bridge across the Cher river 60m long. Henry paid for the work by a tax on church bells! When he was killed in the jousting lists by Montgomery, the commander of his Scottish guard, his widow Catherine de Médicis kicked out Diane and took over. It was she who really made Chenonceau as we see it today. She had a superb park laid out, built two storeys on the bridge which had been intended really as a new entrance to the château, and added buildings beyond. The lower floor of this enclosed bridge is one long beautiful gallery.

Catherine held most spectacular parties here. Girls disguised as mermaids welcomed visitors from the moats along the great avenue leading to the castle, singing nymphs ran from thickets, then satyrs rushed out to disperse them. They in turn were driven off by mounted knights. Banquets, dances, masquerades and fireworks followed. Once there was a naval battle of scaled-down ships on the Cher river.

The greatest saturnalian party was held by Catherine for her gay son, Henry III. One writer suggested that she did it to lure him into ensuring the succession of the Valois dynasty.

Henry, it seems, took his place dressed as was usual, looking more like a woman than a man, his lips and cheeks painted, pearls in his ears, a pearl necklace round his throat. Below sat his friends — his mignons — all painted, hair curled, and wearing little velvet caps fashionable with women. The ladies of the court — Duchesses and Countesses, half naked, served the male courtiers at table and after. Maïtrices de l'Hôtel, they were

called, and most were mistresses of at least one of the men at Court. That was the fashion. One of the maïtrices was Madame de Sauve, later Marquise de Noirmoutier. She showed her religious tolerance by dividing her favours equally between Catholic and Protestant gentlemen including the King of Navarre and the Duke of Guise, who spent his last night in her bed.

One wonders what Henry's devout wife, Louise of Lorraine, made of it all. She was strangely devoted to him. Catherine left Chenonceau to her and there she heard of Henry's death, stabbed by a fanatical monk. She spent years there in the white clothes of royal mourning, praying for his soul. His rooms, his bed, his chairs and praying stool were all covered in black velvet. Her own room was painted black and decorated with white tears. In the village they used to say that her ghost was seen at the windows on moonlit nights, fingering her rosary — 'la bonne reine blanche'.

The car park packed in summer with coaches and cars from all over Europe, the snack bar, the stall selling 'Chenonceau Château' wine and souvenirs, the restaurant in the old stables, the streams of tourists hurrying back and forth up and down the drive with cameras at the ready, as if they have but an hour to see it all before it is demolished, make it difficult to appreciate Chenonceau's atmosphere and beauty. Try to go in spring or autumn, when you can dally in peace along the long approach drive shaded with plane trees and flanked by canals, in the gardens, and beside the river in which Diane de Poitiers delighted in taking her morning bathe.

You cross two bridges, with the stables called Bâtiment des Dômes, across lawns to the right. Then you see the château itself, small, graceful, white with Italian Renaissance symmetry, flanked by pretty corbelled pointed towers and richly ornamented balustrades and roof lights. Diane's five-arched bridge over the Cher, 60m long, enclosed in Catherine's two-storey gallery, is quite delightful. Strange that these two women who hated each other should have had the same passion for this château. When Henry II died, Catherine took away from Diane the jewels he had given her and Chenonceau, giving her in return the château of Chaumont — quite a gesture for those days. But Diane hated it and soon abandoned it for the friendlier château of Anet.

Diane's garden is to the left of the château as you face it, Catherine's to the right.

The château was built on piles in the river which once supported a mill. Catherine Briçonnet's design was really the beginning of the modern house. Gone were the draughty outside spiral staircases, the draughty passages which joined strings of rooms and ante-rooms. She had one central vestibule room, with all the others opening off it, on each floor, and a central straight-up staircase, all arranged for easy service and comfort. It was finished in 1521. Three years later her husband Thomas Bohier died in Milan. Two years after that she died.

Francis I never trusted his treasurers and financiers. After Bohier's death his finances were investigated and it was found that he had financed Chenonceau by 'borrowing' vast sums from the royal treasury. His son Antoine was stripped of everything to repay the debt, including Chenonceau. Francis had added another château to his collection.

The guardroom where you enter was paved with four-coloured majolica tiles now almost destroyed. It is hung with lovely 16th-century tapestries. The chapel alongside with two bays and a five-sided choir has a 16th-century bas-relief of Madonna and Child and two centuries of graffiti on the walls. The scribblings dated 1543 and 1546 were left behind by the Scottish Guard serving Mary Stuart. The stained-glass is modern — the old was destroyed in a 1944 bombardment. The bedroom of Diane de Poitiers is sparsely furnished, though it has a fine 16th-century fireplace by Jean Goujon and Flemish wall tapestries depicting the triumphs of charity and authority. Some cynic has put a 1901 painting by Henri Sauvage of Catherine de Médicis on the mantlepiece. Neighbouring rooms are the Cabinet Vert, with beamed ceiling, fine furnishings and paintings, and Catherine's tiny library. The room of Francis I has a magnificent fireplace, fine Italian furnishings and two notable paintings: Diane de Poitiers as the Huntress Diane (almost certainly by Primaticcio) and The Three Graces by Van Loo — in truth, the three sisters Mailly-Nesle, two countesses and a duchess, all three nude, all three mistresses of Louis XV. It seems that he liked to go from sister to sister. He took two of them with him on his Flanders campaign in 1744 but the Flemings were so scandalised that he had to send them home. As they left, it is said, the people of Menz emptied chamberpots on to their carriage.

In Louis XIII's chamber (or Grand Salon) is a portrait of Louis XIV by Hyacinthe Rigaud (a present from Louis after a visit) and a dramatic painting of Christ and St. John attributed to Rubens. There's a picture, too, of a

Leonardo da Vinci's bedroom at Clos-Lucé, his house in Amboise

beautiful young lady with big brown eyes who was mistress of this house in the 18th century — Madame Dupin.

By the entrance to the long gallery across the Cher are steps to the kitchens. We should like to have eaten a meal cooked here in the time of Catherine. When she came from Italy she found French food far too primitive and brought to France Florentine chefs such as Buontalenti (who indeed seems to have had great talent), with new recipes and new ingredients such as haricot beans and petits pois which we regard as typically French. Catherine's fruit ices were very popular — frozen with ice stored in the ground, fast-flowing cold water and much difficulty.

The upstairs rooms have been recreated in 16th-century style, with exquisite Gobelin tapestries, and in the vestibule are Oudenarde tapestries of hunting scenes and sculptures of Roman emperors in Carrara marble brought by Catherine from Florence.

The room of Gabrielle d'Estrées has been completely restored. Gabrielle came here with Henry IV to see Louise of Lorraine, the widow of Henry III. Henry had a political aim. Her brother, the Duke of Mercoeur, was the last leader of the Holy League, Henry's extreme-Catholic enemies, and he wanted the Duke's submission. A deal was made under which César de Vendôme, son of Henry IV and Gabrielle, should marry the Duke's daughter, Françoise de Vendôme. He

Chenonceau, 'the most beautiful house in the world', still has its lovely gardens

did, and as a result inherited Chenonceau in 1624 — a nice wedding present. His room here is attractive, but he preferred his other estate at Anet. The attics above once housed a small convent of Capuchin nuns who had a drawbridge to pull up at night to discourage visitors.

Catherine's Long Gallery is still the great delight of the château. Its black and white chequered floor is almost dazzling but the views of the quietly flowing Cher from the alcove windows bring thoughts of all the great, the good, the wicked, the sad people through history who have watched the

53

river gliding beneath them. What were *their* thoughts? It is far more evocative than the authentically costumed but inevitably inert figures which you can see in the waxworks museum in the Dômes.

In the 1914–1918 war this gallery was lined with wounded. It was a hospital. In the Second World War, figures passed stealthily down it to disappear across the Cher. The river was the very boundary of Occupied France and Vichy France, and the gallery a passage of escape for those the Nazis were seeking.

One who lingered at the gallery windows was the writer Jean-Jacques Rousseau. After the Court moved away from the Loire in the reign of Henry IV, Chenonceau gradually became semi-abandoned until sold in 1733 by the Duke of Bourbon to one Dupin, Farmer-General of Taxes. Like all tax-collectors of those centuries, he had acquired much wealth. His second wife (the girl in the château portrait) was beautiful, intelligent and charming. She invited Rousseau to become her

secretary and tutor to the children of Dupin's first marriage. He loved it there. He wrote of fine food ('I became fat as a monk'), of much music, of composing pieces for three voices, and of writing a three act play called 'The Dangerous Engagement' which was acted by the family.

Madame Dupin lived here until she was 93. She was very popular with the local people and because of this Chenonceau was protected from harm in the Revolution. George Sand, the writer, was a member of the same Dupin family (Aurore Dupin).

Chenonceau has been very lucky with its owners. Madame Pelouze, who bought it in 1864, knew much about Renaissance architecture and returned the château as nearly as possible to its Bohier design. The Menier chocolate family bought it in 1909 and have spent a fortune keeping it up. And it still looks so deliciously white, cheerful and beautiful.

The old village, which has an 'x' on the end (Chenonceaux), is now mostly for tourists — little hotels, restaurants,

'Brantôme'

Pierre de Bourdeilles, abbot, wit, envoy of Henry II, Chamberlain to Charles IX and Henry III, appointed himself a sort of court-reporter under the pseudonym of 'Brantôme', telling witty and sometimes scurrilous stories of the court scandals, intrigues and junketings.

One story truly shows the jealousy between Catherine de Médicis and Diane de Poitiers (not named but clearly recognised).

The queen had the idea of cutting a hole in her rival's bedroom ceiling, spying on her one balmy night that was tempting for love-making. To her dismay, she saw what she admitted to be 'a beautiful, white-skinned woman, delicate and fresh, half-naked, caressing her lover, and the lover returning her caresses, until they left the bed and disported themselves on the rug'.

The lover was, of course, Catherine's husband, the King.

snack bars. The old Relais du Bon Laboureur is hardly for labourers these days. It is fairly expensive but keeps a good reputation for food.

After Chenonceau, other sites of the Cher valley are something of an anticlimax. There are attractive drives and walks through the minor roads and pathways of the Amboise forest and the riverside town of **Montrichard** has fine old, half-timbered houses of the 15th–16th centuries, clustered around the Romanesque church of Ste. Croix. Here little 12-year-old crippled Jeanne de France, daughter of Louis XI, was married to the future Louis XII, to be so cruelly cast aside later. They loved the gentle Jeanne in Montrichard.

The old fort, the donjon, is crumbling, but you can still get in to climb it in summer for the views, though only four people can stand on its top platform at a time. It was built by the formidable Foulques Nerra (the 'Black' Count of Anjou) during his endless arguments with the Counts of Blois, and strengthened by Philippe-Auguste, enemy of the Plantagenets, who actually managed to drive Richard Coeur-de-Lion out of it in 1188 by courtesy of his famous sappers — 'Taupes du Roy' (the King's Moles). They dug a secret tunnel under one corner tower, removed the stones, replaced them with wooden props, and set light to them. The props burned through, the tower collapsed, the French poured through the breach, and the road opposite is still called rue de la Brèche. The Germans fired guns from the tower in 1940 at the French across the river, who could have used Philippe-Auguste's moles.

Louis XI bought the fort to stay in safety while he went to worship the miraculous painting of the Madonna in the church in neighbouring Nanteuil, now a Montrichard suburb. This church was built in the 12th century by Benedictines near a miraculous spring.

In the Middle Ages there lived in the swamps near this spring a monster who fed on cattle or children who went too close to the wilderness of marsh and reeds. No one would enter the marshes until a brave young monk took the long linen veil from the Virgin in the church, walked into the swamp, and led the monster back, using the veil as a lead! The monster was a huge crocodile and at the holy spring it died in convulsions. That sort of thing happened a lot in the Middle Ages.

Pilgrims came to the church to pray — for courage. Louis XI certainly needed it. He had such a fear of being killed by his enemies that he shut himself finally in the château at Plessis-lès-Tours (see p.38). Philippe-Auguste prayed here, too, for courage in battle.

The square keep of Montrichard looks down over the Cher where there is a place for river-bathing

It seems that he tended to ride away from the most dangerous action, which is surprising, for he fought Richard the Lion Heart and few cowards would tackle such a doughty enemy. Mind you, he was probably just ahead of his time. In more modern times, not many kings or commanders-in-chief have been seen firing in the front-line and a discreet choice of when to retire is now called a 'tactical withdrawal'.

Southwards, find D81 at Céré-la-Ronde and drive on to D11 for an attractive route to **Montrésor**. A gem of a village sloping up in an amphitheatre from the tiny Indrois river and surrounded by country sprinkled with woods. It has an ivy-covered castle, a Renaissance collegiate church, and a 12th-century covered market.

The peaceful early 16th-century château, with mullioned windows and great dormers, is set in a lovely garden walled by the inner girdle of medieval fortifications of a ruined castle which belonged to Henry I and Henry II of England. One wing has wonderful views over the countryside. The furnishings are original, from Renaissance to Second Empire, with French, Italian and Polish paintings. The 16th-century church is Gothic with Renaissance decoration, paintings and lovely windows.

Nouans-les-Fontaines (8km east) is reached along the Indrois valley lined with alders, willows and poplars, with orchards on the slopes. Its 13th-century church contains the primitive 1st-century masterpiece by Jean Fouquet, 'The Deposition', a huge painting on wood, in subdued colours.

A lovely run back through Montrésor, and on past Genillé through the Loches Forest, a Plantagenet hunting ground, takes you to

Loches itself. A charming town on the banks of the Indre with a fine medieval city within; it refuses to be hurried even by masses of tourists. It is one of the most striking and interesting places in France, and you must walk around it, for its narrow lanes make driving almost impossible.

Richard the Lion Heart lived in the château of Loches. While he was a prisoner in Austria on his way back from a crusade, his brother John gave it to the king of France, Philippe-Auguste. On his return Richard was so angry that he stormed it and took it in three hours. When he died, it took Philippe a year's siege to get the English out.

Later it became a sinister place. In the Tour Ronde and Martelet of the château Louis XI kept his little iron cages for those who had upset him. Cardinal La Balue, suspected of negotiating with the enemy in a war with the Burgundians, spent eleven years in one, able neither to stand nor lie down. Ironically, he had been an enthusiast for their use on others. Ludovico Sforza, Duke of Milan, captured by Louis XII, spent eight years in an underground cell. The former patron of Leonardo da Vinci covered his walls with paintings; on release, he died, some say, of sudden sunlight. And two bishops in a dungeon lit by a solitary ray of sunlight hollowed an altar out of the wall.

See these sinister towers first, then the happier scene of the recumbent figure of the beautiful Agnes Sorel, mistress of Charles VII and model for Fouquet's 'Madonna and Child', now in Antwerp. She was called 'Dame de Beauté', a pun on her home town of Beauté-en-Marne. Even Pope Pius II said that she had 'the most beautiful face one could see', but the Dauphin,

Catherine de Medici's gallery at Château de Chenonceau

the future Louis XI, hated her and at Chinon slapped her face publicly, so she moved to Loches to keep out of his way. She died at 28, possibly poisoned, and left her wealth to the convent of St. Ours where she was buried. The canons did not want this 'immoral woman's' tomb, but did want her money. Not until Louis XVI's reign were they able to get it moved to the Lodge at Loches château.

In the great hall Joan of Arc persuaded Charles VII to go to Reims to be crowned, and in the anteroom is a copy of the record of Joan's trial. You can walk round the ramparts (1km).

In Loches' place de la Marne is a statue of Alfred de Vigny, the sensitive novelist, poet and philosopher born here in 1797. He is remembered best for an historical novel featuring the Loire valley, *Cinq-Mars*, rather similar to the stories of Sir Walter Scott. He also translated some Shakespeare plays into French. Loches is a pleasant place for a short holiday break.

6
Amboise to Blois

Although the A10 motorway has taken much of the heavier traffic between Tours, Blois and Orléans, the N152 north of the Loire from Amboise to Blois is still busy in summer. It is an attractive route as far as Chouzy-sur-Cissé, with the Loire to your right and to the left wine villages such as **Mesland**, where the church has a remarkable portal of around 1060 and 16th-century sculptures. It is believed locally that a Gallic temple stood on the spot. The twenty-six heads (barbus) have war-helmets and very protruding eyes. The Gauls used to chop off the heads of their enemies after a battle and keep them pickled, believing that in future fights they could call on their strength and courage. They worshipped a horned god called Cernumnus whom the Romans called Hermes.

Later people of Mesland were regarded as sorcerers by their neighbours because they could divert storms to other villages. When a storm was coming, the most attractive women of the village would run in their nightclothes to the church and pull away at the bells, telling the storm to go away and burst over Seillac and drown Onzain. No wonder Onzain folk objected!

Onzain is a pleasant place with good shops, wine caves and a superb old turreted hunting lodge, Domaine des Hauts de Loire, in a park with a lake. It is now a delightful but expensive hotel.

At Escures on the N152, where the Loire reveals a big sandbank when waters are low, cross the bridge to **Chaumont**, a small town along one street on the river bank, with its château on a hill which is hard work to climb.

It is a formidable pile, built for defence by the Counts of Anjou, over a period of 50 years, and finished in 1511. Partly because of its strength, later because of a quite different usefulness, it escaped wars and demolitions. And now it is known for its luxurious stables.

The first castle was begun in 980 by Odo, Count of Blois, who fortified his wife's cowsheds for defence against the warring Foulques Nerra of Anjou. Pierre d'Amboise, who owned Chaumont in the 15th century, was made to pull down a second castle by Louis XI after he had joined rebellious barons, but was forgiven and allowed to start the present building in 1465. It was completed by his son and by his grandson, Charles II of Amboise, who found such favour with Louis XII that he became Marshal of France, admiral, lieutenant-general in Italy and royal steward. He was helped, no doubt, by his uncle, Cardinal Georges d'Amboise, who was Louis XII's minister.

When she became a widow, Catherine de Médicis bought the castle to exchange with Diane de Poitiers. Not surprisingly, she coveted Diane's château at Chenonceau. A room at Chaumont connected by a staircase to the tower started a story that this was the study of the Queen's Astrologer, Ruggieri, and the tower was where he and Catherine consulted the stars. She is said to have read here in a mirror the future fate of her three sons, Francis II, Charles IX and Henry III, all of whom met violent deaths.

What is certain is that Diane found Chaumont far too gloomy, in spite of the lovely river and woodland views, and soon retired to her old home at Château d'Anet near Dreux.

Madame de Staël, the volatile and brilliant writer, thought the château dreary, too, when her half-printed book *De l'Allemagne* was seized and destroyed by Napoléon's police and she was banished from Paris to Chaumont. But she was strictly a Parisienne who loved the social scene and the limelight, and she probably thought little of Mickleham in Surrey when she was a refugee there with Talleyrand and other French emigrés in 1972.

She was welcomed to Chaumont by the owner Le Ray, Governor of Les Invalides, who had turned part of the castle into a successful business for producing medallions of famous people of the time, hiring a well-known Italian artist, engraver and potter, Nini, to produce them. Maybe it was saved in the Revolution because it was a factory rather than the luxury home of an aristocrat.

Oddly its moment of luxury and glory came from 1875 onwards. A very rich sugar refiner named Say was passing with his obviously spoiled 16-year-old daughter Marie who decided that she wanted it. So he bought it for her. She married a Prince, Amadée de Broglie, who had just as extravagant tastes as she had. They bought superb majolica Sicilian tiles, from a palace at Salerno, showing hunting scenes to grace the grande salle, which had been Catherine's council room, completely modernised the building with electric heating, lighting and piped water, and bought two hamlets and knocked them down to improve the view and extend the park. They did not like the village church either, so they knocked it down and built a new one. They took electricity to the village down the hill and it was one of the first in France to have street lamps and later a cinema.

It is said that Marie's afternoon snack was of foie gras with fresh-baked rolls. To entertain their guests they made such extravagant gestures as chartering a train to bring the whole of the cast of the Comédie Française or even the Paris Opera to Chaumont for the weekend. It must have been great fun to be a guest there. One maharaja was so delighted that he gave Marie an elephant, which she adored.

They were particularly addicted to horses, and the Prince built magnificent stables, including one for the elephant. There were Lilliputian stables for the children's ponies and stables lined with velvet for the family mounts — like plush hotels for horses. The stables include a former dovecote used by Nini as an oven. Here Benjamin Franklin sat for his portrait medallion. The stables still contain expensive harnesses and whips and English prints.

The sugarbeet factory which supplied the money for all this luxury went bankrupt and the manager shot himself. Failing to take the warning, the Prince went on spending, went bankrupt and sold his horses in 1917. Chaumont has been owned by the state since 1938.

With its three surviving wings, the château opens out towards the river. The fourth wing was knocked down in the 18th century because it blocked the valley view. You reach the courtyard over a drawbridge between two close-set towers. The white walls are ornamented with a shell-shaped recess containing a figure of Madonna and Child against a background on which the arms of France are surrounded by the initials of Louis XII and Anne of Brittany, fleurs-de-lys and ermines. A frieze winding round the towers and along the wall has entwined 'Cs' of Charles de Chaumont and wife Catherine, and an emblem of a flaming mountain ('chaud mont'). Along the base of the watchpath are the initials of Diane de Poitiers. The façade of the oldest part of the château, the west building, is flanked by the fine staircase. The gallery was added in the 19th century.

The chapel at the end of one wing, dating from the 15th–17th centuries, has 19th-century windows showing the early days of Chaumont.

Inside, the château is not entirely furnished. It has some excellent Renaissance furniture and tapestries, but many of the rooms are much smaller than in Catherine's day. The big ones were broken up by the Prince de Broglie.

The Broglie family were not all extravagant playboys. The first, born in 1671, was a Marshal of France and a distinguished war commander. His son was French commander in the Seven Years' War and became a Russian commander after the Revolution. His son was guillotined during the Revolution, but his grandson, a Liberal politician and advocate of the abolition of slavery, was foreign secretary (1832–1834), prime minister (1835–1836) under King Louis-Philippe and a writer. And his eldest son was a writer, Academician, Ambassador to London (1871–1872) and twice prime minister. His grandson, born in 1875, won distinction for researches into X-ray and his young brother Louis Victor de Broglie won the Nobel Prize for pioneer work on the undulatory theory of matter.

The road to Blois back across the river is attractive as far as Chouzy, and after that you skirt the forest of Blois. But the advantage of taking the left bank road is that you are rewarded with a superb view of Blois as you approach and you see at its best the long 18th-century bridge with a small hump in the middle topped by a cross. Built by Jacques Gabriel in 1724, it is one of the most elegant bridges in France.

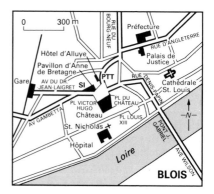

Blois (pop. 49,422) is a magic city. Here in one big château which still totally dominates the city is the story of a series of extraordinary Frenchmen. It is absolutely necessary to spend at least two days exploring Blois to begin to appreciate and enjoy it. It was terribly bombarded in 1940 and set on fire, but the reconstruction was most carefully and lovingly carried out and the bustling centre of the city is a higgledy-piggledy medieval assault course of ramps, twisting streets, alleys and flights of steps.

The old town through the centuries has been an agricultural market. It still is, for wine, wheat, strawberries, vegetables and bulbs. Chocolate is made here and pâtisserie is an art, with superb gâteaux created like edible sculptures. You can see them in the main street of the old town, rue Denis-Papin, which runs from the square by the bridge right up to the square by the castle. Just before it swings left you reach Denis-Papin steps. From the top is a fine view to the south. Strange that this man Papin, so honoured now in Blois, left it swearing that he would never return. Born nearby in 1647, he was a Protestant who had to flee the persecutions after the Edict of Nantes, giving religious tolerance, was revoked. A doctor of medicine and an engineer, he was an inventor who realised, like Watt 100 years later, the power of steam. In England, where he worked with Boyle, he invented the marmite de Papin, the first pressure cooker. In Germany he invented a steamboat which he tried on the river Weser. Local fishermen broke it up because they feared for their livelihood.

Wandering the streets and alleys of the old town, you can see timbered houses and old mansions where you will find treasures by peeping into their courtyards, like the superb staircase at the 17th-century Hôtel de la Chancellerie and the Renaissance sculptures and Italian Renaissance galleries of the courtyard of Hôtel d'Alluye, a mansion built in 1508 for Florimond Robertet, treasurer to three kings — Charles VIII, Louis XII and Francis I.

From the top of Denis-Papin steps, take the eastward road (rue du Palais) to place St. Louis. On the corner is a half-timbered medieval house called Maison des Acrobats. Its posts are carved with acrobats and jugglers. In the same square at the top of rue Pierre-de-Blois is a lovely Gothic house with a timber footbridge spanning the road. It is Hôtel de Villebresme or Denis-Papin House.

Cathedral St. Louis dominates the square. Built in the 16th century, it was almost totally destroyed by a hurricane in 1678. All that was left was its tower, rising above a Romanesque ground floor. Slender columns divide its upper storeys. It is crowned by a double lantern. In the old church Louis XIV's minister, Colbert, had been married to one of the Charron family, and after the hurricane he persuaded the King to hand over quickly the money for rebuilding. The original church on the site was dedicated to St. Soulaine, a Frankish priest, friend of Clovis, who was buried here. His name was associated with *se soûler* (to get drunk) and alcoholics came to his tomb to be cured!

The next road down towards the river from the cathedral is rue du Puits-Châtel where a peep through doors to courtyards will reveal Renaissance galleries, balconies and staircases.

Much lovelier than the cathedral is the church of St. Nicolas, with three spires. Originally a Benedictine abbey church, it is across the road from the river end of the château. It was all built in the 12th century, apart from a 14th-century chapel in the apse and the 17th-century lantern tower. The superb three-storied early Gothic nave was inspired by Chartres cathedral. Behind the altar is a row of attractive narrow arches on Corinthian columns. The abbey itself survives as part of the city hospital facing the river quay.

Westward from the church is the big Poulain chocolate factory, employing 1,000 people, which you can visit on weekday mornings. Auguste Poulain opened it in 1848, and he made a brave last effort to keep the Loire as a trade highway after the railways were built. He had designed a special flat-bottomed, shallow draught steam tug called 'Fram' which pulled a barge carrying cocoa and sugar from Nantes to his factory. But the railways took over after ten years.

The size of the château and its muddle of 13th- to 17th-century styles can bewilder and over-awe. Amid all its ornate embellishments, its portals and carvings, most tourists find the splendid staircase tower the most impressive.

There's no record of the first castle of the Counts of Blois here but Thibault the Trickster is believed to have built it. The Châtillon family, who took over built a medieval fortress from which the Tour du Foix remains. The last of this family line, Guy de Châtillon, old married to a young wife and heavily in debt, sold it to Louis d'Orléans, brother of King Charles VI, in 1397 in a manner worthy of an historic Whitehall farce. First Louis seduced the wife of the old

duke, then he talked her into getting the money to buy it from her old husband, sending him bankrupt in the process. That was just the main plot. Louis had married his cousin, Valentine Visconti of Milan. One of his mistresses was his sister-in-law the Queen — Isabelle of Bavaria. As the Marquis of Sade said correctly: 'He had his cousin for a wife and his sister-in-law for a mistress.' But his wife Valentine was one of his brother the king's mistresses. Definitely a family affair. When Isabelle was trying to insist that her son the Dauphin Charles was a bastard, she named Louis as his father.

When Charles the king lost his reason, Louis' fight to be Regent ended with his murder in Paris. Despite their infidelities Isabelle was so deeply upset that she shut herself up in the Château de Blois for the rest of her life in a room draped in black.

Her son Charles d'Orléans was a literary man and poet, forced into battle against the English and Burgundians and captured at Agincourt. He was imprisoned in the Tower of London and spent 25 years there playing the lute, reading and writing poetry. He was not harshly treated and seems to have quite enjoyed his captivity. His miserable family made no great effort to pay his ransom.

Finally released in 1440, he wanted nothing to do with politics. A widower of 50, he married a 14-year-old girl, knocked down much of his Blois fortress and built something more comfortable to live in. Little remains of the original but a pleasant gallery. Charles held court for writers and artists including the vagabond poet François Villon and good King René of Anjou, another who preferred culture to power and politics.

The magnificent Francis I staircase at Château de Blois was used as viewing balconies for jousts and receptions

When he was 71 his 35-year-old wife had a baby son and Charles did not mind the bawdy jokes, but gave him the royal name of Louis. He became Louis XII and very much a politician. Once he had got rid of poor Jeanne de France and married Anne of Brittany, he extended and improved the Blois château where he was born and moved his court there. It became more of a capital than Paris was.

In 1514 Claude, his daughter by Jeanne, married his cousin Francis whom Louis made Count of Blois and his heir. Anne had died, Louis married Mary of York, sister of England's Henry VIII, a young, lively girl who wore him

out with balls, junketings and late nights so that he soon died and Francis became king.

Poor Claude bore Francis seven children in nine years. She was as frail and timid as her mother, and it seems that she spent her time among her ladies-in-waiting, reading and working tapestries. One of the ladies-in-waiting was a girl who came from Blickling in Norfolk and whose father had been English Ambassador in France. Her name was Anne Bullen. She came back from France calling herself Anne Boleyn and with the polish of the French court. Henry VIII took a quick liking to her, poor girl.

Francis built the most spectacular and sumptuous wing of the château, as one would expect of this great showman. Its rich, unusual decoration, its monumental fireplaces and its wonderful staircases are quite stunning and worth a great deal of any visitor's time. This is where you climb the magnificent Francis staircase. It is in an octagonal cage, with three sides recessed into the building, the other five looking into the courtyard through openwork between pillars.

When Francis started to build Chambord, his interest in Blois waned a little. After all, Chambord was in the heart of hunting country and hunting and women were his passions.

Henry II succeeded to the throne and this brought Catherine de Médicis to Blois. Her room is interesting and impressive. It has 237 panels, four disguising doors to cupboards, opened by pressing a secret pedal in the skirting board. Being Italian and the daughter of a merchant she was despised by the snobbish French court, and the cupboards were said later to be her 'poison' cupboards. But more likely they concealed secret papers, jewels or even her beauty preparations, a fashion she brought into France from Italy. In his book, *Catherine de Médicis*, Balzac had her hiding secret papers there, then caught doing it by her daughter-in-law, Mary Stuart.

On the second floor of the castle's Francis wing, just above Catherine's room, are the apartments of her son Henry III. Here he had the Duke of Guise murdered. Guise was a big, strong man and it took eight armed men to kill him while Henry watched from a hiding place. He went downstairs to tell his mother: 'I have no companion to share with now. The King of Paris is dead.'

You can choose for yourself which of Catherine's reported replies you prefer. Either she said, 'Well cut, my son' or she warned: 'God grant that you have not become the king of Nothing at All.'

On Christmas eve, as a gesture of peace and goodwill, he had Guise's brother, the powerful Cardinal de Lorraine, murdered. The body was burned and what was left thrown in the Loire. Henry himself was assassinated a year later. The new King Henry of Navarre had no interest in the château. But it did have one final royal association which, architecturally, was rather disastrous.

Louis XIII's brother and presumed heir, Gaston d'Orléans, had an enthusiasm for conspiracy. To keep him busy, Louis made him Count of Blois, gave him the château to play with, and lent him the royal architect Mansard (or Mansart). In 1635 Mansard started on the château, intending to pull it all down to build an enormous four-sided classical pile, covering the whole château square. Mansard was the man who invented the Mansard roof with steep lower sides and almost flat higher sides to leave space for rooms. He started by destroying part of the Francis wing and the nave of the chapel of St. Calais. He built a three-storey wing with a big central pavilion and two short wings classical in design with less sculptural decoration than the Francis wing. From the courtyard it compares unfavourably with the earlier buildings. Happily, before he could knock down any more of the Francis wing, a new heir was born, the future Louis XIV. Gaston ceased to be dangerous, and Richelieu lost no time in cutting off his funds. In fact, the interior was unfinished. It was never used until the 19th century and the central staircase of the pavilion was not built to Mansard's plan until 1932. It now houses the city library.

The façade of the château from the esplanade has, on the right, the pointed gable of the 13th-century feudal Chamber of the States General and the attractive Louis XII building with balconies to two of the first-floor rooms — the bedrooms of Louis himself and his Minister Cardinal d'Amboise.

Across the inner courtyard is a terrace with views of the Loire and the Tour du Foix, part of the original feudal walls. Only the chancel remains of the king's chapel of St. Calais after Mansard's efforts, but it does contain some good modern glass windows by the great Max Ingrand.

On the ground floor of the Francis I wing an audio-visual presentation ($\frac{1}{4}$ hour) of the château is given in the summer tourist season.

On the first floor of the Louis XII wing is a fine arts museum, with 16th-17th-century portraits of Marie de

Chaumont castle — feudal grimness with some lighter Renaissance touches

Médicis by Rubens, of Gaston d'Orléans and of Louis XIV by Mignard.

North-west from the château, off av
Jean-Laigret, is Pavillon d'Anne de
Bretagne, an elegant little building,
once in the big gardens of the château.
It now houses the Blois tourist office.

Six kilometres from Blois along the
north bank of the Loire on N152 at
Ménars is a château by the water's
edge. **Château de Ménars** was bought
in 1637, by Guillaume Charron, a wine
merchant. At that time, it was quite a
small house. The Charron family had
built on to it, until it was a grand house
and Louis XIV had given the Charrons
the ranks of Vicomte, then Marquis.
This was not unconnected with the fact
that Marie Charron was the wife of

Jean–Baptiste Colbert, for long Louis'
powerful chief minister. The gardens
were already magnificent.

One Charron lost interest and sold
the property to a lady named Antoin-
ette Poisson, who loved the gardens.
She was the mistress of Louis XV, the
Marquise de Pompadour.

Pompadour stayed often at Ménars.
She hired the king's architect Gabriel,
designer of Blois bridge, to rebuild it.
Her brother, the Marquis de Marigny,
inherited it from her and improved the
grounds even further. Alas, when we
visited last in 1986, it was closed for
renovation. We do hope it will be open
again by the time you go. It is pleasant
to see a château which is a real home,
not a castle-museum.

Henri, Duc de Guise

The defeat of the Armada by the English helped to bring down Henri, Duc de Guise and give Henry III the courage to assassinate him.

Guise was a big man, a good soldier, fanatical in his anti-Protestantism, especially, after his father François de Guise, who regained Calais from the English, was killed by a Protestant during the siege of Orléans.

Henri was even ambitious to be king, and paid genealogists to fake descent from Charlemagne. He was one of the contrivers of the St. Bartholomew's Day massacre of Protestants in 1572, head of the extremist Catholic League and was responsible for the atrocity against Protestants at Amboise château.

To further his plans for the crown, he became a paid secret agent of Philip II of Spain and played a part in the Armada plan. The day the Armada was due to sail (12th May 1588) he disobeyed Henry III's order and entered Paris, secretly infiltrating 2,000 of his Leaguer troops into the capital. His job was to stop the king invading Philip's Low Countries (Belgium and Holland) while the Spanish were away 'subduing' heretical England.

The Armada failed, Philip dropped Guise and stopped paying him and his power dwindled. Henry III took the chance to have him killed at Blois.

Robert-Houdin

On the north side of the place du Château is a museum to another interesting Blois citizen, Robert-Houdin, better known to us as Houdini, but not the same as the American escapologist Houdini, who stole the name. This one was born Jean-Eugène Robert in Blois in 1805, and had several jobs, including helping his father as a clockmaker, before he became a 'magician' by the use of the new electricity and clever mechanical devices. He also invented a periscope, electric clock and the very first electric motor. Twice at her request he gave shows for Queen Victoria at Buckingham Palace. He fooled the warlike Arab chieftains in southern Algeria into believing he was invulnerable by a trick with a gun.

His architect grandson Paul Robert-Houdin, conservateur of the château after World War II, initiated the first Son et Lumière at Chambord in 1952.

7
Blois to Chambord

There is almost a surfeit of châteaux around Blois and on the way to Orléans, so that lack of time and boredom can easily make a traveller decide to skip some of the treasures. Blessedly there are still attractive forests, too, though a large part of Chambord Parc is the National Hunting Reserve, used occasionally by Presidential hunting parties and for entertaining foreign VIPs, to the intense annoyance of some Frenchmen. It is surrounded by a 32km wall, the longest in France. However, a part of the forest to the west is open to the public, with a network of footpaths, including long-distance footpath GR 3 (Sentiers de Grande Randonnée) which links Mont-près-Chambord here on the edge of Boulogne Forest, right through the Sologne countryside all the way to Sancerre, and the GR 3C running through the Sologne to Gien on the Loire, way past Orléans.

There are very pleasant walks, too, through the Russy forest just south of Blois, and drives or walks along the lanes in the valley of the charming little Beuvron river. You meet the Beuvron at Cellettes just past the forest, and either way to Seur or Bracieux the scenery and hamlets are attractive. Many Loire châteaux started as forest hunting lodges. One is **Beauregard**, an unassuming, attractive little château off D956, 9km south of Blois on the edge of Russy forest. It was one of many lodges of that enthusiastic huntsman, Francis I, who gave it to his uncle the Bastard of Savoy. Jean du Thier, secretary to Henry II and a highly cultured man, built the present château. Italian woodworkers and painters from Fontainebleau decorated the inside. A financier Paul Ardier bought it in 1631 and put in the remarkable collection of portraits which you can still see there. There are 363 of these portraits of France's famous people, all the same size, lined up side by side around the gallery walls. There are kings from Philippe VI, the first Valois, to Louis XIII, with portraits of their queens, important courtiers, and some famous foreigners. Louis XII and family, for instance, entertain Amerigo Vespucci, the Florentine navigator, who gave his name to America.

The beamed ceiling and wainscoting still have paintings by Jean Mosnier, and the floor is of 17th-century Delft tiles showing a complete army on the march — infantry, cavalry, musketeers, artillery, all in authentic uniforms of the time of Louis XIII. It is a remarkable and interesting room. The big 16th-century kitchens are interesting too. Many travellers bypass Beauregard, but we

Cheverny apartments are sumptuously decorated and furnished

find it more rewarding than many more famous châteaux.

Cheverny, 7km south of Beauregard, just off D765, is another charming, less famous château. Elegant, white, with almost perfect classical symmetry, it has been described by a French writer as like a haughty woman. But we find it friendlier than that, and the inside is not a museum, like Blois or Chaumont, but a sumptuously decorated home, still lived in, with fine furniture, sculptures, painted panelling, marble, gilt.

Finished in 1634 in white tufa stone, it has a narrow central pavilion between two wings with rounded roofs supporting lanterns. It was built by Henri Hurault, Count of Cheverny, who had owned the previous château, and passed to a cadet branch of the family, the Marquises de Vobraye, who still own it. It is in a fine park with superb trees — horse chestnuts, Wellingtonia, limes, cedars.

Some of the interior decoration is almost overpowering — like a gourmet feast with a little too much richness.

The staircase is carved in white stone fruits and flowers. The pillars and pilasters of the first floor guard room have war themes, with detailed armour and weapons. Ceilings and window shutters are elaborately painted. The fireplace is carved, gilded and decorated with motifs from the story of Adonis by Jean Mosnier, the artist whose work is also at Beauregard. The Gobelins tapestry in the guard room of the Abduction of Helen of Troy is a delight. Mosnier worked here for 18 years, and left some quite remarkable ceilings in fine colours, with figures which seem to be in action. His Don Quixote scenes in the dining room show his sense of humour, too.

Mosnier was the son of a glassblower, born in Blois in 1600. A copy he made when he was 16 of the Madonna impressed Marie de Médicis. She sent him to Italy to be taught and he stayed there for nine years. He worked at the Luxembourg Palace in Paris for Marie, but then returned to Blois and died there.

The grand salon is completely covered with paintings, from wall panels to ceiling. The small salon has five fine 17th-century tapestries from Flanders. Both rooms are furnished with fine Louis XIV and Louis XV pieces. The King's bedroom is lavishly overpowering. No king ever slept in it, but it got its name from the tradition of droit de gîte — right of shelter. When a king gave permission for the building of a château, he took the right of bed and shelter without warning. Kings sometimes stayed at a nearby château when they were too late to get home from hunting or when moving around the country. A bedroom had to be kept ready for the King at all times. The bedroom at Cheverny is still ready, even to a bedcover of 15th-century white Persian silk, embroidered with faded flowers.

For an insomniac the room is full of interest. A series of 17th-century tapestries follow the dramas and terrors of Ulysses' travels. On the ceiling Perseus meets the Medusa. Then thirty painted panels tell an unlikely story from ancient Greece about the misadventures of an Ethiopian princess and her love affair with a handsome Thessalonian who turns out, of course, to be a powerful prince in disguise. It's a classical soap-opera in which the girl is abandoned at birth by her mother, becomes a priestess at Delphi, gets captured by pirates and enslaved and

69

Château de Troussay, near Cheverny, is a delightful little Renaissance manor house

Françoise, became bored. Henri spotted in a mirror King Henry making signs to the courtiers that Hurault was being cuckolded. Without saying a word, Hurault called for his horse, rode home to Cheverny, and found his wife in bed with a page. The page leapt out of the window but broke his ankle. Hurault ran round and killed him, then returned to the bedroom and killed his wife. The king banished him for three years — to his own château at Cheverny, where he married a pretty daughter of his bailiff, had seven children and built the new château.

South-west of Cour-Cheverny village (3km) is the little Renaissance **Château de Troussay**, known for its furnishings, carvings and sculptures collected from vanished local houses, and for its agricultural implements.

From Cheverny take D12 north-east through Cour-Cheverny village. After 6km you reach the little Beuvron river at Ponts d'Arian, which means Hadrian's bridges, for this was a Roman road. The Beuvron and a smaller stream the Bonne Heure, both of which pass through Bracieux, are rich

involved in a war before she and her boy friend just happen to meet again at the court of the Ethiopian king.

The kennels and stables are spectacular, too. In one stable is a museum of hunting, with a picture of the hounds setting off from Cheverny château and antlers everywhere — 2,000 of them, on walls, ceilings, rafters and pillars. From November to Easter, hunts meet twice a week and you can hear the celebrated coiled horns, 'Trompes de Cheverny'. The French are still addicted to all forms of hunting. La Chasse is a national disease.

The stables are built on the site of the original Hurault family château of 1519. The owner in the reign of Henry IV, Henri Hurault, joined the royal army and was away for much of the time, campaigning. His young wife,

The charming Château de Villesavin was built as a house in 1537 for the builder of Chambord

in fish, and you can get a fishing licence for a local lake at a café-bar in Ponts d'Arian.

On the left is the gorgeous little Renaissance château of **Villesavin** which few tourists visit. A visit does not take long and is rewarding. While Chambord was being built nearby, Francis I's works superintendent in charge of craftsmen, materials and finances, Jean le Breton, had this house built for himself. Florentine craftsmen worked on it, and it is Italian even to the Carrara marble. The Italian adornment of the windows is particularly attractive. There is a small chapel with dilapidated frescoes (it was used as kennels for a while), an interesting kitchen with pewter ware, and a dove-cot with 1,500 perches and a rotating ladder for cleaning. In a barn is a little museum of horse-drawn carriages, a horse-drawn bus, with an early tricycle and a children's goat cart.

Three kilometres on is **Bracieux**, a charming little market town on the edge of the Sologne country. On the banks of the Beuvron, it has a superb piece of country architecture in its old covered market, with wooden columns, topped by a 16th-century granary with pinnacle turret. Around here in the Bonne Heure valley are attractive old farms and manor houses, such as Herbault.

From Bracieux northwards, D112 runs through the Chambord hunting reserve to the château. At **Chambord**,

---

Francis I

Those 440 rooms at Chambord might well have been needed if Francis I had lived longer. The whole court always travelled with him: 12,000 horses carried them, their servants, furniture, crockery and baggage. All had to be housed, the horses fed and watered. Artists, writers, scientists gathered round him, too. Brantôme said that anyone who came was received but the King was knowledgeable on almost any subject, so the visitor 'had better not be a fool or ditherer'.

Francis did everything on a vast scale. When he met Henry VIII of England in 1520 at the Camp du Drap d'Or (Field of the Cloth of Gold) near Calais to try to seal an alliance, Francis used 6,000 workmen to prepare the site. His tent was draped in gold. Henry's shone in the sun like a crystal palace. Henry had 5,000 followers from his court, dressed in velvet, satin and gold. Even mules were dressed in crimson velvet and gold.

Cardinal Wolsey, Henry's organiser, took over to France among other items 700 conger eels, 2,014 sheep, 26 dozen heron and four bushels of mustard. They both took their Royal choirs and organists for Mass in the middle of a field.

Francis and Henry jousted every day but one. On that day the wind was too high so they wrestled. Francis threw Henry flat on his back. They still swore eternal peace but Francis went back to the Loire, Henry went to meet the Emperor Charles V, France's sworn enemy, and soon made a treaty with him against Francis and France.

Francis rather overdid his flamboyance. It was really almost a folly. It is dazzling, awesome, beautiful in overpowering way. Francis himself could not finish it for lack of both time and money.

Reactions to Chambord from writers and poets through the centuries are fascinating. Chateaubriand said that it looked 'like a woman whose tresses have been disarrayed by the wind'. De Vigny imagined that it had been snatched magically from the East and whisked away to the Loire valley. Victor Hugo wrote: 'All magic, all poesy, indeed all madness is represented in the admirable bizarreness of this palace of fairy kings and queens.' Our friend Vivian Rowe, that English lover of France, called it: 'The skyline of Constantinople on a single roof.' A French travel writer, J.L. Delpal, described Chambord as 'a shining example of out and out architectural megalomania, prefiguring Versailles in its gigantism but totally lacking in the amenities of pleasant living.'

True; it has 440 rooms, 15 great staircases, including one double spiralled so that two people going up and down never lose sight of each other but can only meet at the top and bottom, and 70 lesser staircases, so it was hardly as comfortable and homely as Chenonceau, nor as easy for the staff to provide quick service. But with its staircases, secretive landings and towers, it must have been a wonderful place for a party. And if it looks bare and barnlike now, that is because it was stripped of furnishings in the French Revolution and allowed to deteriorate

Château de Chambord — the grandiose dream of a showman king

Louis XIV's royal bedchamber at Château de Chambord

in the last century. The French Government's Historic Monuments Department took it over as the whitest of white elephants when nobody wanted it, and has spent a fortune restoring it and re-excavating the moat. It is now doing its best to give it suitable tapestries, trophies and furnishings.

Francis began work on Chambord in 1519. In 1525 he was defeated in Italy by Charles V and taken prisoner. To release himself he gave up Flanders and Burgundy to Charles and gave his two sons as prisoner-hostages in Spain. He went on pouring money into Chambord when he had no money to ransom his sons, his treasury was so empty that he was raiding the treasuries of his churches and he was grabbing his subjects' silver to melt down.

By 1539 enough of the château was finished for him to receive Charles V there. With his usual showmanship, Francis had young women dressed as Greek nymphs run from the trees to spread flowers before Charles' path, which must have impressed the Emperor, for he said: 'Chambord is a summary of human industry.

In 18 years during which Chambord was habitable before his death, Francis is said to have stayed there only 40 nights.

Henry II continued the building. Francis II and Charles IX came often and their young courtiers seem to have had some fine times there. Despite sickness, Charles was a hunting enthusiast. He was said to have stayed in the saddle up to 10 hours a day and tired five horses. His mother Catherine de Médicis was a renowned horsewoman and her rival Diane was so fond of hunting that she was portrayed at Chenonceau as Diana the Huntress. Three hundred falcons were kept at Chambord.

Louis XII gave Chambord as part of the Blois domaines to his scheming brother Gaston d'Orléans. Gaston's daughter, La Grande Mademoiselle, told later how she used to make her father run up and down the spiral staircase while she passed him in the other direction, never meeting him.

Louis XIV loved Chambord and perhaps this was another reason why he built his own Versailles in an inaccessible forest. He brought Molière to Chambord to put on plays for the court. But the building of Versailles was the real swansong of Chambord. Louis XV gave it to his father-in-law, the deposed King of Poland, Stanislas Leczinski, who lived there from 1725 to 1733 and filled in the moat which Francis I had taken so much trouble to fill with water from the diverted river Cosson.

Then Louis XV gave it as a thank offering to Marshal Maurice Saxe, bastard son of the King of Poland who had deposed Louis' father-in-law. Saxe had won France's few victories against Austria, including the Battle of Fontenoy. Saxe was a luxury-loving, conceited, violent and courageous soldier. He kept at Chambord his own extraordinary private army. He set up six cannon captured in battle and two cavalry regiments composed of Tartars, Cossacks, Wallachians and negroes from Martinique. They rode ponies from the Ukraine which ran free and fed themselves in the forest but came to a trumpet call. If any soldier disobeyed the simplest order, he was hanged from a tree in the forest.

Louis XIV and Molière

Louis XIV's power over his court even stretched to dictating their laughter, like a studio audience.

When he first brought Molière and his troupe to Chambord to perform in the guardroom, converted into a theatre, Molière and the composer Lully staged their comedy with ballet 'Monsieur de Pourceaugnac'. Louis was not amused, so nor were his courtiers. Then Lully tried a real slapstick gag worthy of pantomime.

Madame de Maintenon, the royal mistress, reported that Lully got up on the stage, broke into a run, and jumped off, landing on the harpsichord in the orchestra, shattering it.

The gag was a triumph. The king laughed and so did the court.

Next year, 1670, Molière staged 'Le Bourgeois Gentilhomme'. Once again, the court thought that the king was not amused. He looked morose and hardly laughed. But at supper he told Molière in a loud voice how much he had enjoyed it. So the courtiers discovered that they had enjoyed it, too. The second performance was a riotous success.

Saxe was a reprobate who treated women abominably. He was believed to have arranged the death by poison of one mistress, Adrienne Lecouvreur, star of the Comédie Française. Then he took a fancy to another actress, Le Favart. He still had influence in Paris and he made certain that her actor-manager husband could not get a job there. He brought him and his wife to produce and act for his guests at Chambord on the stage where Molière played. Meanwhile he carried the wife off to bed.

The marshal died two years later, officially from a chill. It is more pleasant to believe the court story that he was killed in a secret duel by the prince of Conti, whose wife he had seduced. He had organised a great send-off for himself. The six cannon were fired in Chambord courtyard every quarter of an hour for sixteen days. After that Chambord was neglected. The furniture was looted or sold during the Revolution. In 1809 Napoléon gave the château to Marshal Berthier, who sold the beautiful hardwood timber and never stayed there. After his death it was bought in 1821 by public subscription for the Duc de Bordeaux, posthumous son of the murdered Duc de Berry and grandson of Charles X. When Charles was driven out of France, Louis Philippe, Duc d'Orléans, undertook to be Regent for the little Duc de Bordeaux, but stole the crown. When he too was thrown out the Duc de Bordeaux could have been King Henry V, but he refused to serve under any flag but the white flag of Joan of Arc. Nobody wanted Chambord. No one could afford to pull it down. The state had to buy it.

The lower part of the château looks squat and rather stolid. The top is a whirlwind of planned disarray in carved, decorated stone, a stone garden of turrets, dormers, cupolas, bells, pinnacles and gables, with 365 sculptured chimneys.

From the main courtyard you can see the keep, joined by arcades and two-storey galleries stretching to the corner towers.

The renowned double spiral staircase starts in the guardroom where Molière's stage was set up. It is connected with each storey although originally it was intended to go straight up.

Ground-floor rooms have been partly refurnished. There are fine tapestries — a Brussels tapestry of the Call of Abraham in the Sun Room, 16th-century tapestries after drawings by Laurent Guyot in Francis I's hunting room. There are more tapestries and pictures on the first floor and in the François I tower the royal bedchamber used by Louis XIV, Stanislas and Saxe, with panelling put in for Saxe in 1748.

The Dauphin's suite has mementoes of the Duc de Bordeaux, including miniature artillery which could pierce a brick wall and his manifesto of 5th July 1871 declaring: 'Henry V will not abandon the white flag of Henry IV.'

The second floor has hunting mementoes, animal paintings by 17th-century Flemish painters and some more good tapestries in the Henry V tower.

Son et Lumière started here in 1952. Now it includes a night trip around the castle. And in the lights the château roof shines magically in dazzling light — like lightning.

8
Chambord to Orléans

The D112 road from Chambord through the park to the Loire at Muides is called Route François 1er. At Muides it crosses the river to **Mer**, a pleasant old town, once fortified, with a 15th-century church which has a 16th-century Flamboyant belfry tower.

D15, which runs under the motorway, is flanked for 9km by rose bushes — 10,000 we are told — as far as **Talcy**. Here is yet another château — severe and almost threatening from outside, delightful within. It was rebuilt in 1520 by a Florentine banker, Bernado Salviati, cousin of Catherine de Médicis, contains beautiful items of furniture, tapestries and trinkets from the 17th century to the Directorate, and an interesting 16th-century kitchen. You feel that you would like to live in some of the rooms. In the second courtyard is a huge dovecot with 1,500 pigeon holes, almost too big for the house and, under walnut trees, a 400-year-old wine press still capable of producing ten ̄barrels of grape juice in one pressing.

Talcy has two charming sentimental stories. When Bernado Salviati's blonde daughter Cassandre was 15, the poet Pierre de Ronsard came to stay at the château. He fell for her completely and wooed her with sonnets (*Les Amours de Cassandre*).

But she preferred a man called Jean de Peigne. Twenty years later Ronsard met her again. She was a widow. She still turned him down. But he dedicated 183 sonnets to her.

Cassandre's brother Jean inherited Talcy. In 1571 Diane, his daughter, nursed a wounded Huguenot, victim of the Catholics. He had, it seemed, an operation on the kitchen table. He was another poet, Agrippa d'Aubigné, friend and brother-in-arms of Henry of Navarre. Agrippa had a love affair with his nurse until her uncle, a Catholic, threw out the Protestant poet. By the time she caught up with Agrippa again, he was married, whereupon 'she languished in sorrow and died'.

Back to Mer and along the N152 is Beaugency. To see the nuclear power station at St. Laurent-Nouan, you must cross the river at Mer and approach Beaugency on D951. **Beaugency** is blessedly bypassed these days and it is quite difficult to find a way in and through it, for its little narrow streets have many one-ways and no-entries. Park down by the river bridge and walk, for it has many treasures of the Middle Ages, many of its houses are flower-decked and its green hillside and riverside setting is most pleasant. It is one of the Loire valley's holiday towns, with interesting old hotels (one

Loire Poets

Pierre de Ronsard, poet of love and romance, is regarded as the greatest French poet of the 16th century, as Rabelais was the greatest prose writer. Though he dedicated 183 sonnets to Cassandre Salviate, he wrote passionate and romantic poems to other women, too. Hélène Surgères from Saintonge was one. Another was a girl called Marie from Port Guyet, whom he loved enough to move to Bourgueil to be near her. He was even jealous of the doctor who visited her when she was ill.

He was born at the Château de la Poisonnière in Vendôme in 1524 and served as soldier-diplomat to the Dauphin and the Duke of Orléans. He accompanied James V and his bride Marie de Lorraine to Scotland and stayed three years. Becoming deaf, he abandoned arms for letters, studied at Collège Coquéret with Du Bellay and became one of the seven men of the famous Pléiade, pledged to develop and 'elevate' the French language, which meant really abandoning the vernacular and imitating classical poetry. His first Odes (1550) were much influenced by the Greek poet Pindar and brought violent opposition from critics supporting the growing French nationalism. But he was a favourite of the Court and Charles IX especially poured favours on him. He spent years of happy ease at the Abbey of Croix-Val in Vendôme and the King made him Commendatory Prior of St. Cosne near Tours. This was a perk at the expense of the church whereby an outside layman held a church post and received the church revenues. Richelieu collected such benefices. Many of the priors or even bishops were very much absentee-dignitaries. But at least Ronsard retired to his priory and died there in 1585. The priory, overrun by suburbs, is a ruin but his grave was found in 1933.

François Villon, lyric poet of the previous century and seemingly a great wit, was, alas, also a rogue, vagabond and even a murderer. Born of poor parents in Paris in 1431, he took the name of his teacher. He graduated as Master of Arts in 1452 but by 1455 he was in hiding after killing a priest in a street brawl. Imprisoned he was released and banished. He wandered to Angers and was in prison in Orléans for robbing a church. But he met the Duke of Bourbon at Moulins and was entertained in 1457 by the Prince poet Charles, Duke of Orléans, at Blois, where Charles held court for writers, poets and artists. Charles used to organise poetic debates and competitions and Villon won one, completing a poem of contradictory ideas which began 'I am dying of thirst in front of a fountain'. Charles was so delighted with his poem that he wanted Villon to stay. A pity that he didn't, for Charles was a kindly, patient and understanding man who himself had spent 25 years as a prisoner in the Tower of London because his family would not pay his ransom after he was captured at Agincourt.

Villon was soon in trouble again for brawling and connection with a burglary, for which he was tortured and imprisoned at St. Meung. His 'Epistle to his Friends' describing his suffering and asking why he had been abandoned is regarded as his greatest poem, but best known in Britain and the US is his 'The Ladies of Bygone Days' ('Where are the snows of yester-year?'), probably because it was dramatically translated by Rossetti.

A Royal amnesty saved him from Meung. But back in Paris he was sentenced to death in 1463 for another crime. The sentence was commuted to banishment and he disappeared.

The French literary Establishment is not fond of mentioning him and some reputable guide books ignore him. It seems unlikely that he would have cared about that.

In 1791 the English poet William Wordsworth moved into lodgings in rue Royale, Orléans. He was 21, an ardent admirer of the French Revolution, and attending Revolutionary meetings and celebrations. That did not stop him falling in love with Annette Vallon, 25, a Royalist and counter-revolutionary. She had a baby and 'Mr and Mrs Williams' had their daughter christened Caroline in Orléans cathedral. When war broke out between France and England, Annette persuaded him to flee. They kept in touch, met occasionally, and finally in Paris Annette and Caroline, now grown up, met Wordsworth, his wife and sister Dorothy.

Max Jacob is perhaps better known as an artist than poet outside France. Born in 1876, son of a Jewish tailor in Quimper, Brittany, he went to Paris as a young man, and shared poverty and the great Bohemian life with Picasso, Cocteau and Braque. In 1915 he became a Christian. Picasso was godfather at his baptism. Six years later he went to live in St. Benoît-sur-Loire, complaining jokingly that life was no longer any fun in Paris because as a Catholic he could no longer sin with pleasure. He lived in the main street of Benoît until 1944, when the monks returned to the abbey and he retired there. Not for long. The Gestapo came for him. On the train to a prison-camp he persuaded his guards to post a letter to Cocteau for him. Cocteau got up a petition to the German Embassy for his release, signed by all his friends except Picasso, who said that Max was too smart to need his help. In fact, he was probably afraid of the consequences with the Nazis. The petition was actually successful, but when his friends went to collect him from Drancy prison, they were told that he had died of pneumonia.

Jacob's poems have two qualities the French greatly admire — emotion and clarity, and he has been much more admired in recent times than during his life. His painting and sculptures were always admired, although they lacked the effect of Cocteau or Braque. In the Fine Arts Museum in Orléans, an area is devoted to his work, mostly watercolours of Brittany and sculptures.

in the old abbey)-and across the bridge a huge camp site with a beach for swimming in the river.

In the Middle Ages Beaugency had the best bridge between Blois and Orléans, was highly coveted by armies and was therefore fortified and constantly attacked. In fact, through history the local people must have regarded the bridge as a mixed blessing. The English took the town four times in the Hundred Years' War until Joan of Arc retook it in 1429. Then in the Wars of Religion (1562–1598) the Catholic Leaguers and Huguenots held it in turn. The Protestant Prince of

Condé sacked it, then it was set on fire by more Protestants in 1567 and the abbey badly burned. In 1940 the retreating French blew up part of the bridge, and the town was bombed in 1944. But it has managed to hold on to many of its old buildings, monuments and houses, especially in place Dunois, opposite the church and keep and place St. Firmin, an area which looks delightful at night when lit by old street lamps.

The bridge, 440m long with 22 arches, is one of the many built by that great engineer Satan in a night in return for the soul of the first creature to cross. As happened elsewhere the local people welshed on payment. The Mayor pulled the old trick of bringing along a cat and a bucket of water on opening day and sending the poor moggie scurrying across. Satan laughed so loudly that the top fell off the Tour de César, and that formidable keep is still topless. Spoilsport historians have tried to discredit this story by pointing out that the tower was only built in the 11th century at the same time as the bridge, to protect it.

The Devil likes Beaugency. Along the river quai to the left as you cross the bridge from the south is another tower where he still lives, Tour de Diable. It is right next to the Augustine Abbey of Notre-Dame, which was rebuilt in the 18th century. A neighbour like that must have been disconcerting to the monks. But now that the abbey is an hotel we have not heard of his causing any trouble to the guests. Perhaps they are all exceptionally well-behaved. That is more than can be said of the Protestants who burned down that abbey and brought down the roof of the 12th-century Romanesque church of Notre-Dame which lies close to the

Devil's Tower. Alas, in repairing the roof the Romanesque vaulting was replaced by an imitation Gothic ceiling in wood painted to look like stone — a genuine bodge-up. German bombardment in 1940 wrecked the stained-glass windows but new ones from Orléans are bright and attractive. The sculpture of Joan of Arc is hardly worthy of her but the church remains elegant, with its light columns and radiating chapels.

In 1152, three archbishops, forty bishops and many barons piled into this church for a Council to judge one of the scandals of the Middle Ages. King Louis VII accused his wife Eleanor of Aquitaine of adultery in Antioch while she was accompanying him on a Crusade and wanted his marriage annulled. She did not defend the suit. She wanted rid of him, too, He was a dull man, she was lively, intelligent, beautiful and wayward. She settled for a very dubious compromise — consanguinity, which means that their blood relationship was too close. It wasn't, but legal argument fiddled the facts and they both got their annulment on these grounds. It seems that the Ecclesiastical judges were not too worried about her love affaires. As a result, she married a man she already had her eye on — Henry Plantagenet, who was lively, cultured, could play the troubadour and was wayward. He soon became Henry II of England. So England got Aquitaine and nearly all South-West France which caused France even more trouble than Germany did in modern times.

The castle at Beaugency, right behind the church, was a medieval fortress converted into a residence in the 15th century by Dunois, bastard son of the Duc d'Orléans who was assassinated by the Burgundians in 1404. Dunois was companion in arms of Joan of Arc. He helped her free Orléans. After her death he took Chartres, chased the English from Paris and Normandy, took Bordeaux and Bayonne and sent the English back home to fight in the Wars of the Roses. Château Dunois now contains an excellent Folk Art Museum in its arcade-ringed courtyard and rooms with furniture, clothing, artisanry, souvenirs of local celebrities, games and a good collection of 19th-century dolls and puppets. Rooms are skilfully furnished to different period styles.

Facing the church and château ios the 11th-century fortress-keep, Tour de César, 33½m high without the top which Satan laughed off and with walls 3½m thick, so that Dunois and Joan of Arc took all day and half a night in 1429 to dislodge a very small English garrison, who were able to walk out with their weapons on condition that they did not fight for ten days.

The Hôtel de Ville is a pretty Renaissance building, though 'restored' in 1893, a time when 'restoration' often meant altering. The council chamber is worth seeing for its 17th–18th-century hangings, originally in the Abbey. You can visit, by asking the caretaker and paying a very small entrance fee — 2 francs when we last went there (9–12, 2–5; shut Wednesday).

From N152 above the town, a tree-shaded Grand Mail runs down to the attractive shaded square, Petit Mail, with beautiful views over the valley. *Mail* is the original word corrupted by the English into Mall, as in Pall Mall in London. A mail is a mallet, used in a medieval game, like croquet, played on these avenues. Today you will find the locals playing boules on Petit Mail.

Perhaps because it is usually less-crowded in high summer and smaller, many people find **Meung-sur-Loire** more attractive than Beaugency. A photogenic old fortified town it too has a mail down by the river, and the extra charm of the Mauves, a tributary of the Loire, running between its old streets. Once the Mauves drove many mills and one, Le Grand Moulin, is an art gallery. On the quayside is a statue to Jean de Meung, a remarkable poet and wit of the 13th century. He added no less than 18,000 stanzas to an already popular poem 'Roman de la Rose' written 50 years before, by Guillaume

The Renaissance town hall at Beaugency has been beautifully restored

de Loris, turning it by his wit and satire from a romantic poem to a satirical criticism of conventions and people of his day, criticising even Royalty and Church. He had a strong influence on later French literature. When printing was invented 150 years later, the poem was one of the first printed and became a best-seller.

Another poet, the 'vagabond poet' François Villon, was in prison in the château at Meung for two years from 1459 and was said to have been tortured, including forced water-drinking until near bursting point. It was his usual crime — burglary — which got him there. He wrote some of his most haunting and plaintive poetry here, including his 'Épître à mes Amis'. Luckily for him, Louis XI passed through the town on his coronation celebrations and an amnesty was declared. Released, Villon committed another burglary in Paris, a city of which he was Master of Arts of the University. At one time at Meung he was confined in the oubliette, a well where prisoners were kept on an unfenced ledge half-way down, in darkness, with no hope of climbing up if they fell off. Each day one loaf of bread and a pitcher of water was lowered to be divided among them. It was the Bishops of Orléans who dispensed such justice. Meung was their country seat for 500 years. This oubliette, in the château grounds, was only rediscovered in 1973.

The château is of very mixed styles, from 11th century to the 16th, with interior rooms remodelled in the 19th century. It has some delightful furniture, from French 14th-century to English Chippendale.

Under the 11th-century towers, among dungeons and passages, is a vaulted underground chapel where the local people often lived for weeks during raids or wars.

The church of St. Liphard, in the corner of place Martoi in the old town, is a fine example of 11th–13th-century Romanesque, with a massive plain tower. It was named for a 6th-century saint, son of a King of Le Mans, who became governor of Orléans then gave it all up at 40 to convert the locals, first killing his dragon, in the tradition of Apollo, Perseus, Krishna and St. George. Our favourite dragon-killer was the Celtic saint St. Samson who simply ordered the dragon to start eating its own tail, then drop dead. It did.

Meung is said to have been a market town of the Gauls and a stop for Greek traders on the tin route from the Mediterranean to Cornwall. It became a Roman fortified post called Magdunum. The people had an ancient nickname of 'les ânes Meung'. It seems that Silenus, the drunken, happy, fat attendant of Bacchus, rode into town on a donkey and found the locals so miserable and unfriendly that he turned them into asses. Local historians disbelieve this story and say that the name originated during a famine when men of Meung took a string of donkeys bearing flour to Orléans and the people of the city shouted: 'Voici les ânes de Meung'.

Meung has a pleasant swimming pool by the Loire and is a nice spot for a few days' holiday if you can find accommodation. The simple Logis, Auberge St. Jacques, has twelve rooms.

An attractive suspension bridge takes you over the Loire to **Cléry-St. André**, once a place of pilgrimage. The church with its heavy Gothic tower was given the status of a basilica. In 1280 a peasant ploughed up some ancient weapons, pottery, human bones and the statue of a woman. It was probably of a pagan goddess but the local priest announced a miracle and put the statue in the church as 'Notre Dame de Cléry' and pilgrim business boomed. Alas, the Huguenots burned it, and the one over the altar was made later from oak.

The English commander in the Hundred Years' War, the Earl of Salisbury, allowed his troops on their way to Orléans in 1428 to knock down all of the church except the tower. Shortly after, Salisbury had his head knocked off by a cannon ball. The locals said that the Lady, Holy Virgin or Pagan Goddess, aimed it at him. Dunois, Joan of Arc's friend, her 'gentle Bastard', gave the money to rebuild the church, and he is buried there in the Dunois chapel. The rebuilding was continued by Louis XI, who had vowed to give his own weight in silver in return for his victory over the English at Dieppe. He often stayed in Cléry. Through the lovely Flamboyant door of the sacristy of the church is a spiral staircase leading to an oratory from which he could follow Mass without being seen. He had a vault for his grave dug out while he was still alive and it is said that he used to try it for size by lying in it. Perhaps it was a good thing that the Huguenots took away and melted down the bronze monuments, for the beautiful marble statue which the Orléans sculptor Michel Bourdin made in 1622 to replace them is a masterpiece. The figure is kneeling, but it is the face which tells so much about this cruel, cunning king.

St. James' Chapel is richly, you could say floridly, decorated. It was built as the tomb of the Church Dean, Gilles de Pontbriant, and his brother François who was in charge of works at Chambord.

Follow a little white road just northwest of Cléry through le Trépois hamlet and at les Groisons is a very attractive scene where the mysterious little Loiret river runs into the Loire. Then continue to **St. Hilaire-St. Mesmin**. A side road to the Loiret river takes you to a charming spot. Renoir would surely have painted the terrace of the hotel here, L'Escale du Port Arthur, on the bank of the little river. On a fine day you can sit under umbrellas with an apéritif bottle of Loire blanc de blancs on the white table and become mesmerised into delightful dreams by the fast-flowing river and the gentle movement and sound of the lime trees, big willows and tall birches capped with crows' nests. Swallows dive and weave over the water, ducks hug the banks seeking worms, wavelets slap against the flat-bottomed boats slowly twisting on their ropes by the river bank. In inclement weather, you can drink or eat in the glass-enclosed addition to the dining room, with only the terrace and an old towpath between you and the river, and an open fire in the room to warm you.

It is not a pretty hotel, but it is a place of true quiet and calm, a world apart from the big Loire river, into which the Loiret flows, with its nuclear power station, gravel pits, big camp sites, and beaches with frites vans and snack bars.

From St. Hilaire follow the D14 eastwards to **Olivet**, a little town in a charming setting on the banks of the Loiret where Orléans people have for

long escaped for boating, fishing and picnics. Its river banks with riverside paths are lined with old houses and watermills, mostly turned into houses. There are hotels and restaurants, including our old favourite of yesteryear, now famous, Le Rivage. It has a riverside terrace for fine weather drinking and eating, boats tied up below for fishing or for rowing to work up an appetite, and it serves old Loire dishes like friture of small river fish and river eels in *feuilleté* of puff pastry. Olivet is almost a suburb of Orléans now but still has great atmosphere, and is rich in market gardens, nurseries and fields of flowers. Louis VII gave the land by the river and a watermill to the monks of Mount Sion of Jerusalem whom he brought back from Palestine after the failure of the Second Crusade and they named it after the Mount of Olives.

Continue on D14 and you reach one of the glories of the Loire — Parc Floral. It covers 30 hectares. Open from April to 11th November, it blazes with magnificent colour the whole time. Old trees, fountains, lakes and modern sculptures are surrounded by massed blooms. In April, there are tens of thousands of daffodils and tulips, hyacinths and stocks, at the beginning of May come masses of azaleas and rhododendrons, then a unique collection of irises of many unusual and delicate colours. 200,000 rose bushes bloom in June and July, and in July and August hundreds of thousands of plants of many types and colours — begonias, petunias, etc. In August and September come superb dahlias — some of the finest we have seen anywhere — and more roses, and in early November

Quatre Saisons, a restaurant beside the Loiret at Olivet

chrysanthemums of many colours and sizes. If you get too weary to walk, a little train will take you round in covered but open-sided carriages.

Here in the park, called la Source, is what is called la Source du Loiret, the pretty little river which flows a mere 13km into the Loire. It comes up in a pool where the temperature never changes between 12–15°C all the year and which never freezes so that magnificent flamingos, cranes, ducks and other web-footed friends winter here. Emus and deer roam the park. The water bubbles out at 40 cubic metres a minute and its temperature is a great help to flower cultivation. But this is not the source of the Loiret — that may be at St. Benoît about 17km away — it is a resurgence after the little river has gone underground. Or else the Loiret is an arm of the Loire, going underground at St. Benoît.

Château de la Source, 17th-century, Classical and elegant, houses the offices of the University and cannot be visited. Between 1720 and 1725 it was leased by Henry St. John, Viscount Bolingbroke, who as Tory Foreign Secretary under Queen Anne had negotiated the Treaty of Utrecht, which ended the War of the Spanish Succession to the disadvantage of England's allies. When George I came to the throne Bolingbroke was revealed as a secret Jacobite and he fled to France, where he formed a circle of French philosophers and revolutionary politicians. Among his visitors was Voltaire, who read the manuscript of *Henriade* to the circle. When he thought it was safe to return to England, he looked after the exiled Voltaire, and the young Frenchman later used some of his thoughts in his own work, including his contempt of Christianity as a fable.

Statue of St. Joan in Place du Martroi, Orléans

Near the park is the new University of Orléans and a whole new town.

Orléans (pop. 105,589) was badly damaged in 1940 and although it was well rebuilt and became a pleasant modern city, it has suffered from flyovers, motorway feed-roads and spaghetti junctions, and it is almost as difficult to drive in as Rouen. But the French still believe that 'Paris is the head of France, Orléans is its heart'.

No one can blame the people for making the most of Joan of Arc as a tourist attraction, although there is not a great deal to see of Joan.

Place du Martroi, at the top of rue Royale which joins it with Pont George V (named after the English king), is the focal point of the city. In its centre is an equestrian statue of Joan designed by Denis Foyatier in 1855, with bas-reliefs on a pedestal in Renaissance style by Vital-Dubray showing scenes from her life. Holding a sword, Joan is looking up to heaven giving thanks for her victories. A road made only last century but called rue Jeanne d'Arc runs from rue Royale to the Cathedral of Sainte Croix. Here in the chancel she gave thanks for her first victory over the English. The 19th-century stained-glass windows tell the story of her life. And here is a marble statue of Cardinal Touchet, kneeling before St. Joan's altar. He was the man who fought for years to have her canonised. It was

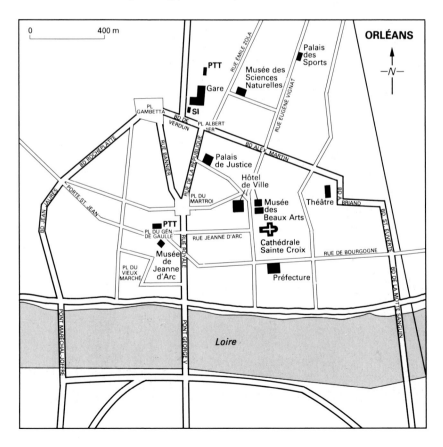

1920 before she became a saint, and soon she was patron-saint of France. There is in this chapel, which is dedicated to her, a marble statue of her by the same sculptor, André Césare Vermare, created in 1912.

The cathedral was begun in the 13th century and building went on until the 16th century when, in 1568, it was partly destroyed by Protestants. They removed the base stones of four pillars, put in hollow logs filled with gunpowder and lit fuses — not unlike the technique of Philippe-Auguste's medieval 'sappers' when dislodging the English from castles.

The Protestant leader Henry of Navarre, having changed to Catholicism to become Henry IV, tried to show the sincerity of his conversion by promising to rebuild the cathedral in Gothic style. He laid the cornerstone in 1601. Building continued through many reigns, but remarkably always in the original Gothic style — a striking contrast to so many other cathedrals which are either a blend or a hotchpotch of styles. Louis XIV was particularly insistent that the transept, built between 1627 and 1690, should be 'in the Gothic manner' and chose a Jesuit architect, Martellange, who obviously knew what was expected of him. Above portals surrounded by columns and pediments he put rose-windows in the form of the Sun King's own symbol. In the centre, as a sort of sun god, is the head of Louis XIV himself, with his motto Nec Pluribus Impar — No one compares with him. One wonders whether Louis really did believe, in applying his policy of absolute power, that he was almost a god, superior to all

other mortals. By 1793 the west front was finished, but during the Revolution there was more damage, and the work of completion stopped. The western part of the nave was not linked to the tower until 1829. Bombs destroyed the tops of the towers in 1944, but they have been restored.

It is an impressive building, large, light and attractive inside, and is loved by the French as a symbol of their continuing history. It is illuminated on

Opposite: *Across the Loire at Orléans*

7th and 8th May for the Joan of Arc Festival, a lavish costume production.

The nearby Bibliothèque Municipale is the former 17th-century Bishop's Palace, with a little garden. Open during library hours, it has a fine staircase and beautiful gallery. Napoléon's Empress Marie-Louise spent her last days in France here in 1814 before fleeing to Austria. Before she left one of Louis XVIII's staff came to relieve her of Imperial jewels and plates she had intended to take away as souvenirs.

Hôtel Groslot, now the town hall, is a large Renaissance building built in 1530 by the bailiff, a merchant Jacques Groslot, but the two matching wings were added last century. The statue at the foot of the steps is of St. Joan looking more feminine than the sword-brandishing warrior of most of her statues. It is a replica of an original in marble at Versailles by Princess Marie

89

d'Orléans, given to the city by her father, King Louis-Philippe, in the last century.

Hôtel Groslot was the royal residence when kings were in the city. In 1560, the 17-year-old François II, his girl bride later to be known as Mary Queen of Scots, his mother Catherine de Médicis and the whole court, including the Duke of Guise, leader of the extremist Catholic League, and his brother the Cardinal of Lorraine came here. Calling an Estates General, the young king demanded the presence of the two Protestant leaders, the Prince of Condé and his elder brother Antoine de Bourbon, King of Navarre. They were promised safe conduct. Condé fell into the trap, was arrested, tried and sentenced to death. The King of Navarre was to be goaded into anger and killed by Guise's men under the pretext of defending the royal person. But Catherine de Médicis warned him and he played his part so coolly that no one had an excuse to attack him. He had the advantage of being a king, even if only a local one.

Condé was saved this time by the death of the young King François in this very house. A growth in the ear reached his brain.

Condé came back to Orléans later with a Protestant army and occupied it. Then Jérôme Groslot, Protestant son of the first owner of the house and city magistrate, got his own back with a reign of terror on the Catholics, arresting and hanging them for their past misdemeanours. But he was killed in Paris in 1572 on the Guise-inspired St. Bartholomew's Day Massacre. Condé had already been taken prisoner by the Catholic Leaguers and shot. Those indeed were the days of terror and violence.

On the modern place Général de Gaulle is a house built by Jacques Boucher, chancellor to the Duke of Orléans, where Joan stayed in 1429. Well, not quite. It was bombed flat in 1940 and the house is a replica! Now called Centre Jeanne d'Arc, it has an audio-visual presentation, models, commentary, costumes and weapons which do give a fair idea of her victory of 7th May 1429 and her entry into the city.

Orléans is very proud of its art gallery, Musée de Beaux-Arts in a new building. It does have an interesting range of pictures from the 15th century through the Italian, Flemish and Dutch schools to the 17th–18th-century French school, with huge ⁻ religious paintings, 19th-century works including Boudin and Gauguin's 'Fête Gloanec' from his Breton days to 20th-century artists including Max Jacob, poet and painter, who lived nearby at St. Benoît-sur-Loire, until his arrest by the Nazis and death in 1940. Pride of the gallery is an early Velasquez of 'St. Thomas'.

Rue Royale, running down to the George V bridge, is a fine and interesting shopping street. It was built by Louis XV with a new bridge called in those days pont Royal, replacing the medieval bridge which Joan crossed. That had 19 arches, and was a hazard to boating. The new bridge was opened by Madame Pompadour in 1760 and a local wit with more courage than most said that it must be safe because it had just borne France's biggest burden. The bridge was renamed George V after World War I to mark Anglo–French entente. So far, the name still stands.

Part Two:
The Cher and the Eastern Loire

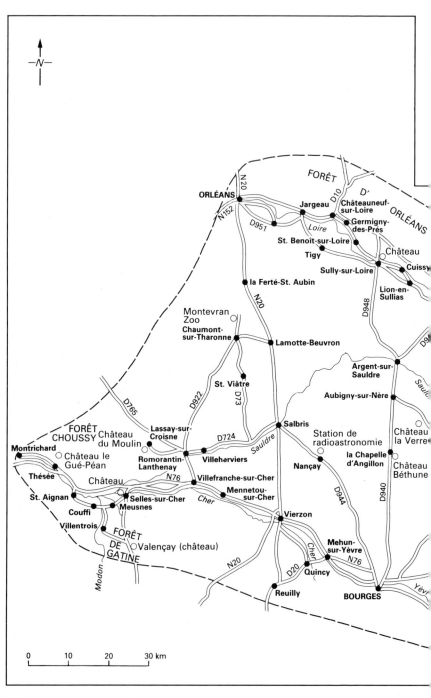

9

The Cher from Montrichard to Bourges

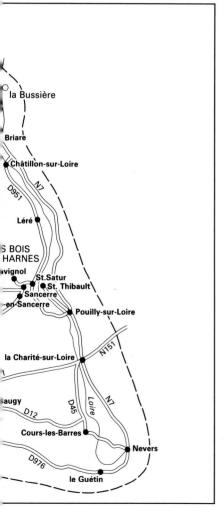

The little-known white Château of **Le Gué-Péan** on the edge of Choussy Forest, 13km east of Montrichard, is the centre for a riding school, which is appropriate to its history. It was a hunting lodge through centuries, very much for the fashionable set of each era. Its guests included several kings, the soldier–priest–writer Fénelon, Lafayette and the less-fashionable Balzac. Though one of its four towers is a solid keep with an interesting bell-shaped roof, it is light and elegant, with two fine Renaissance pavilions with arcades flanking the courtyard. Inside is a little treasure house of interesting items and lovely furniture. The Keguelin family who bought it are a branch of the family who owned it 300 years ago, and their family archives include most interesting documents and souvenirs of Louis XIV, Napoléon and such great writers as Dumas, George Sand, Balzac and the composer Chopin — also of Jean-Lambert, Baron Kainlis, who spent 15 years here studying philosophy. Balzac wrote a novel about him. The tapestries and pictures are excellent and the barrel organ and music boxes still play. There is a small museum of the Resistance, too, for the Marquis de Keguelin was a leader of the Paris insurrection and was decorated by de Gaulle.

You can climb up Château du Gué-Péan's bell-shaped tower and walk along its watch path

the chancel are capitals showing the 'Flight into Egypt' and 'Abraham's Sacrifice'. The Romanesque crypt has wall paintings of the 12th–15th centuries which have kept their colour remarkably for their age.

Although the château is not open to the public, it is worth climbing the monumental staircase opposite the church porch to its courtyard for views over the town rooftops, terraces with fine views of the Cher and its bridges, and to walk around the park.

St. Aignan would be a pleasant stop for a day or two. The caves in the tufa stone hills around here are used for storing white sparkling wine during its secondary fermentation.

Back on D176, running north of the Cher, the cliff overlooking the river just east of Thésée is riddled with troglodyte dwellings and cellars. Then the road joins N76 and moves away from the Cher to the bridge which crosses the river to **St. Aignan**, a delightful little town among forest and vineyards. It spreads itself over a hill dominated by a truly photogenic Renaissance château and ending in a river-port 'resort' with excellent natural sandy beaches, rowing boats, pleasure craft, pedalos for hire and very good fishing in the Cher and Berry canal. There is a riverside camping ground. Among the small streets and squares are half-timbered and sculptured stone houses, and the church built in the 11th–12th centuries is a gem. Through its Romanesque doorway with delicate sculptures is a high nave with capitals depicting fantastic animals and ogival vaulting. In

From St. Aignan it is worth taking D17 past Couffi, turning right on D33 across the border into Indre, then left at Villentrois on an attractive road through the Gâtine Forest to **Valençay**. Here is a handsome château known more for the people who owned it than its history.

It was built by Jacques d'Estampes around 1550. He was a penniless aristocrat who solved his financial problems by marrying the daughter of a financier. He did not stint himself in building his château. It is enormous. Altered through centuries, it is adorned with useless towers to make it look important. It is still surrounded by lovely formal gardens where black swans, ducks and peacocks wander and a vast park in which llamas, deer, kangaroos and dromedaries roam. It is sumptuously furnished, mostly in First Empire style (Napoléon I) but also Louis XVI and Regency. A museum in the orangerie is devoted to Prince Talleyrand. For, at the request of Napoléon, the house was bought in

1803 by Talleyrand, called by de Quincey 'that rather middling Bishop but very eminent knave' and by Vivian Rowe, the English writer with such a love of France, 'the very patron of time-servers and turncoats'.

Charles Maurice Talleyrand de Périgord, son of an officer in the army of Louis XV, was disinherited by his father simply because an accident had made him permanently lame. He left the Sorbonne with a reputation as scholar, wit and rake, and started a career in the Church. By the age of 21, in 1775, he was already Abbot of St. Denis. By 1789 he was Bishop of Autun — quick promotion for a non-believer. Seeing the Revolution on its way, he helped to draw up the Declaration of Rights, and proposed the confiscation of the Church's landed property, which made him president of the Assembly. But he did not like the way the Revolution was going, so he had himself sent to London on a special mission. Then he went to Washington, virtually in exile. But when Robespierre fell he returned to France and became foreign minister. He attached himself to Napoléon and despite disgrace for taking bribes from the British during the American colonial rebellion, he bounced back by supporting Napoléon in a murder.

In 1803 Napoléon told him to buy an outstandingly fine property in which to receive foreign visitors, and gave him some of the money to buy Valençay from a financier who owned it. The first 'distinguished foreign visitor' was ex-King Ferdinand of Spain, deposed by Napoléon. Valençay was his luxurious prison from 1808 to 1814. Talleyrand was made Prince of the Empire but was already planning to desert Napoléon. Though intensely disliked, he became the link between the Allied governments and the Bourbons. He dictated the terms of surrender of Napoléon and made himself foreign minister to the new King Louis XVIII. He deserted Louis when Napoléon returned from his Hundred Days but after Waterloo Louis on his return to the throne was made to take Talleyrand as prime minister by the Allies. As soon as the Allies left France, he was sacked, only to bounce back as adviser to King Louis-Philippe. Then he became ambassador in London. He retired finally to Valençay, having in his old age taken his niece, a Duchess, as his mistress. You can see her elegant room in green, grey and white in the Château. He died in 1838. Only a few rooms are open to visitors. And if the name of Talleyrand is mentioned often in reverential terms by the guides who take you round, that is because the Talleyrand family still lives at Valençay. It is worth going there if only to admire the grounds and to see the luxury in which he lived.

St. Aignan rises in tiers from the banks of the river Cher in the midst of forests and vineyards

Valençay — the 16th-century castle where Talleyrand received princes and diplomats

Back at St. Aignan, the countryside north of the N76 towards Salles and Vierzon is the true Sologne. It is well worth exploring, and we shall go deeper into it a little later. But meanwhile take the quieter and more pleasant D17, through **Meusnes**, where there is a museum devoted to flint knapping. For nearly 300 years muskets were fired by flints, and in the 18th century 500 knappers were employed to supply the French army. The industry flourished in these parts until World War I because of the high quality flint in the chalk. The Meusnes museum is in the Mairie.

There is another museum of flint knapping, combined with an exhibition of old wine growing and making implements, at **Selles**, an ancient, mellow little town. It is prettily placed in a bend of the Cher, with a canal nearby and two little tributaries of the Cher — the Sauldre, coming from the Sologne, and the Fouzon, from the Berry side.

Selles grew over centuries from an abbey founded in the 6th century by a hermit, St. Eustice. Destroyed by the Normans, the church was rebuilt in the 12th and 15th centuries, burnt out in the Religious Wars, partly restored in the 17th century and completed in the 19th century. It's a fine building. There are two châteaux — a fearsome 13th-century fortress, in ruins, on the banks of the Cher, and a 17th-century

Renaissance château. You can visit the furnished rooms, including the bedroom of Marie Sobieska, Queen of Poland, with four-poster bed on a dais.

Follow the little D54 to Villefranche-sur-Cher, a dull place, then take N76 which passes through attractive scenery to Mennetou-sur-Cher and later almost to Vierzon. **Mennetou** is a delight — a sleepy village with steep winding streets, old houses from the 13th–16th centuries and ramparts of 1212 still with three of its five original towers and three gates. Joan of Arc passed through la Porte d'En Bas on her way to Chinon to ask the Dauphin for an army. The church, all that is left of a Benedictine priory, has an interesting 13th-century choir, but it is usually open only for services. The village would make a superb background for a TV thriller or suspense story.

Vierzon is quite different — a thriving industrial town making agricultural and industrial machinery, glass and porcelain, and a water-communication centre, with the Cher meeting the Yèvre river and a port on the Berry canal. It still has some nice old houses on the banks of the Yèvre and some delightful riverside scenes.

Southward from Vierzon on D918 (16km) is the little wine town of **Reuilly** which with Quincy produces the 'poor man's Sancerre' — a dry aromatic white wine made from Sauvignon grapes. It has less individuality than Sancerre or Pouilly Fumé but is much cheaper. Reuilly also produces a little light red wine. Reuilly is in Indre by a few kilometres but its wines are called 'Loire'. At La Ferté 2km away is a fine château built by Mansard in 1636. Try the wine and buy it, perhaps, at the next village to Reuilly, Le Bois St. Denis.

Here young Claude Lafond makes a beautifully fruity Sauvignon white, an elegant and vital (racé) red from Pinot Noir which should be kept four years, and a unique delicate rosé-Reuilly from Pinot Gris. Claude was 18 and studying to be an electronics engineer when he promised his dying dad that he would continue the family's wine-making business. At 35 he has already won gold and silver medals at Paris Concours for white and red wines.

D20 takes you 9km north-east to **Quincy**. Or from Vierzon, D27 takes you direct beside the Cher to the wine village. Quincy white wines are usually smoother than Reuilly. You can taste, and buy if you wish, at Roger Pipet's cave. Roger, fifth generation vigneron, makes light, fine wines with a fresh bouquet 'in the tradition passed down by my ancestors'.

In 4km, D20 reaches **Mehun-sur-Yèvre**, an attractive little riverside town with two towers from a 14th-century castle. N76 or D60 take you to Bourges.

Within a few years, **Bourges** (pop. 80,379) has become an industrial city, caught up in the French technological revolution. It has chemical, aeronautical and metallurgic industries, a Michelin tyre factory and is a military base, too. But industry is around the edges and the centre still has a touch of the days when Joan of Arc's Dauphin was scathingly called 'King of Bourges' because he hid here and had sway over little else in France except parts of the Loire. The centre is extremely interesting but is no place for an impatient driver. Its charm is its narrow streets, many still cobbled. So park (by the cathedral if you can) and walk.

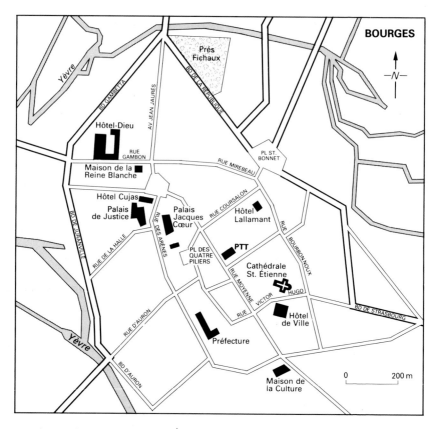

The Gothic cathedral of St. Étienne truly deserves that cliché 'majestic'. It is remarkable and beautiful. Enormously wide, with five great portals on the west front, it has a masterful Gothic uniformity, with repair work through the centuries beautifully matched except for some mistakes in the 19th century. But it is the interior which is so majestic and startling in its effect.

Planned by an unknown architect, it is said to have been based on Notre-Dame in Paris but altered in some respects as building progressed. Begun in 1192, it was consecrated by 1224, remarkably fast for the inevitably slow building methods and transport of those times.

The size and exact unity of the interior strikes you in a flash. It is 110m long (just think of 100m on a running track!), 40m wide and 40m high. Because there are no transepts, you look straight down the nave and choir, and the unbroken line of columns runs with exact precision to the far end. Colonettes make the heavy columns look slimmer, too. The whole is lit by 141 stained-glass windows, including no less than 30 rose-windows, from the 12th to the 17th centuries. The light and colour is worthy of Chartres. Even the organ at the west end dates from 1667. The treasures hidden in the many chapels, the statues, the subjects of the glass, are all too numerous to

Château du Moulin is a 15th-century moated fortress with interesting furnishings

Moulin, captain of Charles VIII's guard, who saved the king's life at the Battle of Fornova (1495). The dining room has a 15th-century sideboard, the salon an interesting painted ceiling, bedrooms have canopied beds and Flemish tapestries. In an enormous fireplace in the vaulted kitchen is a wheel which was pulled round by a dog to work the spit — a method of exercising dogs which would not have appealed to the Royal Society for the Prevention of Cruelty to Animals.

D922 from Romorantin leads to the Cher at Villefranche, while D724 east takes you through the wide Sauldre valley, planted with vines and asparagus, through the asparagus marketing village of Villeherviers, to the N20 at Salbris, on the left bank of the Sauldre.

Fourteen kilometres south-east of Salbris near **Nançay** is the radio astronomy experimental station, which spreads over 2km. A terrace at the entrance, open to the public, has explanatory noticeboards and recorded commentary in English, but the public are only allowed inside at 2.30pm on the second Saturday in each month, except July and August, and you must apply in writing in advance to the station — a long way in advance to have much hope. In contrast, Nançay itself has several artists' workshops, with their work displayed in the Grenier de Vilâtre on weekends.

We shall mention Aubigny-sur-Nère in the next chapter because it is more easily reached from Sully or Gien.

103

10
Orléans to Gien, Pouilly-sur-Loire and Nevers

Many people, including the French, lose interest in the Loire valley east of Orléans. They miss much — interesting small towns and villages, beautiful riverside scenery, river beaches, the Sancerre hills and some of the best vineyards in France.

Leave Orléans by the southerly bank of the Loire, on D951 or better still, if you can find it, by the little road which follows the river bank as far as Sandillon, then on D951 to **Jargeau**. This little town, whose ancient collegiate church dates from the 12th and 16th centuries, became famous to the French when on 12th June 1429 Joan of Arc won her first open field victory over the English. When things were not going well, she mounted a scaling ladder against the castle wall, carrying her standard. A stone hit her helmet. She fell back stunned, but jumped up quickly and called for another attack. The castle fell, the Duke of Suffolk was captured. Joan's mother, Isabelle Romée lived after Joan's death in a nearby farm in the hamlet of Bagneaux, off D951. From Jargeau you can either follow a little riverside road on the left (southern) bank and cross the Loire at Châteauneuf-sur-Loire or cross at Jargeau and take the main road to Châteauneuf.

Châteauneuf was really smashed up in 1940, but time has healed and it has become a most pleasant little market town. Most of the old buildings may have gone but the little that remains is very appealing. One of Louis XIV's Secretaries of State with the splendid name of Phélypeaux de la Vrillière built himself a miniature Versailles here. His magnificent Italian-style tomb is still in the church but all that remains of his château is a rotunda. However, part of his gardens is now a public park with super azaleas and giant rhododendrons at the end of May and beginning of June. There is a formal French garden, too, and a bordering moat with ducks and swans, shady riverside walks, a bathing beach, swimming pool and a picturesque covered market which lures people from many villages around. Built in 1854, it looks much older.

In the basement of the rotunda is the Musée de la Marine de Loire — the history of boats on the Loire and the men who sailed them, with models, tackle and photographs (see box, pp. 106–7). It is vividly presented. In a wild setting among thick woods and tall grasses 11km northwards is a reservoir of the old disusd Orléans canal, called **Étang de la Vallée**. Here you can swim, fish, sail yachts or windsurfers, row or just pdal a pedalo. Boats are for hire. It is near **Combreux**, where there are many ponds and yet another moated château. In the forest of Orléans, which stretches from north-east of the city to about 15km from Gien are masses of attractive pathways for walking, many of them marked.

The D60 from Châteauneuf to Sully is a pleasant riverside drive and much nicer than the main D952. Furthermore, it passes through St. Benoît-sur-Loire, which not only has as its basilica one of the finest Romanesque buildings in France but its history covers much of the story of the Loire from the Druids to the Nazi occupation.

But first you pass **Germigny-des-Prés**, a village with a charming cypress shaded square and a remarkable church built by a bishop in 806, restored in 1869. In the apse is a superb Italian mosaic made of 130,000 glass cubes in gold, silver, azure, purple and green. it represents the Ark of the Covenant.

St. Benoît was the spot where the Druids held their annual council, the Gauls' Stonehenge. With the arrival of Christianity, the church took over the site in the 7th century for a Benedictine abbey called Fleury. The founder of the Order, St. Benedict (Benoît in French) had died in the previous century and was buried in the Monastery of Monte Cassino in Italy, which he had founded. Then the second Abbot of Fleury, Mommole, had a bright idea. Knowing that the Lombards had sacked Monte Cassino about a hundred years before, he sent over a raiding party to Italy in 703. Secretly they dug up the bodies of St. Benedict and his sister St. Scolastica. The journey back to Fleury (1,125km) was not easy. St. Scolastica's

body was wrapped up and propped up on a horse. Monks from Le Mans helped defend the party and in return were given St. Scolastica! The Abbey became 'St. Benoît', the pilgrims flocked in, so did the wealth. It was a master-stroke of medieval tourism. But the Italian monks were furious and legal actions continued until the Pope said that St. Benoît could stay in the Loire.

In the 9th century, when the Emperor Charlemagne ruled so much of Europe, Théodulf, Bishop of Orléans, founded the renowned monastic school at which not only theology but many other subjects were taught — grammar, rhetoric, logic, arithmetic, geometry, astronomy, art, music, medicine, agriculture and industry. Teams of copyists and illuminators compiled manuscripts, writers and historians told the history of the saints and of the times. It was one of the greatest centres of education, culture and civilisation in the world. Several branch monasteries were set up, including one at Minting in Lincolnshire.

Then the Norman raiders came up the Loire in their longboats, but the Norsemen had a long way to row to the abbey and the monks had warning, so they scampered with their relics and treasures behind the walls of Orléans, then came back later to repair the damage. The present church was built from 1067 to 1108 after the old one had been burned down, but the chancel was not finished until the 12th century. By this time the danger of raids had stopped and the abbey became very powerful again.

In the 15th century the system of 'commendatory abbots' was brought in by French kings to reward favourites

Loire Navigation

For around 3,000 years, the Loire river was a major highway. When the Romans came, the Gauls had developed regular river trade in boats exactly suited to Loire conditions. In fact, Greek traders were using the Loire in the Bronze Age. The boatmen had a guild under the Romans and governed their own affairs. Under various names the guild flourished into the Middle Ages, when it was called Communauté des Marchands Fréquentant la Rivière and it dealt not only with rules of navigation but wrecks, dredging of channels (vitally important) and care of widows and orphans. Droits de Boîte, a cargo levy, used to meet expenses, was placed in a quayside box before the boat left.

Richelieu took away some control from the Loire merchants and Colbert, Louis XIV's Minister, took away the rest, appointing 'Intendants' to supervise the channels for the King. They neglected their job, bureaucratic regulations made commerce more and more difficult, and the river began to silt up with sandbanks as the channels were not kept clear. Levies increased so much and there were so many toll points that the cost of a cargo could multiply by four between Nevers and Nantes. And the toll-keepers expected bribes or the boats would be held up. Then the Revolution caused chaos. Napoléon's government did manage to straighten things out (probably because he needed the Loire for carrying military supplies) but the railways came and took nearly all the traffic.

A last ditch attempt was made to save Loire navigation in 1844 with steamboats. Four companies were formed to carry goods from Orléans to Nantes. Competition was fierce. Boats in too much of a hurry blew up their boilers and got stuck in sandbanks, and clouds of black smoke polluted the landscape and dirtied the clothes of passengers. One company launched the 'Inexplosibles' with safety devices to stop boilers blowing up and some large luxury passenger steamships were introduced. But the end was near in 1846 when the Paris–Orléans railway opened, and soon other lines were making river navigation too slow, expensive and so redundant. The river silted up, which is not surprising when you think of all those tributaries bringing silt for so many kilometres (see Chapter 1).

Many types of boat were designed for the Loire's special oddities, such as the *Sapines* which were poled with the current to carry wine to Nantes and were then sold and broken up for their wood, large light *coches d'eau* which carried passengers and were rowed both ways. From Orléans to Nantes took about eight days, and the journey back at least a fortnight. But this was not much slower than going by the appalling roads, was more comfortable and a lot safer. So even kings and courtiers used them sometimes. But the main traffic was carried by *chaland*, sometimes called *gabares*, a name more frequent in the Dordogne. You can see a model of one of these in the Musée de la Marine de la Loire at Châteauneuf-sur-Loire, as well as the tools, sails, tackle and anchors used by the boatmen.

The *chaland* was flat-bottomed, with no keel and with a draught of less than a metre even when fully laden. Its bows were flat and raised, rather like a landing craft, so that they slid on to obstructions instead of ramming them.

Some were as long as 30m, with a beam of 5m but most were about 15m long. The biggest could carry 60 tonnes. They had a single mast, either with a long rectangular sail or main and topsail, and the mast was lowered at bridges by a small winch. There was no rudder. They steered with a sort of oar and with a big pole (*bâton*) which could be attached to the bow and used like the pole on a punt by a very strong man! To tack, they would throw out a big anchor and pole the ship's head round, then haul the anchor in.

If they ran aground when the river was low they could be there until enough rain came. They carried a V-shaped device like a plough to make a furrow so that the current would carry the sand away and free them.

They transported a variety of loads to Nantes, including wine, Orléans vinegar, wool, timber, grain, coal, and returned with fish, fruit, salt, and such imports as sugar, spices, tobacco and rum. The boatmen were said to be tough, hard-drinking, whoring men, yet devout. Inevitably they despised landlubbers, calling the farmworkers 'cow-pat turners'.

and curb the power of the church by hitting it in the pocket. These 'abbots' were often laymen who were granted the church incomes but sometimes took no part in the religious life. The monks of St. Benoît actually refused to receive one such abbot at all until Francis I arrived at the head of troops to persuade them. The abbey declined and then came the cruellest stroke. Its abbot, Odet de Coligny, elder brother of the Protestant leader Admiral Coligny, himself became a Protestant and was able to tell Condé's Huguenots where to find the best loot. The gold was melted down and sold, all the other treasures sold, even the library, collected over 700 years. Magnificent manuscripts were dispersed all over Europe. Some are now in Oxford, Rome, Berne and Moscow.

At the Revolution, the abbey, almost closed, was shut completely. Everything except the church was knocked down under Napoléon I and the church became a wreck. But it was restored as an historic monument from 1835 and the monks returned in 1944. That was the year when the poet and artist Max Jacob retired there, only to be arrested by the Gestapo and taken to his death in prison. He used to conduct visitors around the abbey. He said of the basilica, 'There is something more than the lines of its beauty, something more than the colour and light of the countryside. There is the spirit. The spirit reigns supreme over Saint-Benoît.'

It is certainly an imposing building and it is difficult for an admiring layman to understand how some critics have called it 'austere'. It must have been even more imposing when the towers were taller. The Romanesque 11th-century belfry porch is superb, despite looking a bit unfinished. Its top crown was knocked off by Francis I's troops in 1527 when the monks had shut themselves in the tower. It was replaced in 1661 by a lantern tower. The stone, turned golden over centuries, was brought down-river in boats from the Nivernais.

Inside the porch you can see some strange carvings on the capitals of the columns — leaves and plants alternating with Apocalyptic scenes show-

*The moat at Sully — the château where
Voltaire wrote plays and had them staged*

ing humans, goblins, devils and weird animals, no doubt suitably frightening, hideous and malevolent to peasants in the Middle Ages but looking quite amusing now.

The high-vaulting of the nave and white stonework make it light. The dome in the transept carries the central belltower. The Romanesque chancel, built between 1065 and 1108, has a floor paved with a Roman mosaic brought from Italy in 1531 and the tomb of Philippe I, who died in 1108. Alas, the radiating chapels of the ambulatory are not open to the public. The crypt looks much as it must have done in the 11th century and is rather beautiful. Large round columns leave a double ambulatory with chapels surrounding a central pillar supporting the High Altar above. In a little cell cut in the pillar the relics of the saint are laid.

The basilica is known for its Gregorian chant. Mass is at noon or 11am on Sundays, Vespers at 6.15pm. A monastery shop to the right of the porch hires out audio guides from Easter to 1st November, when the basilica is open to visits from 9–11am and 3–5pm. In winter it is open only on Sundays.

Sully-sur-Loire is a charming town with a river beach on the edge of the Sologne. It faces, across the Loire, its medieval château, surrounded by water. Both have been restored after heavy damage in 1940–1945. A long graceful suspension bridge spans the river. The fortress looks dark and sinister but inside its outer walls is a pretty Renaissance Petit Château, altered later by Henry IV's statesman,

the Duke of Sully, who built the tower. The château contains the finest medieval timber roof in France, erected in 1363.

Maurice de Sully, the Paris bishop who built Notre-Dame, was born here in 1120. Charles VII sheltered here with his mistress Georges de la Trémoille while Joan of Arc fought the English at Patay for him in 1429, and she hurried here to persuade him to go unwillingly

to Reims to be crowned. A year later, having failed to take Paris, she returned and was kept a virtual prisoner for a month.

But Sully is remembered mostly for the man who took its name as duke, Maximilien de Béthune, who bought it in 1602. Successful commander of Henry of Navarre's Protestant forces at Coutras and Ivry, he became the first of the great statesmen who made France great and rich. When Henry took the crown as Henry IV, he became minister of state, attending to finance, industry, agriculture and public works. His greatest achievement was persuading the French actually to pay their taxes. In a dozen years he doubled the state's income.

His fussiness and attention to detail must have tried the patience of his staff and friends. He wrote down every

The basilica of St. Benoît-sur-Loire is one of the finest Romanesque buildings in France

penny spent and even had a written contract with his odd-job man for the building of three rabbit hutches. He spent his later days dictating his memoirs and had them printed secretly on a press in one of the towers of his château, but the imprint was of an Amsterdam printer. No one knows why he used this subterfuge but, after all, Henry IV was dead, Protestants were extremely unpopular in court circles and Maximilien de Béthune had led Henry's Protestant forces to victory, and as a Protestant he had refused to follow the tradition of Lords of Sully of carrying the Bishop of Orléans' chair when he entered the city. Such a Protestant with a private printing press might have been in very great trouble.

The château is a feudal fortress and very imposing — rectangular, with round towers at four corners, two with

pepperpot roofs. Almost derelict, it was bought by the state in 1962 and very well restored. Now it is clean, neat and very cold. Once it stood in the Loire but Sully had an embankment built to protect it from floods, and now it is reflected in the little river Sange tributary which feeds the moats. Though light on furnishings, the rooms give the impression of the comfort which Sully provided. The upper hall of the keep has a remarkable timber roof, put up in 1363 yet still with no worm or rot: the wood is chestnut from trees that were around 100 years old at that time. Only the hearts of the trees were used. They were weathered under water for years, dried for several more years and disinfected before being put up.

In the huge hall on the first floor, Voltaire watched his plays being performed. He sheltered here in 1716 after being exiled from court for his biting epigrams. He was 22 and still called by his real name, François Marie Arouet. He left verses on people's plates before dinner and wrote his first play, *Oedipe*, which was performed by guests of the Duke, great-great-grandson of the first Duke. He chased many of the young women guests, whom he used as actresses. One was Suzanne de Livry, from near Sancerre, who became a more regular mistress. When he was allowed back in Paris, the play was a huge success at the Comédie Française, but then he let Suzanne play the lead and the audience laughed heartily at her incompetence. Obviously quite besotted by her, Voltaire gave her the lead in his next play, *Artémire*, which he also wrote at Sully. She was hooted off the stage. She left him and went to London, to be hooted off the stage there. But she married the

French ambassador, the Marquis de Gouvernet.

During the French retreat in June 1940, the centre of Sully was wiped out by German bombardment. In 1944, to stop the German retreat, a formation of US Flying Fortresses hit St. Germain, the old quarter of the town, whilst aiming to cut the bridge. The rebuilding has been remarkable.

There is good river fishing across the river from the château.

Sully is on the edge of the Sologne, and becomes livelier when shooting parties arrive in season. Twenty kilometres southward by D948 past Cerdon is **Etang du Puits**, a big stretch of water in woodlands with beaches, pedalos and rowing boats, children's park and fishing for carp, bream and pike. Regattas are held here.

Sixteen kilometres farther along D948 and D940 signs reading 'La Cité des Stuarts' lead you to **Aubigny-sur-Nère**. A town of old houses with steep pitched roofs in higgledy piggledy streets and big squares, it now makes lingerie and electric motors. For long it was a Scottish town; Charles VII gave it in 1423 to John Stuart of Darnley for helping him fight the hated English, and Scots craftsmen set up glass-making and wool weaving. The Stuarts, prominent in French diplomacy and war, stayed until 1672, when the last male heir died. The Stuart château is now the town hall, and their arms are on the vault of the church. The most interesting old house, Maison du Bailli, was

Gien arose from the ruins of terrible bomb damage in 1940 and 1944

La Verrerie — the lonely Sologne château given by a French king to a Scot

theirs, too, as was the isolated lakeside **Château de la Verrerie** (11km SE). You can now stay there as a paying guest.

Louis XIV gave all this property to Louise de Kéroualle, the baby-faced Bretonne who became mistress of the English Charles II, Duchess of Portsmouth and mother of Charles Lennox (Duke of Richmond). A later Duke of Richmond sold it in 1834.

Château de la Verrerie is said to have inspired part of Alain-Fournier's novel, *Le Grand Meaulnes*. Alain-Fournier wrote hauntingly about the Sologne. Killed as a young man in the 1914–1918 war, he is revered still in France though little known in Britain or America except among scholars of French literature. He was born at La Chapelle d'Angillon, 14km south of Aubigny, which is the Ferté d'Angillon of his novel. His house is on the left along D940 towards Aubigny, his name is among the War dead in the village church of St. Jacques and the audio-visual presentation at the feudal Château de Béthune tells his story. This was another Duke of Sully château.

You could cut across country to Gien on the D940 from **Argent sur-Sauldre**, an interesting little town with a 15th-century château with large round towers, terraced gardens overlooking the Sauldre, and several very small industries, including dress-making, pottery, dairy and furniture. But from Sully there is a delightful run alongside the Loire to Cuissy and Lion-en-Sullias along the embankment road (levée) then on to the D951 to Gien.

Gien is a masterpiece of post-war reconstruction, a cunning blend of old and new styles and materials. This little peaceful, appealing town decked in flowers much of the year, gives no hint of the terrible devastation of World War II. It is beautiful again.

In June 1940, to cut off the retreat of the French army, the Germans bombed the town for three days, setting it on fire. It burned for many days more. Luckily heavy rain finally put out the fires before they reached the château. In 1944, the Allies tried to cut the railway bridge. Fifty US Flying Fortresses pattern bombed the target. Alas, they missed it and knocked down a lot more of Gien. The road bridge was cut by one RAF Mosquito from one of the specialist pin-point bombing squadrons. It just cut one arch away, which was enough and made repair reasonably easy after the war.

Rebuilding the church took longer, but a masterful job was made of it. The architect was André Gélis, chief architect of Historic Monuments, and he will surely be remembered for centuries. One square tower was left from the 15th-century church. The rest had to

be completely rebuilt. On a framework of reinforced concrete, pink brick walls were made from bricks baked in wood-fired kilns. The effect is beautiful, especially inside the nave, where the bricks are lit from stained-glass windows by Max Ingrand. With Braque and Cocteau, who designed far fewer, Ingrand has left France with some absolutely superb works of art in glass. We are amazed how often French guides, even guides to art treasures, leave out his name and simply say: 'Some fine (or beautiful) modern glass', rather like calling a Renoir 'a fine painting by a modern artist'.

The effect of the windows, brickwork and narrow pillars with decorated capitals is uncommonly warm and light, for the decoration is in coloured Gien earthenware pottery showing events in the life of Joan of Arc, to whom the church is now dedicated. Round the walls the stations of the cross are shown on coloured plaques from Gien's own pottery factory.

Gien's pottery factory (Faïencerie) was started in 1821, using local clay and sand. It is on D952 Orléans road just west of the town. It is known especially for dinner services and objets d'art, but it has made many of the town's attractive street name plates of coloured faïence. The traditional pottery in fact was introduced in the late 19th century in bleu de Gien — deep blue enhanced with yellow-gold decoration. But it produces also delightful many-coloured designs of animals and birds, and also old-style brown-glazed pottery called *vieux grès*. A museum at the factory (open 9–11am, 2–5.30pm) shows hundreds of pieces from the 19th century and also production techniques.

Gien's château had to be much

repaired after the Fortress raid. It contains an International Hunting Museum which the French love and which does have enough interesting items and fine paintings to lure even a passionate anti-hunter.

The château was built from 1484 to 1500 on an old fort of Charlemagne by Anne de Beaujeu, favourite child of Louis XI, who made Gien her chief residence. She was a clever woman and was so successful as Regent for her young brother Charles VIII that Brantôme called her 'one of the great kings of France'. She was only 23 when she became Regent. She gave Gien its beautiful bridge and the church.

The Musée International de la Chasse has a lavish collection of hunting weapons from pre-history to the present — crossbows, powder horns, arquebuses, sporting guns. But it is an art museum, too, with tapestries, paintings, porcelain, pipes, sculptures, and a collection of about 5,000 ornamental buttons from hunting jackets. The large hall with fine timberwork ceiling has a collection of paintings by animal painter, François Desportes (1661–1743), painter of the hunt to Louis XIV. Alas, his lively and dramatic pictures too often show cruel combats set up for Louis between wild animals and dogs. More appealing are the bronze sculptures and engravings of Florentin Brigaud, animal artist of this century, and delightful tapestries designed by René Perrot in our own time showing a great love and understanding of nature.

Gien is a charming place to spend a few days. It is on the edge of the Sologne, too.

Little **Briare**, 10km upstream from Gien, has a famous bridge across the Loire built by Eiffel of Tower fame, which is almost as spectacular as his tower and certainly more useful and more beautiful. It carries a canal, not a road. It is nearly 640 metres long, and there is a wide pavement with stone balustrade so that you can walk across it, with views up and down the Loire river and to woods and countryside.

It was the Duke of Sully in Henry IV's reign who ordered the construction of the Briare and Loing canals to join the Loire to the Seine. The Briare–Loing canal is 104km long and has 52 locks. It joins the Seine at Saint-Mammes, extending the Canal Latéral in effect to the Channel, North Sea and many waterways of North Europe. The barges had to cross the Loire through the river's currents, which was risky. So in 1890 this remarkable Pont-Canal was built.

To the north of Briare and Gien is pleasant countryside with lakes, woods, little streams, market gardens and good fishing. Ten kilometres north of Briare at la Bussière, beside a lake and moat, is an angling museum, open every day.

From Briare follow the busy N7 for 4km then turn right over the Loire to Châtillon-sur-Loire on to D951. At Léré take D751 and D955, a very pleasant route past les Bois de Charnes, to Sancerre.

At St. Satur, just before you reach Sancerre, the D183 takes you in 4km to **Chavignol**, a charming, picturesque wine-growers' village producing one of the best wines of Sancerre and a superb goat's milk cheese, with a pungent smell — crottin de Chavignol (literally goat's droppings — see page 21). Both Sancerre's great gifts to gastronomy, the flinty wine and the powerful cheese, can be bought at cellars dug out in 1972 for this purpose

Wine Tasting

At Domaine Henri Bourgeois, Chavignol, the Bourgeois family have been producing Sancerre wine for ten generations and also make, bottle and mature good wines from other properties. Quite one of the best white Sancerre wines is their 'Côtes de Mont Dâmnés' from south-facing slopes which have been known as far back as the 11th century when lordly local landowners squabbled over them. Now they are in Bourgeois hands, and produce a delicious, strongly fragrant wine, with a taste of its own which stays in the mouth for ages. 'Vigne Blanche' is a fresh, vital wine with a flowery smell. 'Duc Etienne de Laury', which needs to be kept in bottle for a year or more, is another very fragrant wine, produced from 25-year-old vines. Red 'La Bourgeoise', from Pinot Noir vines planted 56 years ago, is the best red Sancerre we have tasted. Matured in oak barrels, it is full bodied and fruity and it would be criminal to drink it young. 'La Bourgeoise' white should be kept a while, too. It is powerful and easy to recognise after a few bottles. You can taste and buy every day 8–11 am, 3–7 pm. English is spoken.

Tasting in Pouilly is not quite so straightforward but is possible. Opposite Relais Fleuri, where there is a good choice at reasonable prices, is the Co-op (Caves de Pouilly-sur-Loire). Its tastings are really for professionals but their wine is worth buying and if you have a genuine interest and are not time-wasting, they will usually let you taste. The 'Les Moulins à Vent' Fumé is dry and fruity, the 'Vieilles Vignes' has more body. They also make a light Pouilly-sur-Loire, and three little-known wines from around Gien and Cosne-sur-Loire (Coteaux du Giennois) — a fresh light Gamay red, a heavier Pinot Noir red and a rosé. Cheap and good value. (Open Mondays–Saturdays 8–12 pm, 2–6 pm.)

Some of the best Fumé wines are produced by Domaine Fernand Blondelet and Domaine Tinel-Blondelet (notice on left, 250m past Relais Fleuri going towards Pouilly). Fernand Blondelet is one of the most respected producers in the Loire. The younger generation runs Tinel-Blondelet Domaine (open 8am–12.15 pm, 1.30–6.30 pm; phone if possible — 86.39.13.83; English spoken).

— Caves de la Mignonne, between St. Satur and Sancerre. Alas, tastings are given only on special occasions. The best place to taste and buy Sancerre for quality and choice is Domaine Henri Bourgeois at Chavignol (see box on Wine Tasting, above).

Sancerre is a beautiful old hilltop wine town with gables and turreted houses lining narrow, steep streets. It has an enormous tower, last remains of its castle. From its lime-shaded terrace are unforgettable views of vineyard slopes, the Loire, and a curved viaduct taking a road to bypass the very old village of St. Satur. In 1534 Protestant Sancerre withstood a Catholic siege for seven months. The people ate powdered slate and leather. Perhaps even these were palatable with the local wine.

The attractive Château de Boucard near Sancerre is still surrounded by a moat and canals

A diversion from Sancerre north-west takes you in 12km to **Château du Boucard** (open daily), a moated castle built in the 14th and 16th centuries. It has many interesting features inside, including beautiful pewterware and a slanting hole in the chapel so that the Princess de la Tremoille could attend services without leaving her bedroom.

St. Satur, still a port on the Canal-Latéral, grew round an Augustinian convent established in the 12th century. The monks planted the surrounding hillsides with vines and began Sancerre vineyards. Their wine was so popular that they grew rich and in 1362 started to build a fine Gothic church. You can see from all that was built, the vast chancel and apse, how ambitious their plans were. They had based it on Bourges cathedral. But the

English marauders arrived before the tower was built. They demanded a ransom of 1,000 gold écus, and refused to believe that the monks did not have this much money. They looted the abbey and church, then locked the senior monks in a tower and set light to it. They tortured the younger ones to reveal where the treasure was hidden, failed, so tied them in sacks and threw them in the river. Not surprisingly the abbey never recovered.

St. Thibault, adjoining St. Satur, was a thriving Loire port until 1860 for exporting Sancerre wine. The little junction canal through to the Canal-Latéral has been restored for pleasure craft. From St. Thibault take the attractive little D243 to Pouilly-sur-Loire, or the busier but equally attractive D920 and cross the river to Pouilly on the D59.

Do not judge this little wine town of **Pouilly** by what you see from the N7. Go down towards the river and savour its wines and food at the Relais Fleuri. Chef–patron Jean-Claude Astruc cooks superbly, especially duck, chicken and river fish, knows a great deal about Pouilly Fumé wines and keeps a fine cellar (for information on wine, see page 28; for tastings, see box, p. 115). Pouilly is a typical tiny wine town and a good place for a night or two because of its good restaurants. L'Espérance has a deserved Michelin star for its regional cooking but is considerably dearer than Relais Fleuri; La Vieille Auberge is cheaper and good value.

Follow the busy N7 to **la Charité-sur-Loire** (only 13km), which produces a drinkable red wine. Here Joan of Arc had her first setback. She laid siege to the town in 1429 but this time the Heavens were on the side of the Burgundians and she had to retire. To

The rolling wine hills of Sancerre

avoid any more N7 traffic, cross the river here on to D45, a fairly minor road, as far as Cours-les-Barres, then left over the river to Nevers.

Nevers is another city which has joined the recent industrial and technical revolution, and the old city on the hill is flanked by tall modern blocks and

117

The Ducal Palace at Nevers, a Medieval and Renaissance blend, is now a courthouse

factories, although the older part of the city still dominates the skyline. Its cathedral contains a sample of every architectural style from the 10th to the 16th century, and is really two churches knocked into one. A few craftsmen still keep up the tradition for pottery and you can buy it in the town, at a price. The first craftsmen came in 1565 from Italy. It is enamelled earthenware fired at extremely high temperatures to make it hard and almost like porcelain. Called majolica in Britain and many countries, it is called faïence by the French, Faenza in Italy where it originated. The Municipal Museum, transferred to an old Benedictine Abbey at 16 rue Saint-Genest, has fine examples of the work tracing changes through the centuries. It has also some fine modern paintings, including Dufy. It is shut November, December and January and on Tuesdays.

The Convent of St. Gildard here is where Bernadette Soubirous spent her life as a nun after her visions at Lourdes. Her body is preserved in a glass casket in the chapel.

Nevers is at the meeting of the Loire and Nièvre rivers and is in Burgundy, but you can hardly miss it if you explore the Loire this far. On small interesting roads you can cut right across the lower Sologne to Aubigny-sur-Nère.

Taking the Bourges road D967 west from Nevers, you cross the Allier river and reach Le Guétin. Here the Canal-Latéral crosses the Allier, too, by a stairway of locks, three up, three down. Nearly 2km away at Le Bec d'Allier the river joins the Loire after a 345km journey from the Cévennes and the two rivers have created sandhills, now clothed with willows — a bird watcher's delight, with egret, terns, nightingales, warblers and long-tailed tits among the trees and on the waterline. Here too the meeting of the waters can lead to the birth of many Loire floods.

Part Three:
The Central Loire

11
Langeais to Chinon

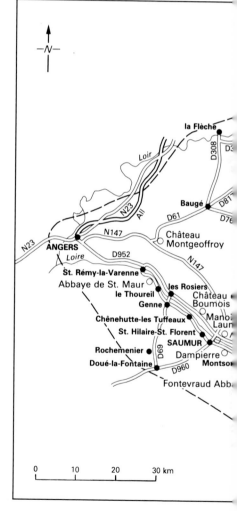

Chinon is a small, smiling, prosperous wine town. Though busy in working hours, it is really a leisurely place and to enjoy it you must explore it at a leisurely pace. Its streets of old houses and shops rise steeply from the tree-lined river Vienne to the still formidable remains of a medieval Gothic fortress — one of those built for power and defence before Touraine and Anjou became the playground of the French court, and Gothic piles were replaced by charming Renaissance châteaux made for love, parties and intrigue and for the hunting of game and bed companions. To us Chinon still looks like a medieval city — a stage-set for a swashbuckling film.

Chinon has a near-surfeit of history. It is only 16km from the meeting of the Loire with its tributary the Vienne, and, like the Loire, the Vienne is a capricious river of fitful moods. In summer the water barely washes the piles of the 12th-century bridge. But in early spring and late autumn it becomes a raging torrent, and you know why a solid river wall defends the quays and the attractive riverside road lined with shops and restaurants.

You have two main choices of routes from Tours to Chinon. The direct D751 takes you to Azay-le-Rideau and its magnificent castle (see

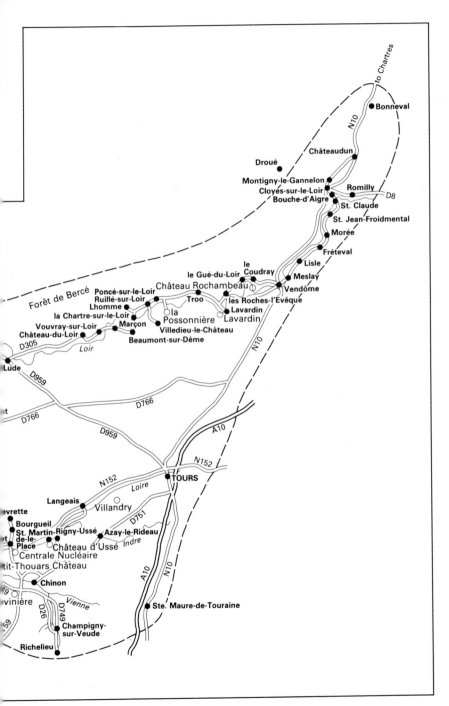

page 42) and then through the lovely oak and pine forest of Chinon where once kings hunted wild boar. In a vast clearing in the forest called Landes du Ruchard in 732, the history of Europe and Christianity was changed. The Arabs, who had crossed the Straits of Gibraltar 20 years earlier, brought an army up to the Loire valley, but here they were defeated and driven back to Spain by the Franks under Charles Martel. The Muslim prisoners were interned and settled in the Véron between the Vienne and the Loire. For centuries the people were said to be much darker than others around here.

You can wander in Chinon forest and picnic. St. Benoît-la-Forêt, where Louis XI kept his falcons, is a pleasant village. But don't stray too deep into Ruchard moorland. You might be shot by the military.

An interesting Tours–Chinon route is to take the N152 from Tours on the north bank of the Loire to Langeais, a busy route for traffic but with river views of many little green islands which grow in size as summer turns the Loire into a friendly stream and shrink in winter rains and in spring floods which cover many completely, leaving their trees fighting to stand up and keep their heads above water.

Langeais is a busy, pleasant little town with a charming suspension bridge, useful for crossing the river without getting mixed up in the traffic of Tours or Amboise. The main square lies hidden from the riverside road and here on Sunday mornings is a big important shopping market to which even wine-makers come from Bourgueil, Chinon and Vouvray to sell their wines in vracs and bottles, and mountains of Langeais melons are piled on stalls in season.

It is still a Loire fishing town, and there are bathing beaches across the river, but Langeais is visited mostly for its 15th-century castle, built strictly for defence in 1465 for Louis XI by Jean Bourré, finance minister to three kings of France. Stuck away on a hill among houses with three thick conical roofed towers and a drawbridge proclaiming its warlike purpose, it is not beautiful but very interesting, for it hides its treasure in its courtyard and rooms. From the courtyard garden it looks more like a huge house than a fortress, with slender staircase towers and attractive slim dormer windows.

Structurally it has hardly been altered over centuries and the interior was brilliantly restored with the help of artists and scholars by the last private owner Jacques Siegfried before he bequeathed it to the Institut de France in 1904. Its flamboyant Renaissance decoration and furnishings give a superb idea of aristocratic life in the 15th and 16th centuries, for when originals were missing, Siegfried had exact copies made by artists and craftsmen in France and Italy. It is unlike other Loire châteaux. You feel that Charles VIII and Anne of Brittany, who married here, might suddenly walk in.

There are lavishly and superbly decorated chests and cupboards, costly carpets and hangings, fine paintings and sculptures, and lovely Flemish and Aubusson tapestries of subjects as wide-apart as hunting scenes and the creation of the world. The chimneys are fanciful. The great hall rises through two storeys to a chestnut timber roof in the shape of a ship's keel. Even the gardens are replanted in 15th-century form. And in them are the ruins of a tower built in 994 by the truculent Count of Anjou, Foulques Nerra.

In a first-floor room is the marriage chest of Duchess Anne of Brittany, ruler of what was then an independent Dukedom. She married Charles VIII here in 1491 when she was 15 — surely one of the strangest 'secret' marriages in history. She was already married by proxy to Maximilian of Austria, whose daughter was engaged to Charles VIII! But Charles had no intention of letting Austria get hold of Brittany and he besieged Rennes to persuade Anne to marry him. The people were starving, and to save them Anne agreed to meet him. He was not handsome but they got along well. They had to marry secretly to avoid her abduction by the Austrians or by Bretons who wanted to stay independent. But she turned up for her wedding in a litter covered in gold cloth and with a wedding dress with 160 sable furs, so she hardly slunk in the back door. The castle's owner, old François Dunois, son of Jean Dunois, Joan of Arc's companion, had known her since childhood. He was so excited at seeing her again that he died.

Downhill from the castle is an attractive creeper-clad hotel with a good restaurant, Hôtel Hosten. Alas, a lorry drove into its salon recently, so rebuilding has been done and Jean-Jacques Hosten, taking over from his father Jean, has leaned towards light modern, nouvelle cuisine dishes. For those who still favour old-style bourgeois cooking at much lower prices in an old-style Logis with the cosy atmosphere of the 1930s–1940s, there is the Hôtel Duchesse Anne, 275m away.

The charm of Langeais for us is that along the side roads to the north you can escape within 5km from the traffic and summer visitors to little agricultural hamlets with small farms, unpretentious old cottages, old-style village shops and bakeries, village bars and relais where they serve four-course lunches of dishes like home-made soups and pâtés, rabbit in wine, farmyard chicken or pot-au-feu with lots of fresh vegetables, local cheese and fruit tart, with a litre of red wine, at unbelievably low prices. We have rented a house here on a track and the local people were oblivious to what went on in the Loire tourist area.

Over the bridge from Langeais, take the tiny D16 along the south bank of the Loire, past a string of islands and the quiet, attractive village of Bréhémont, a port in the days when the river was the main road. The road turns south at Île St. Martin across the Indre river to the unbelievably pretty **Château d'Ussé**, an impressionistic blend of Gothic sternness and Renaissance poetry. Topping a ridge overlooking the Indre river, with terraced French gardens in front and a background of the dark cedars and firs of Chinon forest, it is built of white stones in a medley of towers, pointed rooftops, beautiful curves, lofty pinnacles and tall chimneys spanning architectural styles from the 15th to the 17th century, from a military fort to a graceful home. You can see it best from the bridge across the Indre 183m away, and if you should happen to see it in early morning light or in mist you will know right away why Charles Perrault was inspired to use it as a setting for the Sleeping Beauty. Those dark trees could so easily spread around to hide it until the prince came to awaken the princess with a kiss.

The Duchess of Duras who owned it from 1807 had no fairy-story ending to her love life. After her husband was beheaded in the Revolution, she fell for

High above Chinon stand the ruins of the château where Joan of Arc asked the Dauphin for an army

the writer and politician Chateaubriand. Her son was influential at Court after the restoration of the Monarchy and Chateaubriand used her influence to secure himself the post of Ambassador to London. It seems that he gave her little in return except the row of cedars lining the avenue. Then she helped him to become Foreign Minister and he rewarded her by dumping her for younger and more exciting mistresses. The poor dowager Duchess

wrote to him: 'I have stopped the hands of all my clocks so as to no longer hear the striking of the hours at which you will no longer be coming.'

Ussé is the home of a count, but there are guided visits to part of it from mid-March to 1st November. It contains some interesting items, including Charles X's English-made sporting guns and swords, a delightful Mansard 17th-century staircase, and a suitably ornate Royal Bedroom prepared for Louis XVI who did not come. It is hung with red and white Chinese silks and the voluptuous four-poster bed is canopied like a crown. You visit, too, the charming late-Gothic chapel of 1520 standing separately in the park, with Renaissance décor, some magnificent Italian wood sculptures and a Virgin by Della Robbia. Alas, we never saw the priceless Aubusson tapestries of the life of Joan of Arc. They were stolen in 1975 and have not been seen since. No doubt they will turn up mysteriously at an auction next century.

From Rigny-Ussé, the village, take little forest roads south to St. Benoît and on to D751 into Chinon.

The charms of **Chinon** seduce you almost instantly, whether you wander its old streets with little shops still busy with customers or stroll its more

Langeais — the Sunday morning market

modern riverside road to the place de Jeanne d'Arc. Park your car here or in place du Général de Gaulle to walk the old streets, and stroll first along rue Voltaire. In a side turning is a wine museum and at the end of rue Caves Peintes, which looks out over vine-covered slopes, are the cellars, made from Roman stone quarries, where Rabelais' character Pantagruel used to drink a few glasses of cold dry white. The Chinon wine syndicate still keeps wine in its 1½km of cellars and if you want to throw a big party, for about 400 friends, you can hire the big gallery. Rabelais was a local lad, of course, and wine merchants and restaurants quite properly keep his name alive. A favourite old hotel in Chinon for tourists is the Gargantua, called after Rabelais' greatest character. It is housed in a 15th-century mansion in rue Haute Saint-Maurice and its Flamboyant turret and gable are a delight. Its old-style regional dishes in old-style portions are for hearty eaters.

Rue Voltaire is rich in beamed houses of the 14th and 15th centuries and you find many more as you reach Grand Carroi, centre of the town in the Middle Ages. Some seem to be leaning as if they have over-indulged in Chinon wine.

Beyond here is the Hôtel of the States General, the mansion where Joan of Arc's Dauphin, Charles VII, called meetings of the Estates General in 1428, when the English had taken much of France, including Paris, were besieging Orléans and Charles VII had fled here from them with his court. It was in the castle up the hill that Joan told him of her voices calling her to lead an army to relieve Orléans and save France. The mansion is now Chinon's museum, with relics of Joan

and a portrait by Delacroix of Rabelais. The story that Richard Coeur de Lion died here after being mortally wounded by an arrow at Chalus is almost certainly untrue.

However, the castle was built largely by Richard's father, the Plantagenet Henry II of England, Count of Anjou, in the 12th century. And here he died. This once-great king, who had obtained whole areas of France by marrying Eleanor of Aquitaine when her marriage to Louis of France was dissolved because of her tendencies to embrace other men, caught her at her old tricks and imprisoned her. But she turned their sons against him, and two fought him for his crown. Then unbelievably his third son Richard Coeur de Lion joined with the new, stronger French king, Philippe-Auguste, to fight against him, and, defeated by Philippe, very ill and dispirited, he retired to Chinon castle where he heard that even his fourth son, his favourite John, had abandoned him. He gave up and died. His servants immediately stripped him of his jewellery and rich clothes and made off with them.

Richard became King and strengthened the castle. Philippe could rarely take castles from Richard. But when he died, and John became king, Philippe took many, Chinon among them. The siege lasted a year, mind you, and the castle fell finally to sappers undermining the walls until they split.

Much of the castle was removed on the orders of Cardinal Richelieu, who bought it in the 17th century and dismantled even the great hall (where Joan was received) to use the stone for his new château and town of Richelieu 19km south-east.

The castle of Chinon was in three

parts, separated by dry moats. Fort St. Georges, named for England's patron saint, is now dismantled. Across a moat, you enter the Château du Milieu (Middle Castle) under a tall, thin 14th-century clock tower with a bell from 1399 which still rings on the hour. You can visit the gardens, from which there are fine views over Chinon, the Vienne and its valley. We find that this view alone repays the climb to the fortress. Another bridge takes you over to the Fort de Coudray. The only way you can see the Logis Royaux (Royal Lodge), against the wall of the Château du Milieu, is by guided tour, which takes half an hour. The ground floor is restored and houses a museum, with a model of the castle in the 15th century and a beautiful 17th-century tapestry showing Joan recognising the Dauphin.

All that is left of the great hall is the fireplace. It is difficult to imagine the scene when the peasant girl from Lorraine walked in among scoffing courtiers to tell the Dauphin Charles that God had sent her a message that he was to give her an army to defeat the English and save France. The Dauphin had played a trick on her. He had dressed as a courtier to fool her. But she recognised him, and after much cross-examination was given her command. Charles was probably so desperate by then that he would clutch at any suggestion. She put new heart into French soldiers just at the moment when the English were exhausted, suffering from sickness and from short-age of troops. She took Orléans, returned to Chinon and persuaded the chicken-hearted Charles to go to Reims to be crowned King of France.

From the château ramparts over-looking the Vienne river you get an aerial view of the island which supports the bridge. It is an innocent-looking isle with a path around it. But in 1321 the Jews of Chinon, 160 men, women and children, were burned alive here, accused of poisoning the wells. The wells were probably contaminated by typhoid but, to people of the Middle Ages, the Jews were always a ready scapegoat for their anger.

A happier view is from Clos de l'Echo on the north side of the château, which produces a distinct echo. Here the men of Chinon tease their ladies with some leading questions. 'Les femmes de Chinon, sont-elles fidèles?' 'Elles?' asks the echo. 'Oui, les femmes de Chinon.' 'Non', says the echo.

And on a south-east facing hillside you can see Clos de l'Echo vineyards, producing one of the great wines of the Loire. Once it was owned by Rabelais' family. Now it is owned by the Couly-Dutheil family, who have a shop at rue Diderot by the castle car park where, by phoning ahead (47.93.05.84), you can taste the wine if you are serious about buying it. It is a full-bodied, fruity red wine aged long in cask. Greatest vintages produce a superb wine called Baronnie Madelaine. Try also Domaine du Puy, but keep it until it is five years old.

Chinon produces dry white, a smooth, light rosé and red wines, and the red are now fashionable in Paris. The owner of a Michelin-starred restaurant on the Seine told us that he was buying Chinon now because good Bordeaux was over-priced.

Traditionally red is made with the Cabernet Franc grape (like Bourgueil from across the Loire), called locally le Breton. It gives a herby, fruity wine which traditionally was kept up to ten years, when it is smooth and simply delicious. But the modern fashion is to

The dream-like Château of Ussé inspired Perrault to write 'The Sleeping Beauty'

drink it young, cold and fruity with modern light dishes, which pleases producers who do not have to mature and store it, and also get paid quicker. We like it old. Much Touraine Sauvignon is also produced now.

Another good place to try the wine is le Thélème in place Mirabeau near place Jeanne d'Arc. Here you can buy a glass, a bottle or a dozen bottles of many Loire wines, especially Chinon, and also cheeses and Loire specialities. There is a little restaurant, too.

The Indre river at Ussé

The flag carrier of Chinon wine is Gatien Ferrand at a fine old house **Château Ligré**, marked on the local Michelin map just off D749. The red wines are vital, subtle and superb, the white fine and fruity. Rabelais would have approved. Six kilometres south of the same road is a superb 15th-century château with dunce's cap turrets which he probably knew — **Château Marçay**, which blessedly survived all wars to become an hotel and restaurant with superb classical cooking and a good choice of Chinon and Bourgueil wines.

Nearby off D759 south of Chinon is **la Devinière**, country house of Rabelais' family where he was probably

Rabelais

François Rabelais, satirist, monk, wit, connoisseur of wine and eminent physician, was almost certainly born in the farmhouse La Devinière outside Chinon, although his father, a Chinon lawyer, had a town house in Chinon's rue de la Lamproie. His writing has all the uncouth vitality of the early Renaissance, with coarse humour, a love of the fantastic, witty comment on life and a healthy contempt for pedantry which got him into trouble as a monk. Voltaire called him 'a drunken philosopher'. He was sent to a Benedictine Abbey at nine years of age then entered as a novice at a Franciscan monastery at Fontenay le Comte where the large library enabled him to become a renowned scholar of Greek and Hebrew. But the Franciscans did not believe in new-fangled learning and took away his books. So he fled to a Benedictine house near Orléans and obtained the Pope's permission to switch orders with the help of a bishop. He studied medicine at Montpellier University, became a doctor at Lyon, where he wrote the first of his great satirical stories, *Pantagruel*. Then he wrote *Gargantua*, the story of a giant who could perform prodigies in battle and had an enormous appetite, told in larger than life style which never used one adjective where a dozen could be fitted in and with fantastic and earthy anecdotes thrown in. For instance, when Gargantua goes to visit the Sybille of Panzeau, a wise old hag, to get advice, he cannot resist turning her round and lifting up her skirt.

His character Brother Jean des Entommeures, as a reward for helping Gargantua in a war, is allowed to build the Abbey de Thélème, cloisters which are exactly the opposite from the monasteries where Rabelais had lived. Thélème is to be pleasant and luxurious, have no walls, no clocks, no rules except 'Do what you will' and to admit women. It was obviously Rabelais' own idea of what an abbey should be like. His satirical wit was turned against all pedants, garblers of the French language, intellectual snobs and fussers over detail, rapacious lawyers, and both zealous Catholics and Protestants. On a voyage of discovery his hero reaches the isle of Papefigues (Protestants) and the isle of Papimanes (Catholics), but he prefers the isle of Messire Stomach (the Epicureans).

Behind the fantasy and coarse jokes there was very serious comment on the changing times from medievalism to the Renaissance.

Thanks to his patron, Cardinal Jean du Bellay (uncle of a poet), he enjoyed the income of two parish livings, but resigned both before he died in 1553.

born and which he used as a background to part of his story Gargantua. (A local story is that he was born in a field on the way there because his mother had eaten a surfeit of tripe!) Devinière is a stone farmhouse of great character and is now a Rabelais museum. The local village Sevilly has troglodyte houses (cave houses) down its main street.

The D749 passes Rivau castle and Champigny-sur-Veude to Richelieu. **Rivau**, built in the 13th century, fortified in the 15th, still has its drawbridge and some beautiful Gothic and Renaissance furniture in its rooms paved with white tufa. It is worth seeing but although it is open from 15th March–31st October, you must apply in advance to see it (47.95.71.15). More pleasant than D749 is a lane D26 the other side of the little river Veude. It leads to Champigny, but you can still cut across to Rivau on the way.

Champigny, in the attractive Veude valley, has a magnificent Renaissance chapel — all that is left of its château built in the early 16th century by Louis I of Bourbon. He accompanied Charles VII to Naples and came back with the same love of Italian Renaissance architecture. The ruthless Cardinal Richelieu bought the château from Gaston d'Orléans and had it dismantled because he wanted no competition for the new château he was building for himself at Richelieu. But Pope Urban VIII stopped him knocking down the Sainte-Chapel. And the farm of the château which remains looks as spectacular as many other intact châteaux. For Gaston's daughter, Anne-Marie-Louise of Orléans, known as the Grande Mademoiselle, got the remains back and transformed it into the charming classical house you can see from outside but not enter.

The chapel's stained-glass windows from the 16th century are superb in their elegance and their glowing colours which enrich the whole interior. The focus is the moving picture of the crucifixion on the central window of the choir. Below is St. Louis, who reigned as Louis IX from 1226 to 1270 and died while on his way back from a Crusade. He was patron-saint of France until Joan of Arc took over in 1920. There are portraits of members of the House of Bourbon-Montpensier and a series telling the story of Louis' life and death, including some vividly colourful groups of Crusaders and their tents decorated with family arms. For delicate elegance these are some of the finest stained-glass windows in the world.

It is amusingly ironic that all that remains of Cardinal Richelieu's great château, in the town of **Richelieu** 6km down the D749, are a domed lodge-pavilion, canals, two more pavilions, an orangery (hot house) and wine cellars at the end of formal gardens. The works of art with which this powerful despot filled his palace are spread around many museums, with a sculptured group 'The Slaves' by Michelangelo in the Louvre in Paris; twelve paintings showing the victories of Louis XIII are in Versailles and other major works in the museums of Poitiers, Tours, Orléans and Azay-le-Ferron. After the Revolution, when the château was confiscated and stripped of many treasures for the Museum of French Monuments, Richelieu's descendants sold it to an asset stripper named Boutron who knocked it down to sell as building materials. But the great park which surrounded the palace remains — 475 hectares crossed by straight avenues lined with chestnuts or plane trees. And there is a large statue of him.

Richelieu himself had knocked down or allowed to decay nine other châteaux, including the royal palace at Chinon and the great fortress of Loudon, to avoid any competition with his ostentatious palace.

In 1621 he was still just Armand du Plessis when he bought Richelieu, then a village and manor. He had the estate raised to a Duchy. When he became Cardinal and First Minister of France, and one of the most powerful men in

New trees are still planted in the old Chinon forest: this is a plantation near Ussé

Europe, he commissioned Jacques Le Mercier, architect of the Sorbonne and the Cardinal's palace (now Palais-Royal) in Paris, to build him not just a palace but a wall-enclosed town so that his court would surround him. It was the first example of real town planning. When he was 12, Louis XIV visited it and later built something similar at Versailles. The town was built in a rectangle 700m by 500m. The entrance gatehouses still

stand, topped with tall roofs. So does Grande-Rue, lined with 28 absolutely identical houses with monumental doorways. The whole town was planned with geometric precision, orderly and lacking any individuality — predecessor of modern Manhattan, perhaps. Opposite Notre-Dame church (Classical–Jesuit style, in white) is a fine 17th-century covered market roofed in slate. The town hall, once the law courts, has a Richelieu museum (closed Tuesdays and Sundays out of tourist season).

Work on Richelieu town ended with his death in 1642 and it was too far off the map to become important. Now it is a market town for cattle farmers and holds cattle fairs. And it is the terminus of a little steam railway that runs to Chinon with stops at Champigny-sur-Veude, Coutureau and Ligré-Rivière every weekend between 25th May and 15th September, taking 1½ hours for the journey.

The prosperous wine town of Chinon, seen from the Vienne river

12
Chinon to Saumur

Take D751 west from Chinon and you come to an entrancing little château where you can taste the wine of one of France's most distinguished families. The Counts of **Petit-Thouars** have owned and made wine at their château overlooking the river Vienne since the 16th century. The present count, Comte Yves du Petit-Thouars, makes a delicious Touraine Appellation Contrôlée wine which is matured for a year in old chestnut barrels in fine old caves cut in the hillside. You can taste and buy.

One of his ancestors, an Admiral, finished a distinguished career at Aboukir against Nelson. His leg was shot off, so he ordered his men to stand him in a barrel of sawdust to stop him from bleeding to death. But die he did, shouting, 'Don't lower the flag!' The present count, Yves du Petit-Thouars, has just written a book on *Wine and Women*.

Just westward is the historic royal abbey of *Fontevraud*, where for centuries an abbess ruled over both monks and nuns, which infuriated some monks. Nearly all the abbesses were royals.

Here you can see some of the warring Plantagenets lying at peace with each other at last. Here lie Henry II of England, great legal reformer and opponent of the Roman church's interference in civil government, whose chance remark led to the murder of Thomas à Becket at Canterbury; his beautiful, wayward queen Eleanor of Aquitaine whose first husband Louis VII of France had divorced her and whose second, Henry II, had imprisoned her for her affairs and who had retired to the abbey; her beloved son Richard the Lion Heart who rebelled against his father, and Isabella, wife of the unreliable King John. They are all buried here, and lie together in stone effigy. There is more to see, especially an ingenious medieval kitchen.

The Vienne river from Petit-Thouars to its meeting with the Loire at Montsoreau is attractive, with several islands. **Candes-St. Martin**, a very old town on a hillside sloping to the bank of the Loire, has a fine church of the 12th-13th centuries on the spot where St. Martin died in 397 (see page 11). At 80 he had come to Candes to settle the quarrel between monks of Poitou and Touraine. They then quarrelled over his body, but the monks of Tours removed him in secret to his own abbey.

Montsoreau is the river port for boat trips running between here and Chinon from April to October. Take the little

Nuclear Power

Following D749 north from Chinon you see an enormous silver-sphere alongside the river before the Port Boulet bridge. This object which might well have fallen from space, 55m in diameter, is part of the Avoine-Chinon Nuclear Power Station. Put into service in 1963, it was the first nuclear power reactor in France to generate electricity. This prototype EFD 1 was shut down in 1973 but not destroyed. Two units called EFD 2 and 3 have a capacity of 540,000 kilowatts and annual production of 3,500 million kW. Four new production units (Chino B 1–4) have a capacity of 900,000 kilowatts and produce 24,000 million kW annually. A belvedere has plans and models to help us understand what goes on. Groups can be shown around by arrangement (minimum notice 2 weeks — 47.93.04.50).

It was a crying shame to put these plants right alongside such an attractive part of the river, where the Vienne meets the Loire and islands have formed. But a lot of water is needed for nuclear plants and in the 1970s and early 1980s the new technology of France stood way above the environment in French Government priorities. It probably still does.

There are great arguments about what the nuclear plants on the Loire do to fish and fishing. The warm water from the plant is said to make some fish grow very big indeed, but there is no doubt that the water reaches temperatures beyond the tolerance of many fish, and we are told that this includes trout. We have also been told of oxygen impoverishment and toxic poisoning of algae and the appearance of strange micro-organisms.

St. Laurent-des-Eaux Nuclear Station is built on an artificial island in the Loire, reached from the left bank 10km downstream from Beaugency and 30km from Orléans off D951. An information centre explains the workings and the problems of nuclear energy (open 9am–6pm daily). Between St. Laurent-Nouan and the station is a big experimental fish farm and greenhouses using heated water from reactors to find out what happens to fish and vegetables.

Another nuclear station is at Dampière-en-Burly, 13km west of Gien (3-hour guided tours with 1½ hrs of films, by appointment — 38.29.70.04).

steep road alongside the auberge Diane de Méridor (excellent cooking) to the attractive little village overlooking the castle. Elegant old houses are decked with flowers in summer, and the village seems to have stepped aside from the traffic below. Steps take you to a high belvedere for fine river views over the village and château to the meeting of the Vienne and Loire.

For centuries this hill road was the main highway and until 1820 the castle walls were lapped by the river. Finished in 1455 by Jean de Chambes, one of Charles VII's chamberlains, the château is a fort from outside, a country house within. The Chambes family were a tough lot of warriors with conniving women. One lady of the castle became mistress to the Duke of Berry, brother of Louis XI, and they formed the League for Public Good (Ligue du Bien Public) aimed at doing good to the Duke by putting him on the

Wine from the vineyards around Chinon has won the admiration of Parisians

throne. Louis found out and had them assassinated. Another Chambes was one of the most ferocious killers in the massacre of Protestants on St. Bartholomew's Day, 1572.

The novelist Alexandre Dumas told the story of the lovely, fickle Françoise de Montsoreau in *La Dame de Monsoreau.* He called her Diane de Méridor and was as brazen in his twisting of the story as she was in her love affairs. She fell for Louis de Bussy d'Amboise, a bully, formidable swordsman and duellist and an instigator of the St. Bartholomew massacres. He boasted of his conquest even to King Henry III who made a joke about her husband: 'Our Master of the Royal Hunt has let his own quarry fall into de Bussy's snares.' Her madly jealous husband forced her to arrange a meeting with de Bussy at the

The Sainte-Chapelle at Champigny-sur-Veude is pure Renaissance

now-vanished château of la Countan-cière across the river and killed him before her eyes. She was not too overcome with grief, it seems, for she lived happily with her husband afterwards and bore him six children.

Oddly, the château has a Goums museum devoted to the Conquest of Morocco and to the Goums, cavalry units recruited in Morocco by the French and used effectively in two world wars, especially in Italy in 1944. Goums means Knights. Brave and superb horsemen, they were hardly chivalrous, especially to any young ladies they met while campaigning. The museum was moved here in 1956 from Rabat, the Moroccan capital, when Morocco became independent again.

Cross the Loire shortly after Montsoreau — the N152 is far more attractive than D947, and approaching across the bridge this way gives you a superb view of Saumur and its château.

Saumur (pop. 33,953) is a delightful town that grows on you. Its 14th-century compact and massive castle, standing on a sheer cliff overlooking the town, is softened by the terraces of gardens garlanded with vines that step down the castle slopes.

With its heights overlooking a good river crossing, Saumur was fought over by the counts of Anjou and Blois for centuries. Thibault the Trickster, Count of Blois, left a fortress there when he died in 877 and it was a problem to Foulques Nerra (Foulques the Black), the warring Count of Anjou. So when he heard that the Count of Blois Gelduin had left it to attack one of his fortresses, he rushed all his troops there and attacked. The defenders were too few to defend every gate, so

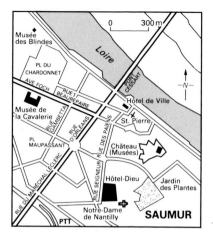

the monks within suggested that the holy shrine of St. Florent should be left to defend the east gate. Their faith was unjustified. Foulques had his men pick up the shrine reverently and take it to safety, then he marched in. So the Counts of Anjou ruled Saumur and, as the title fell to the Plantagenets, the English ruled it. And they and the Dutch got a taste for Anjou wines, which were exported from the port.

Though Louis Philippe took Saumur for the French crown in the 12th century, the port thrived still on exports, and people and ideas reached the town from all over Europe. Thus it became a great centre of Protestantism, and finally Henry III gave it to his Protestant ally Henry of Navarre as a stronghold. It became more than that. Henry appointed as Governor Duplessis-Mornay, a great soldier and scholar and ardent Protestant. He fortified the castle, which had been built in the 14th century by Louis I, Duke of Anjou, and made more comfortable inside by the last Anjou Duke, René I, the man who preferred scholarship, culture and relaxation to power, politics and war. Then Duplessis-Mornay,

Wine

Across the Port Boulet bridge beside the Nuclear Station north of Chinon is the Bourgueil wine country. Here the wine is made mostly from the Cabernet Franc grape, like Chinon red, but the wine is different.

Chinon produces a clean, fruity wine, with a flowery smell, which the trade calls 'violets', and should have a beautiful ruby colour. It is pleasant drunk young at cellar temperature to taste the fruit, but can be a revelation when kept for five years or so and drunk at room temperature.

In Bourgueil some wine is also made from Cabernet Sauvignon on which most of the best Bordeaux wines are based. On different soils, two types of wines are produced — one light and fruity, with a pleasant smell of raspberries, the other is heavier and needs time to mature. Often the two are blended, producing a wine which when kept up to 10 years produces a delicious drink with a clean, no-tannin taste but enough acidity to stop it collapsing. The kinship to Médoc tempted some Bordeaux wine merchants to use the wine for blending to stretch claret many years back. Wines from the nearby village of St. Nicholas-de-Bourgueil are said to keep best, but that may have been successful local propaganda. At Chevrette, ½km north of Bourgueil, is Cave Touristique de la Dive Bouteille, a cave set up by dozens of local growers and wholesalers. The ancient cave is charmingly illuminated and includes big wooden wine presses dating back to the 14th century. You pay 9 francs for the visit and tasting of one glass of good wine. For tasting of many more wines, go to Maison Audebert, avenue Jean Causeret, Bourgueil, owners of several vineyards covering 28 hectares who also raise and sell other growers' wines from Bourgueil, Chinon and Saumur-Champigny (telephone 47.97.70.06 if possible; English spoken).

St. Hilaire–St. Florent, suburb of Saumur on the south bank of the Loire along D751 towards Angers, was the centre for wine long before it produced mushrooms and riding instructors.

In 1811 Jean Ackerman from Alsace, who had worked in Reims, introduced the Champagne method of making sparkling wine — the first time it had been done outside the Champagne. Red grapes are allowed in Saumur Mousseux but one difference from Champagne is that the white grapes must include at least as much Chenin Blanc as Chardonnay or Sauvignon. They are some of the best quality sparkling wines, whether crémant or fully sparkling. Ackerman Brut Royal is especially good.

Ackerman Laurance caves are open for guided tours 1st May–30th September, including weekends.

More than two-thirds of Saumur wines are white, dry or demi-sec. The dry are fruity. Demi-sec are called Coteaux de Saumur and as they come from the same chalky-clayey soil they are rather like Vouvray with a bouquet of honey and flowers. They go very well with fish and light meat, such as veal or pork. Saumur AOC red wines are light in colour, low in alcohol and fruity. But Saumur-Champigny, made from Cabernet Franc, are much better. They have a smell of raspberries, smooth palate and nice after-taste. The modern tendency is to drink them under two years old at cellar temperature. We prefer them 5–10 years old at room temperature — the way they were always drunk until recently.

See Wine Tasting list (pp. 211–213) for other tasting caves.

known as the 'Protestant Pope', set up a Protestant Academy which drew scholars from all over Europe and rivalled Geneva. Protestant craftsmen arrived, too, and Saumur really prospered. But when the Edict of Nantes guaranteeing freedom of religion was revoked, the Protestants fled abroad, leaving Saumur almost deserted.

The château became a prison, then a barracks. When the town authorities took it over it was in a sorry condition. But it still looks magnificent, with its roofs and pointed gables standing out against the sky. And it contains two interesting museums. The Museum of Decorative Arts, helped by a substantial bequest by a local scholar, Comte de Lair, in 1919, contains fine medieval and Renaissance pieces: Limoges enamel, furniture, painting, pottery and porcelain of the 17th–18th centuries and superb tapestries from the 15th–

The Abbey at Fontevraud where Plantagenet kings and queens of England are buried

ings by George Stubbs, and a remarkable glass model, done by an enamelwork artist who lived to be 100. It shows the Cavalry School in the 19th century. But the pride of the museum is a skeleton. It is of an English horse, the super-stud Flying Fox, who died in 1911 aged fifteen, at the height of his career as a seducer. With an enormous stride, he won the Derby, Two Thousand Guineas and St. Leger in 1899 for the Duke of Westminster. His owner died next year, the heir was on army service in Africa and could not be found, and the crazy executors put Flying Fox up for auction. A delighted Edmond Blanc who owned Monte Carlo Casino bought him and many great French horses were descended from him. It would have been no surprise if the young Duke on returning from Africa had horsewhipped the executors. It was Blanc who, asked if he knew a winning system for his casino, said: 'Sometimes Noire wins, sometimes Rouge wins, but Blanc always wins.'

Saumur is known for its cavalry school, its wines, its mushrooms, and its carnival masks, the best in France. The Cadre Noir, in black uniforms with gold and curious two-cornered hats, was formed in 1763 as a cavalry regiment from the best horsemen in the army from all over France. It was not called the Cadre Noir until 1814 under Napoléon. Its great buildings which are headquarters of the Cavalry Academy were built in 1767 but now they train armoured officers and NCOs in tanks and jeeps. Since 1972, the Cadre Noir

18th centuries, including some which used to decorate the lovely local Romanesque church Notre-Dame de Nantilly. The church still has plenty left. A strange exhibit is the workshop of a Gallo-Roman carpenter, dug up at St. Just-sur-Dive.

The Museum of Horses is interesting even to anyone whose interest in horses is mainly aesthetic. There are horseshoes and harnessing, prints, paintings, a fine collection of engrav-

Good King René

Just over the bridge from Saumur, a mere 3km eastward along N152, is a little road left leading to Manoir de Launay, which is marked on the Yellow Michelin map. Alas, you cannot enter but you can peep from the lane at this oblong house with a fat tower and pepper-pot roof. Here good King René, born in 1408, last of the Dukes of Anjou, used to hide like a sensible man with his best friends from his castles at Saumur and Angers, from cares of state and political squabbles. They held friendly tournaments in the surrounding fields and sat around in the sunshine playing music, singing and listening to each other's poetry.

René had one of the most cultivated minds of his time. He was a friend of Charles d'Orléans, the poet, whom he visited at Blois. Besides being Duke of Anjou, he was Count of Provence and, through conquests by an earlier Duke, King of Sicily and Naples. He became King of Naples but failed to take the crown of Sicily. How much this upset him is debatable.

He was married when he was twelve to Isabelle de Lorraine, and one of his titles was Duke of Lorraine. Anjou had taken as its symbol a double cross which had been brought back from Constantinople in the 13th century. Thus it became the cross of Lorraine, which General de Gaulle chose as his symbol for the Free French Forces in Britain in World War II.

René was married a second time to a girl of 20, Jeanne de Laval, who was a very popular queen. Towards the end of his reign, his nephew Louis XI annexed Anjou for the French crown and he retired happily to Provence to improve the local agriculture and write Provençal poetry. He died aged 72 in 1480.

His daughter Margaret was not so fortunate. She was married to Henry VI of England, who was weak and sometimes had mental breakdowns. She had to manage her husband and virtually rule England. The word got around that a secret part of her wedding contract was to hand over Maine and Anjou to France, and that made this foreign queen very unpopular in England. They blamed her for the loss of Normandy in a war. When she was 25 her husband became totally insane and Richard, Duke of York, became Protector. Henry recovered, fell ill again, and the Wars of the Roses began. After a brave struggle of nearly 20 years, she was finally beaten at Tewkesbury in 1471 and lay in the Tower for four years. Louis XI was in no hurry to ransom her, though he had stripped her father of nearly all his possessions. At last he did pay the money and she returned to France. She did not join her father. Instead she lived in a house at Souzay owned by one of her father's old servants, François de la Vignolle, then at Château de Vignolle at Dampierre, where she died at 54. She was called 'unhappiest of mothers, unhappiest of wives, unhappiest of queens'.

Dampierre is 4km south-east of Saumur along D947. The manor house where she died, cut into the hillside, is charming — a lot better than living in the Tower of London.

has been part of the National Riding School, training riding instructors, both civilian and army. It is in a modern building at St. Hilaire-St. Florent, the wine-making suburb of Saumur. But the superb horsemen still take part in the great tattoo in July on place du Chardonnet, these days joined by a motorised rodeo of tanks, armoured cars, motorcycles, jeeps and helicopters, with sham battles.

The story of the Cavalry Academy is told in the Cavalry Museum on avenue Foch. Here you can see superb porcelain figures from Sèvres and Meissen in uniforms of Napoléon's Army and the Imperial Guard, jewel-studded swords and Egyptian sabres, plus a history of the French cavalry through two world wars and the Indo-Chinese and Algerian campaigns. It is open afternoons 15th April–15th October except Mondays and Fridays, and on Sunday mornings.

Musée des Blindés (Tank Museum) in place du Chardonnet, has 150 armoured vehicles, from France's Renault tank of 1918 to German Panthers, Soviet T34s and the British Conqueror (open daily).

You can visit also the National Riding School at St. Hilaire — a very modern, automated stables for 120 horses, with a conveyor-belt for removing horse dung and an automatic distributor which pipes correct amounts of grain to each horse at fixed hours. There is a good commentary.

Another interesting museum, 2km west of St. Hilaire, is Musée de Champignon (Mushroom Museum). As Paris grew, mushroom growers emigrated from the Paris suburbs to old tufa quarries in the hillsides around Saumur, although the mushrooms are still called Champignons de Paris. There are 800km of growing tunnels, producing over 120,000 tonnes of mushrooms a year. The tour shows you methods of growing, from the old system using stacks of straw to more modern methods with wooden crates and plastic bags (guided tours 15th March–15th November).

Saumur has several attractive and interesting churches. St. Pierre and, particularly, Notre-Dame de Nantilly are well worth visiting for their very beautiful tapestries. And there are fine old half-timbered houses alongside 18th-century houses with wrought-iron balconies in place St. Pierre.

Overleaf: *The formidable castle of Saumur stands on a sheer cliff looking down on the town*

143

13
Saumur to Angers

Instead of the D952, which is busy here, take the little D229 from the other side of the railway station at Saumur towards Angers. As the road joins the D952 just before St. Martin-de-la-Place, **Château de Boumois** lies hidden in the trees about 300m back. It is a handsome Flamboyant Gothic castle with a moat and fat jovial towers which are machicolated. Through their parapet and holes, defenders could pour down boiling oil or tar to discourage attackers. As so often with Loire châteaux, the feudal exterior in white tufa stone hides an inner house of graceful elegance. Boumois was another seat of the powerful Dupetit-Thouars family (see chapter 12) and the admiral Aristide Dupetit-Thouars, who died so bravely fighting Nelson at Aboukir in 1798, was born here in 1760. The château contains some mementoes of his short but very adventurous life. It was he who organised the massive Pacific Ocean search for survivors from the two lost ships when the French explorer the Count of Lapérouse lost his life in 1788. His nephew, also an admiral, took over Tahiti in 1842 and made it a French protectorate. The family, despite their several châteaux and vast lands, had survived the Revolution by keeping out of politics.

The château is very light inside. A turret staircase leads to the living rooms, enclosed behind a door with Renaissance motifs and a great wrought iron lock. In the great hall on the first floor is a collection of 15th–16th century arms and you can walk the parapet. The Flamboyant chapel with a pointed roof is beautiful, the dovecot enormous. It has 1,800 nesting holes, 300 more than Villesavin, so the revolving ladder for collecting eggs and for cleaning was needed. It was built in the 17th century and shows how much land the owner must have possessed (see box). Though not so impressive or historically important as some of the big châteaux, Boumois is charming and shows how people lived.

St. Martin-de-la-Place is a pleasant spot to relax. An old port, it still has its slipway, a quay, grass, trees, and sands when the river is low in summer. It looks across the river to **Chênehutte-les-Tuffeaux**. The quarries at Chênehutte were dug to provide stone to build many châteaux of the Loire; now mushrooms are grown in them. The 16th-century priory, which commands the river with splendid views, is now a beautiful Relais et Château hotel in wooded grounds of 15 hectares. It has a Michelin star with prices to fit. You

Dovecots

Dovecots were a sign of wealth and power in feudal Europe, and huge dovecots like those at the Châteaux of Boumois and Villesavin showed that their Lords owned vast areas of land. The right to keep doves and pigeons (called *fuyé* in France) was limited strictly to the nobility and to one nesting hole for each artent (about ½ hectare) of land they owned. These birds were used not only as meat for the Lord's table but for shooting practice. Clay-pigeon (la Trappe) shooting did not take over until fairly modern times.

But what infuriated the peasant farmers was that the lords did not feed these birds and the peasants were not allowed to shoot them. So they fed all the time off the peasants' crops — in the case of Boumois, 3,600 of them. This was one of the peasant grievances which led to support for the Revolution.

can cross it by the bridge between Les Rosiers and Gennes, and the roads from St. Martin and Chênehutte to this bridge are almost equally pleasant.

A long, attractive suspension bridge joins the two little towns of Les Rosiers and Gennes. We are very fond of **Les Rosiers**. It is a typical little Loire riverside town, with old-fashioned small shops, and a church with a Renaissance belltower by the Angevin architect Jean de l'Espine. And it is a good place to eat. There are two good cheap restaurants, Van de Loire and La Toque Blanche. The expensive favourite of Queen Elizabeth, Britain's Queen Mother, is named after Jeanne de Laval, the wife of good King René. Her statue stands in the square. Alas, our friend Albert Augereau, one of the great classical chefs of France, is dead, but his son Michel keeps up the tradition which will outlive all fashions — the best, freshest ingredients, immaculately cooked in butter, varying with the market and seasons.

Gennes, over the river, is more like a village than a town. It is built on the sides of a steep knoll, topped by the

ruins of St. Eusèbe church, with wide views. Part of the church choir and transept date from the 11th century, the steeple from the 12th century, the rest of the choir from the 15th century. The sad but proud graves at the base of the south wall are from June 1940 and are of cadets from Saumur Cavalry Academy. Colonel Michcon, commander of the Academy, and his staff and cadets were so ashamed of the deal Marshal Pétain had made in capitulating to Hitler that they ignored orders to withdraw to Montauban. Their little force of 1,200 men and 800 cadets decided to hold three Loire bridges, armed with two ancient field guns, a few old tanks, World War I machine-guns, practice rifles and hand-grenades. Their stand was called 'comparable with the Charge of the Light Brigade', but although it was as courageous as that death charge, it was not so futile. For the Academy stand not only gave others time to escape and hide in the south of France, so that later they could join de Gaulle's Free French in Britain, but set an example for French resistance to the Nazis at a

low moment when their government had given in.

The bridges they held were at Gennes, Montsoreau and Saumur. At midnight on 19th June the first German tank crossed the Saumur bridge. It received a direct hit from a cannon fired by a cadet. Six more tanks and two lorries got the same treatment. The Nazis brought up high-speed armour and rushed the bridge. It blew up. All three bridges had been mined. It took the Germans 24 hours to bring up reinforcements and pontoons. They crossed at last and in hard fighting the Academy force had hundreds of casualties and ran out of ammunition before giving up. The Colonel was accused of wasting young lives. But one officer who survived told Arthur in a German prison-camp: 'We were French soldiers. We were fighting an evil for France and the World. How could we walk into a prison-camp without firing a shot?'

In the hills behind Gennes are four prehistoric dolmen (passage graves). The best, **La Madeleine**, is on the D69 Doué road just outside Gennes. Last century a farmer used it as a bakery, with an oven in the main chamber. That should have awakened the dead.

The D69 runs through Milly forest which is still recovering from being felled in fairly recent times. To the right at **Rochemenier** (1km along D177) is an interesting underground museum. Until the 1930s the villagers lived in chalk caves, and the museum shows how troglodytic farmers lived and worked. **Doué-la-Fontaine**, an old and

new town built above caves used for storage, is famous for rose nurseries and has a Jardin des Roses open to the public on the Soulanger road. A rose festival (Journées des Roses) is held in mid-July in an arena made from open quarries back in the 15th century when rows of seats were cut out of the rock. It is used for plays and musical performances. In the Vendéen wars the Vendée prisoners were kept in the caves below. Doué also has an 8 hectare zoo in pleasant surroundings among quarries, grottoes and tunnels, with some birds and animals running free. Troops of rare apes roam freely on islands.

The D132 along the left bank of the Loire towards Angers is another attractive route, leading to the charming little former port of Le Thoureil and the abbey of St. Maur.

Behind **Le Thoureil** apples and vines still grow. On the quayside you can see some splendid Renaissance houses, built by Dutch merchants who liked to live on the spot so that they could be sure of getting the best wines for export. In days of river transport the local boatmen used to take the apples and wine upstream to Nevers and through the canals to Paris, where they would tie up at one of the quays and turn their boat into a shop until they sold out, then they would return with a cargo of barrels and staves. The boats were a cross between canal barges and the Loire flat-bottomed shallow-draught *chalands*, and were called *bâtards*. Some houses still have nautical graffiti cut into stone. Now it is a place for sailing, fishing and watersports.

Four kilometres along the road is the abbey of St. Maur. He was a Roman disciple of St. Benedict who came here

Château de Boumois, home of a heroic admiral who died fighting Nelson

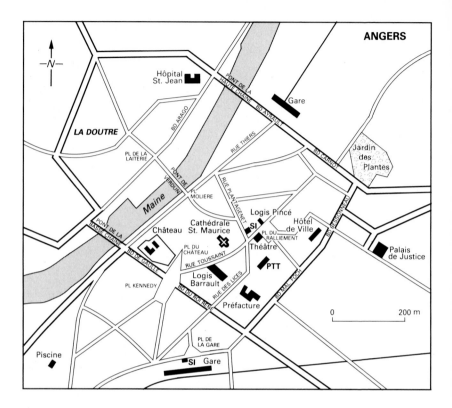

in the 6th century and founded a monastery on the site of a Roman fountain dedicated to nymphs. A 12th-century chapel survives and remains of the 16th-century abbey. It is now an international ecumenical centre welcoming all people of good will.

Just after St. Rémy-la-Varenne recross the river for a drive into Angers with some fine river viewpoints. **Angers** (pop. 141,143) is not a city which appeals to visitors immediately. Its surrounding 'new city' in white, its heavy traffic, hide the delights of the old city. Furthermore, Angers seems to be turning its back on the Loire river, for it stands on the banks of the Maine, formed by the meeting of the Mayenne and Sarthe. But take to your feet in the

pedestrian precincts and narrow streets of the old town and you will find treasures galore.

Start at the castle, which truly dominates Angers. With its seventeen huge bastion towers and awesome enclosure walls 600m long, it is a fearsome sight. Yet it must have been even more dominating before two storeys and the pepperpot roofs of the towers were cut down to the curtain of walls in 1585 under the orders of Henry III. In fact, tiring of squabbles between Catholics and Protestants, he had ordered the château to be razed, to be 'shaved down to the ground so that no niches or cubby holes remain to harbour man or beast'. He wanted to stop Protestants or Catholic Leaguers

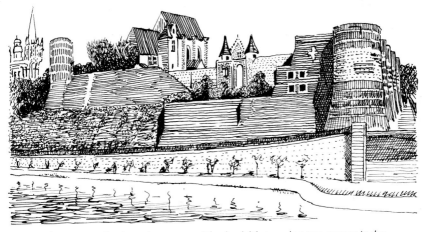

Angers from across the river; the towers of the feudal fortress lost two storeys in the Religious Wars

using it. The Governor stalled long enough on the demolition job for Henry to die and the orders to be forgotten. But the RAF nearly carried out Henry's commands in 1944 when they bombed the castle because the Germans were using it to store munitions. They hit it, but luckily for Angers the Germans had hurriedly removed anything explosive.

Foulques Nerra had a wooden fort on this site. But fifteen years after Philippe-Auguste confiscated Anjou from King John of England (John Lackland), his grandson Louis IX (St. Louis) rebuilt in stone, in record time, between 1220 and 1240 because he feared the return of the English. Parts of the interior have been demolished and rebuilt over the centuries. Yolande of Aragón, mother of good King René, had the chapel built entirely in white tufa stone because she did not like the old one. In the Napoleonic Wars this chapel was used as a prison for British sailors. The stripe-effect on the towers comes from the use of the local dark shale alternated with bands of white limestone. This shale and the dark slate of the roofs gave Angers the name of 'Black Angers' until light relief came from the whiter buildings lining the wide boulevards of the modern city.

The sinister appearance of the castle is relieved these days by gardens planted with lavender, marguerites, hollyhocks and vines between the inner and outer walls and the deer which live in part of the moat where King René kept his menageries.

But the joy of the château is its tapestries. There are four delightful 15th- and 16th-century Flemish tapestries in the royal apartments (Logis Royal) built by King René's father, Duke Louis II of Anjou. The 'Lady at the Organ' is very pleasing. So are the two scenes of animals, birds and plants from Audemarde. Tapestries have been called 'the wallpaper of the Middle Ages'. What wonderful wallpaper!

The 'Apocalypse Tapestry' in the Grand Gallery is the wonder of Angers. It was commissioned by Duke Louis I of Anjou and made in the workshops of

Nicolas Bataille in Paris between 1373 and 1380. But the designs were by Henniquen of Bruges, and are now in the Bibliothèque Nationale in Paris. The original was 130m long and 5m high. Alas, only 75 pictures have survived and these are inevitably faded, but they do show the vast scale of the work, the clear and pure composition and design, the crispness of line. Considering the extraordinary story of the tapestry, we are indeed lucky to have so much.

When he left for Provence, turned out of Anjou by his nephew Louis XI, the last of the Dukes of Anjou, King René, gave the whole tapestry to Angers cathedral. It was brought out only at festivals and then suffered the fate of much Gothic art and was stowed away. The church even tried to sell it in 1782 but found no buyers (Christies would have found one!).

In the Revolution, Angers was on the side of the people. The cathedral was sacked and turned into a Temple of Reason. The tapestry was thrown into the streets and local citizens cut off lengths to use as carpets, bedspreads, even horse-blankets and cart covers. In 1843 a Bishop started a search and recovered about two-thirds of it. Most was found on a rubbish dump.

The story of the tapestry follows fairly closely the Revelation of St. John and opposite each of the pictures is the relevant verse from the Bible — in French. You can hire a taped commentary in English but we find these can distract from the enjoyment of a work of art. The pathos and terror in the faces must have frightened the simple folk of the Middle Ages back on to the straight and narrow path for a time after looking at them. But it all leads to the victory of Christ shown in prophetic vision and, of course, the triumph of the church. The modern tapestry 'Le Chant du Monde' by Jean Lurçat in another Angers museum prophesies a different ending to the world. But Lurçat was a humanist and an opponent of nuclear arms.

It was in the castle at Angers that in 1598 Henry IV ended the troubles with the extremist Catholic League by betrothing his four-year-old son by his mistress Gabrielle d'Estrées, César of Vendôme, with the six-year-old daughter of the Duke of Mercoeur, leader of the Leaguers. A week later at Nantes he issued the Edict giving freedom of religion. It was, of course, revoked on his death, followed by the St. Bartholomew's Day massacres of Protestants and subsequent fighting all over France. But the most difficult period for Angers came with the uprising of the Vendée Royalists against the Republic in 1793, when Republican Angers was in constant danger from the Royalists of the silent countryside to the south, les Mauges. The peasants of the Vendée were genuine Royalists and were upset at the execution of Louis XVI and the persecution of their priests, but what really upset them was an order for conscription to fight on the east front against Austria. The fighting was bloody and bitter, with atrocities by both sides, typical of civil war. Ten months after the uprising, effective Royalist resistance was shattered by defeat at Savenay, and thousands of Vendéens were executed in Angers on place du Ralliement, the busy centre of the town now lined with shops.

Angers castle with its 17 huge defence towers is still a fearsome sight

The old town of Angers may not have been so well preserved as some other cities of the Loire but it is pleasant, with much of charm and interest. Take the side street opposite the castle, mount steps and you come face to face with the Cathedral of St. Maurice. Gothic, dating from the 12th to 13th centuries, its façade has a handsome door topped by three towers. Over the west door is a tympanum of Christ risen, with figures of saints and biblical characters looking at the throne in wonder. Way above the door is a frieze of St. Maurice himself with his 'companions' in medieval military uniforms — rather anachronistic, for they were Roman legionaries of Diocletian's reign. We cannot read the Latin inscription but we are told it says, 'Bring peace in our time, Lord, and scatter nations who want war' — a laudable prayer. You need binoculars to see these sculptures properly. Maurice was an officer in Diocletian's elite Theban Legion, recruited from the East of the Empire. Ordered to attack a Christian settlement in Gaul and exterminate its people, they all refused, so the Emperor had one in ten put to the sword, until there were none left.

As with many Loire churches, the glory of this cathedral is the original stained-glass. Blessedly, as at Tours, it survived bombing as well as earlier wars. There are precious 12th-century windows in the wide nave, gloriously coloured windows of the 13th century in the choir, a breathtakingly beautiful 15th-century rose-window in the left transept, and dozens of others all round the cathedral from two dozen medieval to modern windows in the chapel of Notre-Dame-de-Pitié. To the right of the chancel is a window showing the life of Thomas à Becket. Among the treasures is a green marble Roman bath used as a baptismal font for the Dukes of Anjou.

Behind the cathedral is Maison d'Adam, an attractive 16th-century half-timbered house, with posts decorated with curious small carved figures. Its name comes from an apple tree below a corner turret. Adam and Eve were there, too, but disappeared in the Revolution.

Along rue Toussaint towards boulevard de Gaulle is the David of Angers Gallery in a former 13th-century abbey church. Jean-Pierre David (1788–1856) a local lad found fame as a sculptor with a prolific output of lifelike portrait statues, busts, reliefs and medallions, only often much larger than life. Each time he completed a piece, he gave a plaster cast copy to the museum. So here are monumental statues including an outsize King René, a giant Jean Bart, Breton corsair who raided Plymouth in 1689, was taken prisoner, but escaped three years later, and busts of famous people of David's time — Victor Hugo, Balzac, Paganini, Goethe, Chateaubriand. His 'Young Greek Woman' is beautiful. David led something of a revolution in French sculpture from classicism to more-popular realism.

South of the church is the Logis Barrault (Fine Arts Museum) in a lovely 15th-century house. In the 17th century it became a seminary and later Talleyrand was a pupil. On the first floor is a collection of medieval and Renaissance furnishings, including gorgeous carved chests, sculptures and exquisite enamels and ivories. Paintings on the second floor include fine primitives, a good small portrait of Catherine de Médicis, and an outstanding collection of paintings from the

Jean Lurçat (1892–1966)

Though known mostly as the reviver of the art of tapestry — he left behind about 1,000 tapestries now scattered all round the world — Lurçat was a noteworthy painter, an artist, litho-artist and a very distinguished ceramic artist.

Born in the Vosges in 1892, he set out in 1911 to study medicine but switched to the Art Nouveau school at Nancy, then went to Paris where he studied with many well-known artists. He became friendly with the fresco painter J.P. Laffitte. Home on sick leave from the trenches in the 1914–1918 war, he persuaded his mother to work his first embroidered tapestries. He travelled extensively after World War I in Spain, North Africa, Greece, Asia Minor, had his first exhibition of paintings in Paris, designed embroidered tapestries and costumes for the theatre. He became interested in cubist surrealism, had his first exhibition in New York in 1928 and his first *woven* tapestry made at Aubusson in 1933 ('L'Orage'). He stayed in New York several times in the 1930s and designed scenery and costumes for Russian and American ballet.

When World War II broke out, he was at Aubusson, tapestry-making with Dufy. He was in the Resistance in the Lot from 1941 and after the war he bought St. Laurent Tower, former fortress at the lovely little town of St. Céré in the Dordogne, where he lived until he died in St. Paul de Vence in 1966. You can see much of his work in St. Céré in the nicest surroundings. The Casino bar is decorated with his ceramics, cartoons and tapestries which you can admire with a glass of wine in your hand. And in the charming hotel, Coq Arlequin et de Paris, you can eat gastronomic meals while admiring some of his tapestries, including the famous 'Coq Arlequin', a brilliant tapestry of a puffed-up cock in a coat of many colours. Hotel owner Gérard Bizat, whose family have owned the hotel for five generations, is himself an artist, formerly professional, and was a close friend of Lurçat. Apart from 1,000 tapestry designs, Lurçat left behind 600 paintings, 300 gouaches and several hundred ceramic designs. We have found his tapestries in many places, from Orly airport to the Burgundy wine museum in Beaune and a small hotel in Portugal.

18th-century French school. Boucher's 'Reunion of the Arts', showing plump children playing with paint brushes and musical instruments, is delightfully frivolous. Fragonard's Rococo 'Nymph' is bright — almost dazzling. 19th-century works include a pleasant large view of 'The Seine at Paris' by Jongkind and Millet's 'St. Barbara'.

One of the finest areas of Angers is over the river — the quarter of La Doutre, from 'd'Outre-Maine', beyond the Maine. Inhabited since the Middle Ages, it was the snob area of nobles and affluent bourgeois until the Revolution, then fell on hard times. But the old timber-framed houses are in good repair, the fine 15th-century mansions of the pretty place de la Laiterie have been restored and there are more fine houses, along rue Beaurepaire which joins this square to Pont de Verdun, especially No. 67, decorated with statues. It belonged to an apothecary.

The finest building on this side of the Maine is the former St. Jean Hospital, now the Lurçat Museum. The hospital was founded in 1174 by Henry II of England and Anjou and his Seneschal Etienne de Marçay and cared for the sick until 1854. The beautiful 12th-century hall for patients has three naves with graceful Angevin vaulting. As with many old hospitals in France, such as Beaune, it was arranged so that patients in bed could all see the altar at the end of the hall. Now Jean Lurçat's tapestries called 'Le Chant du Monde' (The Song of the World) line the walls.

Lurçat (1892–1966 — see box), the artist who revived the great old art of tapestry, first saw the 'Apocalypse Tapestry' in Angers in 1938 when he was already 46. He was profoundly impressed. Nineteen years later he started his own masterpiece. He was a humanist and held strong views on nuclear warfare, so many critics called it his 'answer' to St. John's prophecy of the end of the world in Revelations. Having known Lurçat and talked to him, we do not think that he saw it that way. It was a modern version, an update of what he called 'The Great Threat'. But he was adamant that his was not a disdainful or gloomy view of life. His original title was 'La Joie de Vivre' and he wrote: 'It has not taken me long to be convinced that life for one who tries to live correctly is sweet and salted, mild and bitter, convulsive and serene.'

He wanted to show the menace of the atomic bomb ('La Grande Menace'), and the first tapestries are devoted to it — the bomb itself; an inhabitant of Hiroshima, burned, stripped, emptied, all reason for living

shattered; the 'Charnel House of Death' (influenced, he said, by his experiences in the trenches near Verdun at the age of 20); the 'End of Everything' — no more sun, stars, fish, birds ... no more men ... the great emptiness, eternal silence. He showed this by snow on a black background and one last plant, broken and dying. But then he started to show 'man and our reasons for living'. He showed 'Man in Glory in Peace'; 'Water and Fire', the source of all life; a gloriously joyful, bubbly tapestry called simply 'Champagne', a magnificent panel called 'Conquest of Space'; a charming panel called 'Poetry', and finally 'Ornamentos Sagrados', brightly coloured jewels. One trouble is that Lurçat never finished his work. What we have is 80m long and he intended to design tapestries up to 125m. So his story of peace and life as opposed to war and death was never finished.

The work has been called enigmatic, terrifying, a stirring cosmic fantasy, and, by a current British critic, 'undistinguished'! Another Briton, Richard Wade, called it 'a riot of modernist platitudes in a disordered dream'. Surely not such a 'disordered dream' as John's Revelation? Many people have seemed puzzled and called it 'obscure' or 'difficult to decipher'. It should not be. There are notes beside each tapestry, a recorded documentary, and, above all, an excellent illustrated pamphlet by Lurçat himself and translated by himself into English ('It is courteous to explain oneself to one's public'). One thing seems certain — the form, beauty and above all the colours make it a work of genius. But even the colours do not appeal to everyone. Lurçat uses black backgrounds to bring out the riotous

Cointreau

Cointreau, the liqueur with a piquant-sweet flavour, is made in Angers — and it is named after a family. To quote the company publicity of a few years back, the liqueur 'was born of the happy marriage between the alcohol of Angers and oranges ripened under the sun of the tropics'. And it was first produced by the brothers Edouard and Adolphe Cointreau in 1849 and the family ran the company for several generations.

Originally the family called the drink Triple Sec Curaçao, but so many companies stole the Triple Sec tag that they put their name on it.

Cointreau is the joy of cocktail mixers. Most famous of its cocktails is the Sidecar (shake with ice one part Cointreau, one part lemon juice, one part Cognac — or two parts Cognac if you are a brandy addict). Less known is Silent Third — as above, but replacing the brandy with Scotch whisky. And there is White Lady (¼ Cointreau, ¼ lemon juice, ½ gin).

and glorious colours of his deep and bright blues, reds, orange and gold. It is almost his artistic trademark. But one critic has called that 'sombre'. The truth is that Lurçat's personal beliefs did not please many churchmen or politicians and they objected to the message in this work.

With so many superb interiors to see, Angers needs some open spaces where you can get fresh air and sun. It has very attractive landscape gardens (Jardin des Plantes) to the east and on the left bank, park-like ('English style'), with fine trees, a lake, and an exotic plant garden. And beside the Maine river to the north is Maine Lake, excellent for sailing, water-skiing, or just watching others do the same.

Angers is also a good centre for river cruises. Cruisers run on the Sarthe, Mayenne and Loire. The Loire cruisers Roi René I and II are similar to the Seine's Bateaux Mouches, with huge panoramic windows, bar and gastronomic meals. They start from Quai de la Savette across the Maine from the Château (41.88.37.47). All other cruises and self-drive boats (80 boats available) on Maine, Sarthe and Mayenne, information and bookings from Maine Reservations, Maison de Tourisme, place Kennedy, 49000 Angers (41.88.99.38).

Angers is one of the biggest fruit exporting centres in France. You can buy at the big daily food market on rue St. Martin, east from the Préfecture.

There is plenty in Angers to interest most people for at least a three-day visit. So don't be put off by the traffic and hurry, which is un-Loire-like.

14
The Loire from Angers to Châteaudun

The **Château of Montgeoffroy** (just off N147 east of Angers) is a delight to visit. It is no museum. Montgeoffroy is still the home of the de Contades family, whose ancestor Marshal de Contades rebuilt it in 1775, and if the old soldier who died in 1795 were to walk in now, he would find hardly anything changed. Every piece of furniture stands in the place for which it was designed, and even the backgammon table awaits players. King Louis XVIII played on it when he visited the family.

The Marshal, whose enemies said that he had received his rank for 'successfully losing the Battle of Minden', was as meticulous as you would expect of a soldier. He seems to have ordered all his furniture from Paris in one batch, from leading furniture makers such as Gourdin, Garnier and Durand, whose signatures appear on some pieces. He had an inventory made which still exists. A French writer Pierre Verlet published it in full in 1966 in his book *La Maison du XVIIIe siècle en France*. There are fine pictures by Desportes, Van Loo, Rigaud, Drouais and the younger Pourbus, and beautifully matched carpets, curtains, wall-panelling and tapestries. Although only certain ground floor rooms are open to the public (large and small salon, billiard room, dining room and

Madame Hérault's apartments), they give a vivid picture of the way that a nobleman lived in the 18th century.

It seems to be a miracle that all these treasures survived the Revolution. But, as Vivian Rowe said in 1969 in his book *The Loire*, a clue lies in the apartments which the Marshal gave to Madame Hérault of Séchelles. Her son, Marie-Jean Hérault, whom Carlyle called 'one of the handsomest men in France', was a member of the National Assembly after the Revolution, helped draft a new constitution and was twice President of the Convention. Furthermore, he had the protection of no less a man than Danton, the greatest of the Revolutionaries. But Danton fell and they met at the bottom of the guillotine. Danton nodded at the basket. 'Our heads will meet in there,' he said, and they did. The old Marshal was left alone until he died next year. Then the Directory took over and the house was kept safely by a local lawyer until the family returned.

The Marshal's cenotaph is in the chapel of 1543 which he left intact when he rebuilt and which has a fine 16th-century stained-glass window. He left also two round towers and the moat. In one tower is a superb collection of the family's old coaches and carriages. The present château, which was designed by the Paris architect Nicolas Barré, stands at the top of a long gentle slope amid a park and fruit orchards. A handsome building, it has an almost-military symmetry, with a huge central pavilion 2½ storeys high and two wings at right angles. Its only three-dimensional decoration is the Contades coat of arms.

Pick up the little D61 road northeast of Montgeoffroy, turn right and you reach **Baugé**, a peaceful little town with fine houses seemingly almost as undisturbed as Montgeoffroy. It might surprise Yolande of Aragon and her son King René, who personally supervised much of the building of the château in 1455, to find that it is now the town hall. René loved it; but then he always preferred little manor houses to his great castles at Angers and Saumur because he disliked ceremony. It is attractive but simple and its main feature is a cleverly built spiral staircase.

There are fine old mansions in the quiet streets of Baugé, especially in place de la Croix-Orée. Near the 16th-century church, on rue Girouardière, is the Filles du Coeur de Marie Chapel (once the Chapel des Incurables). It houses a 13th-century relic said to be part of the True Cross. There are plenty of these in Europe, of course — enough to build a house — but this one is unusual. It is large and it has two cross-arms. It was brought from Constantinople in 1241 to the now-vanished Abbey of la Boissière and ornamented in the 14th century with gold crucifixes on both sides and precious stones. Then it was taken to Baugé for safe keeping.

This double-armed cross became the heraldic emblem of the Counts of Anjou and as René became Count of Lorraine, it was adopted there as the heraldic emblem, too. So it became called the Cross of Lorraine, chosen by Charles de Gaulle as the emblem of the Free French Forces in Britain in 1940. And while de Gaulle lived, it was almost a national emblem.

The shorter and more pleasant way from Baugé to the remarkable château of Le Lude, which boasts the biggest and best of Son et Lumière, is along the small D817 and D305 roads. But that way you miss the little town of la Flèche and it is really worth the extra 14km, taking two sides of a triangle on main roads, to see this interesting place.

La Flèche runs along the Loir river, which passes through as much attractive scenery as almost any in France. The town was born around a medieval fortress in the river. It grew after a priory was founded, and was given as part of a dowry to Charles de Bourbon, Duke of Vendôme. When he died in 1536 his widow came to live at la Flèche and built herself a Renaissance house. Fifteen years later her son Antoine de Bourbon and his wife Jeanne d'Albret took it over. Their son Henry was conceived there and, although he was born at Pau, spent much of his happy childhood at la Flèche. He was Henry of Navarre, who became France's favourite king, Henry IV. When he became a Catholic and King he gave the house to the Jesuits as a college. One of their pupils was Descartes, called by some 'the father of modern philosophy', though many of his findings as a scientist and a philosopher have been superseded. His belief in logical argument based on an undeniable premise has had an effect on French thinking and education for centuries, and is still the basis of much education. He was a pioneer of analytical geometry, which was his major gift to the human race.

The Jesuit priests from la Flèche set up early missions in French Canada. Three were massacred by the Iroquois and later canonised. Another graduate, Monseigneur de Laval, became the first Bishop of Quebec. After the expulsion of the Jesuits from France in 1762, the college became a military school. Then Napoléon turned it into a Prytanée, for the sons of officers and higher civil servants, which it still is, with pupils in uniform.

La Flèche has charming gardens by the river (Carmes gardens) and is a market town for fruit from the Maine. Recent industrial development has been kept carefully away from the older town. Five kilometres away, just off D306 Tours road, is a zoo in a forest 'Le Tertre Rouge') with a natural science museum.

The D306 is the road to **Le Lude**, a small town of narrow streets on the south bank of the Loir where they make dairy products and furniture, have a nice riverside beach and a château which frankly bewildered us when we first saw it some years back. It is not so much the diversity of architectural styles which is obvious but the lack of intent by the various builders and restorers. None seemed to be quite sure what they wanted the house to be like.

Le Lude was the natural place to build a castle, for it controlled two important roads and the Loir river. Foulques Nerra (971–1004), the belligerent Duke of Anjou, and ancestor of the Plantagenets, was a great strategist and held off his powerful rivals, especially his arch-enemy the Duke of Blois,

by building castles at strategic points. He placed them so that his army could march quickly from one to another. It was inevitable that he would build at Le Lude. But his was a wooden fortress and was replaced in medieval times by a stone castle which in the 13th and 14th centuries repelled attacks by the English. The English did take it in 1425 but the French got it back four years later. In 1457 Jean de Daillon, friend from childhood of Louis XI (he did have some), acquired it and his son started to make it into a home. Basically, it is a square fortress with a plump round tower at each corner. The south face is mid-16th-century and attractive. Round towers have Renaissance refinements, with pilaster-framed windows, dormer windows, medallions and carved ornaments. To the east is the Louis XVI façade, Classical style in white tufa stone, symmetrical and severe. To the north is a Gothic façade, the earliest, built under Louis XII, but with stone balconies and a statue of Daillon added last century.

Inside, the house is charming and richly furnished, with the usual idiosyncrasies of a home which is lived in. Fairly modern pieces are mixed with fine decorations and furniture from the 15th to the 18th centuries. Three 16th-century Flemish tapestries are on the dining room walls, a 17th-century Gobelins tapestry on the library wall. The ballroom has been restored in 15th–16th-century style. The house is the home of Countess René de Nicolay. It is open in the afternoons (3–6pm) from 1st April–30th September, but the gardens are also open in the mornings, and they are delightful — lawns and park divided by a lovely stretch of river and capped on the hilltop by woods. The Son et Lumière show in summer is on the banks of the Loir. And it is what the old-timers of Broadway would have called 'a million dollar spectacular', even if Michelin does call it just 'a memorable evening'. A cast of 350 in period costumes follows five centuries of the castle's history amid changing lights, vivid sounds, and 300 luminous fountains. There are fanfares from red-coated huntsmen, cavaliers, a state barge on the river, ballet and, on Fridays and Saturdays, a great firework display. It is called 'Les Glorieuses et Fastueuses Soirées au Bord du Loir' which they translate as 'Sumptuous Nights on the Banks of the Loir'. It is formidable in any language.

The medieval castle at **Vaas** just upstream was once almost as important at Le Lude, and kept changing hands between French and English, but now the little town is known for its riverside leisure beach and watersports. It has an old riverside lavoir where some local women still do their laundry. It's as sociable as a laundrette and not so noisy.

All that remains of the once-important château of **Château-du-Loir** is a keep, from which there are views of this very pleasant countryside. And all that remains of the priory given to the poet Ronsard as a benefice in the 13th–14th centuries is the Church of Guingalois, which has a 17th-century terracotta Pietà in the chancel by de Mello. The pleasant old town clusters round it.

From here the Loir valley becomes even more attractive. There's lovely country a few kilometres northwards, too, with fine walks and drives in the Forest of Bercé. For a lovely run to La Chartre-sur-le-Loir, missing most traffic, take D64 from Château-du-Loir then right on D61 to Marçon and Beaumont-sur-Dême, then D62 to La Chartre.

This is Coteaux de Loir wine country, and 3km east of Château-du-Loir is **Vouvray-sur-Loir** which confusingly produces a Vouvray wine — dry and white, but not with the superb flowery bouquet and fruity flavour of the *real* Vouvray from the Loire. Loir wines are more acidic, though made with the same Pineau (Chenin Blanc) grape, and improve if kept a little while. You can taste this Vouvray in the Cave Municipale in the Mairie. The reds have a nice colour and are fruity. The Loir wine that is rather like Loire Vouvray is Jasnières from the communes of Ruillé-sur-Loir and Lhomme, just east of La Chartre. In good years it has the natural sweetness of honey, like a Vouvray demi-sec, with delicacy and finesse, but in poor years can be green and acidic. It is difficult to get because here on the Loir climatic conditions are awkward and yield is low. There are troglodyte houses along D64 and some former dwellings now housing wine.

La Chartre is a very pleasant holiday spot, especially for anglers, walkers and sailing enthusiasts. It has a fine outdoor swimming pool. The pleasant traditional Hôtel de France, with lovely garden, was used by the great Aston Martin and Lagonda teams when Britain used to win the le Mans 24-hour race regularly.

The D305 is very attractive all the way from below Château-du-Loir to Pont de Braye, but after La Chartre there are interesting things to see on both sides of the Loir river, so a few short cross-river excursions are rewarding. If you cross at the wine village of Ruillé, for instance, a 6km drive takes you to **Villedieu-le-Château**, an attractive village in a lovely setting, its ruined ramparts and houses with pretty gardens surrounded by slopes of fruit trees and vineyards. Recross the river for the drive to **Poncé-sur-le-Loir**, where there are two craft workshops and an interesting Italianate Renaissance château. The first workshop (Atelier de la Volonnière) is for leatherwork, painted furniture, painted silk and antiques (open weekends). The second, by the river (Centre Artisanal du Poncé), is for glassware, pottery, ironwork, weaving, woodwork and candle-making (open 9–12, 2–6; Sunday afternoons).

The château, probably of Francis I's period, had originally two pavilions joined by a central staircase-tower, but one pavilion was replaced in the 18th century by a dull building. The wing was burned down in the Revolution. But the staircase is remarkable. As at Azay-le-Rideau and Chenonceau (both designed to the wishes of women), the staircase goes straight up, not in a spiral. It has six flights, and the coffered ceilings are all decorated with 130 mythological and allegorical sculptures of elegance and sharpness of detail. They are quite beautiful. The gardens, which are also open for strolling and resting, have 'lawns, tree-covered walks, and a terrace with an avenue of limes. There is a dovecot, too, with revolving ladders reaching 1,800 nesting holes.

Just past Poncé is yet another château, la Flotte, overlooking an attractive valley. Marie de Hautefort, first love of Louis XIII, was banished here from court by Richelieu. but the château was rebuilt last century.

Across the river (2km by D57) is the manor house **La Possonnière**, where the poet Pierre de Ronsard was born in 1524. Alas, it is a private house and all you can do is to study from the outside the engraved Latin tags which Ronsard's father, a soldier, had engraved in stone when he built it. You are unlikely to be able to read these unless the family are away and you have applied successfully in writing to be allowed into the gardens, for the house is surrounded by a wall, though its white stone shows clearly on the wooded hillsides. We respect the right of the owners to keep strangers out of their home, but are sorry we did not visit it when it *was* open.

Troo is still called the 'cave-dwellers' town', for its troglodyte dwellings in rue Haute are still fully equipped houses, some with terraces on which flowers grow in pots and, from above, their chimneys sticking from the rocks look extraordinary. They are built right into the tufa rock, which is honeycombed with a maze of galleries — *caforts* (cave forts) fortified as hideouts in medieval wars. The houses rise in tiers, joined by staircases, alleys and tiny passageways.

Montoire-sur-le-Loir is an anglers' town, for the river is rich in fish here. And you can swim or hire a boat. It is a pleasant place, with a venerable chapel, St. Gilles, which once belonged to a Benedictine priory given to Ronsard as a benefice. He had three of these priories presented to him to keep him in the manner which few poets could hope to sustain, but at least he took a real interest in their welfare and was not just an absentee landlord, like many men who were allowed sine-cures, to indulge themselves on church funds. The chapel has some famous murals, which experts date from the first quarter of the 12th century. The most significant is of Christ sitting in judgement surrounded by angels, with frightening details of the Apocalypse.

Standing on a rocky spur, the ruins of the 11th-century castle are quite romantic. There is a stone and flint wall and a square keep from which there are fine views of the surrounding countryside, the Loir and the keep of the old castle of Lavardin. There is a model in the town hall of how Montoire castle used to look.

Poor Montoire achieved historic notoriety on 24th October 1940. In a railway carriage at the station, Adolf Hitler, at the height of his power, met Marshal Pétain, French hero of the 1914–1918 war, head of the new Vichy Government, and a bitter old man. Pétain was one of those men (and women) through history who have believed that what they thought and did was for the good of their own country. They are still around. He sold the North of France for a non-existent peace. The Nazis were to occupy France north of the Loire. The 'Government' of France would operate from the beautiful spa town of Vichy. The people of the north, abandoned to the rule of occupation, the Gestapo, deportation for forced labour in Germany and concentration-camp trains, thought less of Pétain than those south of the Loire, most of whom were behind him. But at least he refused Hitler's demands that France should fight against Britain. The Germans guessed that the peace was illusory. They placed Hitler's train by the mouth of a tunnel as a precaution against a visit from the RAF!

Lavardin, 2½km up river from Montoire, old, tiny and very picturesque, has the romantic ruins of a huge feudal fortress towering above the village on a rock, like a skyline silhouette. No wonder even Henry II of England and Richard Coeur de Lion failed to take it in 1188 for it covered more than 4 hectares, had triple walls, with each circle of walls rising above the other up the hill. Not a place to storm with impunity. The square keep remains, and there are superb views from the top (26m high) across the countryside, but when we last saw it the tower was in a bad state and restoration work had started.

In the 12th century the castle was on the borders of the territory of the Kings of France (the Capets) and the Dukes of Anjou — particularly of King Philippe-Auguste and his great enemies the Plantagenets Henry II and Richard Coeur de Lion, who twice sacked the little town. The castle was pulled down on the orders of Henry IV in the Wars of Religion after the Protestant Prince of Condé had driven out the Leaguers. The ruins are open in spring and summer school holidays.

The church of St. Genest is very early Romanesque and may have been part of a 9th-century priory. Its mural paintings are superb and well cared for. They date from the 12th–16th centuries and were rediscovered during church repairs in 1914.

Les Roches l'Evêque, on the Vendôme road, has charming cave houses with wisteria and lilac around windows and doors, and beflowered terraces. They are remarkable because most were cut deliberately out of the rock when a housing shortage had filled the natural caves.

The D24 from here is more attractive than the D917. It leads to **Le Gué-du-Loir** where the Loir meets the Boulon river amid reeds, willows, poplars and green countryside. The

Renaissance manor of La Bonaventure belonged to Antoine de Bourbon-Vendrôme, father of Henry IV, and later to the family of the poet Alfred de Musset. Here Henry forded the river carrying his mistress, Gabrielle d'Estrées, on his shoulders. No wonder he was called 'Le Vert Galant'.

The little D5 to Vendôme is very attractive. Across a bridge at Le Coudray a little road takes you in 2km to **Château Rochambeau**, built in the 16th–18th centuries. This was the home of Jean-Baptiste Donatien de Vimeur, Marquis de Rochambeau, the Marshal who led the French forces in the American War of Independence, and gave George Washington much help at Yorktown. The house has two classic buildings joined by a more modern construction. It is still a home and you cannot visit. We hear rumours that it contains some historical treasures among records of the Marshal. He is buried at the cemetery of the nearby village of Thoré. He has never had the same publicity as the flamboyant Lafayette, but he rendered the American Revolutionaries just as much service.

Vendôme, though now somewhat industrialised, manufacturing machinery, car parts, aircraft instruments and plastic, is nevertheless a town of charm and interest. We like to wander around. The Loir breaks up here into a number of narrow arms which meander around under bridges as if the river is reluctant to leave, making the city a series of islands. One of the bigger arms laps the public gardens, which give a pleasant view over the city.

Abbaye de la Trinité at Vendôme was founded by Geoffroy Martel in 1040

There is nothing very exciting to see, but the atmosphere is attractive. The novelist Balzac, who entered the old Oratorians' College as an 8-year-old in 1807, found nothing pleasant at all. The College had been founded in 1623 by César of Vendôme, son of Henry IV and Gabrielle d'Estrées, and had a very old-fashioned discipline, which did not appeal to young Balzac. In trouble for rebellion, he spent much time in the punishment cell, reading in peace. He got his own back by describing the school in his book *Louis Lambert*. Now it is a Lycée named after the local poet, Ronsard, whose house is in the same street — rue St. Jacques. They could hardly call the lycée after Balzac! But let us hope that it has rebellious pupils who read what they want and become magnificent writers.

The old abbey church, founded by Geoffroy Martel in 1040 after he had seen flaming swords falling, is a higgledy-piggledy mixture of architecture from the 11th–16th centuries. The isolated 12th-century campanile, both a belltower and used as a keep in times of danger, of which Vendôme had many, has a square base but ends in an octagon capped with an iron cross, in all 79m high. The church has a Flamboyant façade with exquisite stone lacework. It was built in the 16th century by the architect of the Clocher Neuf at Chartres cathedral, Jean de Beauce, before he built at Chartres and may have been the model. In one of the absidial chapels is a famous 12th-century stained-glass window, the Virgin and Child.

The monastery buildings suffered considerably when the Rochambeau Regiment (12th Light Cavalry) was billeted in them but the part which remains has a superb staircase and an

165

interesting little museum, with a harp whose strings were plucked by Marie-Antoinette, some good furniture and paintings from the Middle Ages and Rennaissance, reminders of local crafts and artisanry, and a super reconstruction of an old country house, complete with peasant and wife in costume. We find these reconstructions of old cottages, showing how people used to live, more interesting than houses turned into museums, with exhibits in orderly rows.

The castle is in ruins, too. It was another dismantled by Henry IV in the Religious Wars after he had taken it from Leaguers. For Vendôme was strongly Catholic. The Ancient Gauls had a town here, then the Gallo-Romans. In the 10th century it had become an important centre under the Capet Kings, then it passed to Geoffroy Martel, Count of Anjou, through whom it became a Plantagenet city under the Dukes of Vendôme and so got bloodily mixed up in the Hundred Years' War. The English sacked it in 1361. Fourteen years later it passed by inheritance to the House of Bourbon. When Henry IV inherited it, it was in the hands of the Catholic Leaguers, but he recaptured it in 1589, hanged the Catholic Governor, and knocked down the castle. Its ruins stand on a hill called la Montagne with fine views over the river but there is little worth exploring except perhaps the graves of Henry IV's father and mother recently discovered there.

Henry gave the town to his son César, who became Duke of Vendôme. When his father died, Protestantism was banned in France and Louis XIII and Richelieu ruled, he used the town as a centre for conspiracy, spent four years in prison in Vincennes and was then exiled. The last of his family, Louis Joseph, a great soldier who fought the Duke of Marlborough and great glutton, died in 1712 and Vendôme passed to the King. It became the front-line in the Franco-Prussian War of 1870 and in 1940 a German air attack wiped out one of its central districts, which was later skilfully rebuilt.

One of its treasures is Porte St. Georges, at the bridge of St. Georges, the entrance to the old town over the main southerly arm of the Loir. Built in the 14th century, flanked by two great towers, it has some almost impish sculptured decorations of Renaissance gargoyles added in the 16th century by Marie de Luxembourg, Duchess of Vendôme. A superb portal.

Unless you are rushing to Chartres or Paris without a moment to spare, there is small advantage in taking N10, and even if trying to hurry you may be caught up in heavy traffic. Take the little signposted Route Touristique on the opposite side of the Loir through Meslay and Lisle to Fréteval — a road just away from the river but charming, with fine houses and little churches. **Fréteval** is on the river and is famous for good fishing. Richard Coeur de Lion beat the French under Philippe-Auguste here in 1184. Beyond it on the way to Morée by N157 are professional fishermen's huts and pretty little houses. Take D19 then right on an attractive little road close to the river to the bridge at St. Jean-Froidmental and St. Claude. A lovely little road D145(7) goes to Bouche-d'Aigre and the D8 to Cloyes-sur-le-Loir. The D8 runs along the tranquil valley of the Aigre, little tributary of the Loir, and just eastward is the truly sleepy village of Romilly, 'Rognes' of Emile Zola's novel La Terre. He made the little moated

Dunois

Joan of Arc's one trustworthy friend and true companion in arms was her 'gentil Bâtard' — Jean, Count of Dunois. He was the one commander who took her seriously and asked her advice. He was the man who led a small force into Orléans to hold it until Joan forced the English to give up their siege. He was the commander who continued her work after she was dead, freeing Paris and finally forcing the English out of France.

He was the natural son of Louis, Duke of Orléans (brother of Charles VI), who was assassinated by the Burgundians, allies of the English. His own father called him the 'Bastard of Orléans'. He was handsome, generous, intelligent and brave. He left the family château at Châteaudun to fight the English in 1417 when he was 15 and ten years later beat an English army at Montargis.

He and Joan became friends as soon as they met. After Orléans, they won together an equally important victory at Patay, taking prisoner the English commander Sir John Talbot, hero of 40 previous victories, and a man who still has a great French wine named after him. Then he marched through areas overrun by the English, taking the fortified towns.

As if in revenge for Joan's death, he took Chartres, the key to Paris, forced the Earl of Bedford to raise the siege of Lagny, and chased the enemy from Paris. English guides usually attribute these victories to his monarch, Charles VII, Joan's timid Dauphin.

He was given the fief of Beaugency for his services and built the château there in 1440. He drove the English from Normandy, taking Caen from the Duke of Somerset in 1450. Then he freed Guyenne, Bordeaux and Bayonne. The English had nothing left in France but Calais.

For joining the League of Nobles in revolt against Louis XI he was deprived of all his possessions but was given them back in 1465 under the Treaty of Conflans. As befitted a friend of Joan, he was a deeply religious man and joined with Louis XI in the rebuilding of the basilica of Notre-Dame at Cléry, ruined by the English under Salisbury in 1428. They are both buried there, Dunois in 1468 in the chapel which he built. He built also the Sante-Chapelle at Châteaudun.

Though he won no great individual set-piece battles like Agincourt or Crécy, Austerlitz or Waterloo, his string of victories was remarkable and he is still one of France's greatest heroes, if too little known outside.

château a 'ruin'. Foresight, perhaps — it was badly damaged in 1940. Zola lived in Cloyes while he was collecting material for this book. It is a pleasant place, though at the river crossing of the N10, and has some old houses and a church with a 15th-century belfry.

The nicer route now is across the Loir on D23 to Montigny-le-Gannelon, between the river and a cliff-face pitted with cave dwellings and a restored 15th-century château, **St. Hilaire**. Recross the river at Duoy, then take D111(4) to Châteaudun.

Even up here on the placid lazy Loir amid the rich agricultural countryside of Beauce and La Perche, you cannot get away from fierce strong castles which dominate town and river. **Château de Châteaudun**, rising vertically above the river, is awesome in its massive, austere strength and not at all the sort of place where you would choose to live, unless pursued by dangerous enemies. Its power is accentuated by contrast with the picturesque Loir, which here winds softly, covered often with grass and water lilies, amid clumps of trees and meadows.

Châteaudun town belonged to the Dukes of Blois from the 10th century until 1391, when it was sold to Louis d'Orléans, brother of Charles VI. His bastard son Jean (the Bastard of Orléans), Joan of Arc's companion in arms, lived here until he was 15, when he left to fight the English (see box on p. 167). He took his title, Comte de Dunois, from this district.

Thibault le Tricheur (the Trickster), Count of Blois, built a fort on this steep spur in the 10th century. It was enlarged by successors, who built the impressive keep (45m high) in the 12th century. Dunois, back from the wars, built the late Gothic Sainte-Chapelle between 1451 and his death in 1468. It is more elegant than the rest of the château. The upper chapel, with a fine wooden ceiling, was reserved for servants. The lower chapel oratory has a large wall painting of the Last Judgement, and round the walls are superb lifesize statues of the Virgin and various saints, in polychrome, put there in Dunois' lifetime. His son put in two smaller saints and a statue of Dunois himself in armour.

The château has two wings at right angles. The Gothic wing was built by Dunois and has a turreted medieval staircase. The Longueville wing built in 1510 by his son François d'Orléans-Longueville is early French Renaissance (described to us by a French architect as 'Gothic lines with Renaissance decoration'). The central pier of its Renaissance staircase is delicately sculptured.

Inside, the château is sparsely furnished, though ground floor rooms are hung with tapestries put in by the French Government and the rooms themselves are interesting, including the monumental chimney pieces in the guard room, attractive wooden ceilings, and the basement kitchen, pantry and bakery. The covered sentry-walk around the top storey gives plunging views. The château has been beautifully restored by the State. The Duc de Luynes, who owned it until 1939 and loved it, left it in a very bad condition because he could not maintain it. The roofing had partly gone, rain had ruined beams, which had to be dug out like a canoe and reinforced with iron joists, and every floor had to be dismantled.

The town of Châteaudun has suffered a number of disastrous fires. The worst in 1723 nearly burned down the whole town. In 1870 the Prussians pillaged the town after a brave resistance by the French and in 1940 German incendiary-bombs rained down, especially on and around the 12th-century church of La Madeleine. Surprisingly, a number of old houses have survived on roads leading to La Madeleine.

From Châteaudun to Chartres, there is little alternative to the N10 unless you are prepared to wander east far from the river, and those routes, though smaller and quieter, are not outstandingly beautiful.

Bonneval, bypassed by N10, is a pleasant little old town on the river, which feeds moats under the old town wall. A town gate, Porte de Boisville, and the four-arched bridge date from the 13th century. So does the pure-Gothic Notre-Dame church.

Although it is technically in Eure-et-Loir, we have always thought of Chartres as being attached to Paris and Île-de-France, and so have nearly all French guide books, so a full description will appear in the book on Paris and its Environs. But if you have never seen this glorious city and its superb cathedral, it is worth driving 43km from Châteaudun to see the cathedral (see box on p. 170), simply as an apéritif for visiting all its other treasures at some time.

Chartres Cathedral

'Chartres is the very mind of the Middle Ages in visible form', wrote Emile Malé. That could be said of several cathedrals, including York, and is fair comment from the architectural viewpoint. From the religious view, Chartres Cathedral is an inspiring place of worship, and to the traveller who knows little of the technicalities of church architecture and who is not deeply religious, it is a building of inspiring beauty from outside and within — a place which is difficult to leave and which leaves you with a warm feeling that such beauty created by men which has survived almost miraculously over 700 years despite all wars, holocausts and tempests will take the next 700 in its stride.

If you believe in miracles, its survival *is* a miracle, for since it was rebuilt in the 13th century following a fire which destroyed its predecessor, it has been in the heart of so much trouble that you would have expected at least several 'restorations'. Like York, which has survived almost as much, its major tragedy was a fire which destroyed much of the roof. This happened in 1836, and the ancient wooden roof was replaced with one of metal.

Edward III of England besieged Chartres in 1360. England held it from 1417–1432 as the key to Paris until Dunois retook it. In the Religious Wars it was besieged by the Huguenots in 1568 and in 1591 by the Protestant Henry of Navarre, but the cathedral was unharmed. And when Henry became Catholic, he chose to be crowned Henry IV here, the only king except Louis VI not to be crowned at Reims. It survived the Franco-Prussian War despite being the centre for five months of German operations against the Loire Army. Incredibly, it survived bombing and fighting in World War II except for minor damage when the Americans freed Chartres in 1944.

The three entrances are all majestic, with beautiful rose-windows over each doorway, but the west façade is the most inspiring and this is the delightful way to approach on your first visit. The triple Portail Royal (Royal Doorway) survives from the previous church and is magnificently decorated with statues of the life of Christ. The North and South doorways have projecting porches with a multitude of sculptures. The impressive North porch is decorated with 700 figures of the Old Testament and the coming of Christ. The prettier South porch has a profusion of sculptures and decorations of martyrs and apostles around a central figure of Christ the teacher. Piers are decorated with figures representing virtues and vices.

Inside, the cathedral is 130m long. The nave is the widest in France (16.4m), its grandeur superb, which would be even more impressive if it were lit more often in dull weather. We have complained about this before. Now the *Blue Guide to Paris and Environs* is complaining, too. It must be a matter of cost. But it is particularly important, for the sheer joy of this cathedral is its stained-glass. There are 173 windows, nearly all medieval, which bring light in a mass of glorious colours — scenes of the legends of saints and of old trades, presented by the trade guilds of the Middle Ages. Two windows in the 15th-century Vendôme chapel lost their glass in 1791. One was replaced in 1954 with a window of St. Fulbert given by the Institute of American Architects. The other is a Window of Reconciliation given by the Germans in 1971.

Part Four:
The Sarthe to Le Mans

15
The Sarthe to Le Mans

The best scenery of the Sarthe Valley starts nearly 50km north of Angers at the forest of Pincé. Farther south, the best views of the river are from the cruise boats which run between Angers and Sablé-sur-Sarthe from mid-June to mid-September. Take the D107 north from Angers, crossing the river to Cantenay and continue on this little road and D108 to **Le Plessis Bourré**. The big 15th-century castle here on a plain of meadowlands is truly striking. The moat which surrounds it is so wide that you must cross a many-spanned bridge of 43m to reach its gatehouse with a double drawbridge and four turrets. Obviously, not everyone was welcome in the old days. The gate protects a low square building in white with blue-grey slate roofs and round towers with pepper-pot roofs at each corner. Beyond the entrance archway is a large courtyard with arcaded gallery, and turret staircases. As you enter you seem to be moving from a fortress into a country mansion. The wooden guardroom ceiling is painted with funny pictures, such as a ham barber and his suffering patient and a man trying to wring the neck of an eel. The library has a collection of fans.

The château was built by Jean Bourré (1424–1506), who was obviously a very clever or very honest man, for he succeeded in remaining the favourite minister of the devious and often vicious Louis XI and was Financial Secretary and Treasurer to Louis XI, Charles VIII and Louis XII without once being disgraced or imprisoned for having his hand in the till. He must have been well paid, for he built at least two other châteaux — at Jarzé, near Baugé, and at Vaux, north-west of Miré and Châteauneuf-sur-Sarthe — not to be confused with the great Château of Vaux-le-Vicomte in Île-de-France, which was so sumptuous and exotic that Louis XIV sent its owner Nicolas Fouquet to prison for life. Fouquet was *his* Finance Minister, and Louis assumed that any man who could afford a rival to Versailles must be fiddling the books. The château which stood here before Bourré was called le Plessis-le-Vent, which shows how windy this plain can get (*vent* = wind).

Join D768 to the west and at Champigné take D770 to rejoin the Sarthe at **Châteauneuf-sur-Sarthe**, a good place for hiring boats or picking up a river cruise. Old mills and a big church make the riverside attractive. The old Hôtel du Sarthe by the bridge has a nice riverside terrace. Cross the river south-east on D859, then very soon take D52 left which meets the

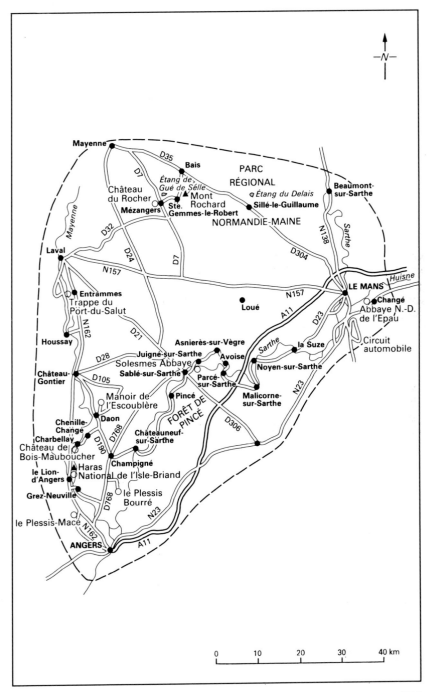

In the Abbey Church of Solesmes by the Sarthe you can hear the Gregorian chant at Mass

river at Morannes and pick up D159, an attractive road skirting the little Forest of Pincé to Sablé. **Pincé** is a very pretty village of under 200 people, with charming flower-decked houses strung along the river.

Sablé is a delightful place, too, in a pretty spot where two tributaries, the Vaige and Erve, flow into the Sarthe. It is another good place for boating or to join a river cruise. Do not let the gloomy Colbert castle discourage you. There are some pleasant old houses on the way up to it, but you cannot go in because it is used by a department of the National Library. Jean-Baptiste Colbert, Louis XIV's highly efficient bureaucrat, who saved France's finances when Louis had wrecked them making unsuccessful war against England, rebuilt France's fleet to combat England's, reorganised the

French colonies of Canada, Martinique and St. Domingo and founded the colony of Madagascar, and was heartily disliked by the French people not only for his punitive taxes but his arbitrary rule. He was one of Louis' bourgeois administrators put in to curb the power of the aristocrats, but he pined to be an aristocrat himself, and bought what remained of a 13th-century château here for the title of Marquis which went with it. It was his nephew, Colbert de Torcy, who rebuilt the château in 1711. Sablé has small metal industries, such as nuts and bolts and screw cutting, but is known mostly for dairy products and its small shortbread biscuits.

Solesmes Abbey is just 2km up river — centre of art, religious art and religious music, and what the experts say is the finest Gregorian Chant to be heard in the world. You are allowed in to hear it at Mass (10am Sundays, 9.45am weekdays; Vespers at 5pm). Otherwise you may only enter the Abbey church.

Frankly, the abbey looks like a towering medieval prison in granite. The main part was built between 1896 and 1901 to what the architect believed to be a 12th-century design. Founded in 1010 as a modest priory, it grew in wealth and power until ruined by the Revolution. The monks returned in 1833 but were driven out again in 1880 in the French wave of anticlericalism. They returned in 1896 to rebuild what was left of the old abbey and add the massive granite pile which hovers over the river. They were driven out again in 1901 and went abroad to start other abbeys, including Quarr in the Isle of Wight. In 1922 they returned.

The church has an old nave and

transept (11th–15th centuries), with 1896 additions. In the transept are famous groups of carvings called 'The Saints of Solesmes', dating from 1496 to 1550. They can tell you the names of the priors who commissioned these works. In the 'Death of the Virgin' one of the priors appears holding the shroud. But no one knows who designed or carved them. They have been attributed to Italian artists and to the monks. Both could be true. Italian monks did, after all, branch out from the great Italian monasteries to many countries. But whoever was responsible, they are really excellent.

There is a pleasant winding drive through interesting villages along the Sarthe Valley to Le Mans, much of it beside the river. Cross to the north bank at Solesmes, from where the abbey looks better, then follow D22 to **Juigné-sur-Sarthe**, a charming village with old houses on a spur jutting across the valley and splendid views of the Sarthe from the church square. Follow D22 to **Asnières-sur-Vègre**, one of the oldest and most picturesque villages, with a 12th-century bridge, 11th–14th-century frescoes in the church and a 13th-century courthouse. Then go right on to D57 past Avoise to cross the river again to Parcé-sur-Sarthe, a lovely run beside the river. **Parcé** is another charming village, built round a Romanesque belfry. Follow D8 beside the river on the south bank, then left on a little local road V1 through Dureil which still hugs the river, rejoining D8 for a nice little stretch into **Malicorne-sur-Sarthe**. The bridge has nice views of a mill and banks lined with poplars, and you can take boat trips from the port. But it is best known for faïence pottery, especially reproductions of period pieces. The Tessier workshops

and museum are open daily except Sunday in winter, Monday all year. The 11th-century church has some interesting pieces and the local 17th-century château in a park is encircled by moats and crossed by a quaint 17th-century humped bridge, but is not open to the public.

The D41 follows the river to Noyen-sur-Sarthe, where the river is wide, with a canal alongside. The little town is built in tiers above the river bank, with an island in midstream. D229 takes you to **La Suze**, where you cross the Sarthe on a bridge of nine arches built under Henry IV. The church is the 15th-century chapel of the now-ruined château. D23 takes you into Le Mans.

Le Mans (pop. 150,331) traffic can be very discouraging, and many people avoid the city, which is a pity if they have not been to the medieval town, le Vieux Mans, which has many treasures.

The greatest of these is St. Julien's Cathedral, though purists shake their heads in disbelief at its architectural idiosyncrasies. 'The cathedral is absurd

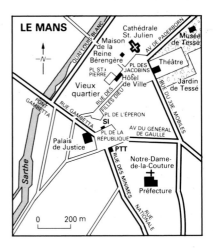

St. Julian's Cathedral at Le Mans is one of the most impressive churches in France

and I have very great affection for it,'
wrote Vivian Rowe. 'It attracts the
same kind of sympathetic affection as
does a mongrel dog, who all too
clearly shows his mixed descent.'

It stands proudly on top of a hill,
approached by steps from place des
Jacobins, and it actually breaches a
Gallo-Roman wall. We are too
cowardly to describe the architectural
mixtures of styles, for they break so
many rules. For instance, the nave is
Romanesque but has Gothic-like
pointed arches. And various builders
seem to have stuck on odd bits, like the
unlovely south porch which covers a
doorway with 12th-century statues
similar to the Royal Doorway at

Chartres in their themes. The choir is
way higher than the nave and is
awesome with a double ambulatory
and twelve chapels in a half ring
around it. Here are the superb 13th-
century stained-glass windows in vivid
reds and blues — not quite up to the
standard of Chartres but nearing it. And
hanging over the choir stalls, which
have wood carvings of the life of Christ
from around 1560, is a series of 16th-
century tapestries showing the lives of
St. Gervase and St. Protase.

From the outside, you can see three
definite parts to the cathedral — the
Romanesque nave from the 11th–12th
centuries, the Gothic choir finished in
1254 and the transepts joining them

from the 14th–15th centuries.

A major reason for the oddities of architecture is that the cathedral was deeply involved in the quarrels of history. The Romanesque part of the cathedral had been completed even to its transept towers when in 1063 the fiery William the Bastard of Normandy seized the city from the Count of Maine. He made the mistake of depriving the citizens of special privileges and while he was away conquering England and gaining for himself the twin titles of William the Conqueror, William I King of England at Hastings, they rose against him. Three times in all they rose, three times he repossessed Le Mans. He noticed that the transept towers stopped the view from the upper windows of his palace across the square to the cathedral, so he could not see what the citizens were up to. So he had the towers knocked down. His granddaughter Matilda married Geoffroy Plantagenet, Count of Anjou, who thus added Normandy and Maine to his lands. He often lived in Le Mans and was buried in the cathedral in 1151. His son, Henry Plantagenet, later Henry II of England, was born in Le Mans and gave the townspeople back their privileges. He intended to spend his old age there, but his rebellious son Richard Coeur de Lion, in alliance with the King of France, Philippe-Auguste, drove him out. Richard's younger brother John, called Lackland for obvious reasons, succeeded him as King of England and took back Le Mans — one of his very few victories. He lost it again, and Philippe-Auguste gave it to Richard's widow, Queen Berengaria, who founded nearby Epau abbey. The choir was built in 1217 after a fire. The cathedral is floodlit inside and special organ music is played on Saturday evenings from 15th June to 31st August (9.30–11pm).

There are many fine old houses in the winding streets and stepped alleys of the old town, among restaurants and little shops — half-timbered houses from the 15th century, attractive Renaissance façades, elegant 18th-century houses with wrought-iron balconies.

Place St. Michel, by the south door of the cathedral, is quite delightful. Here at No. 1 in the cathedral precincts lived the poet and satirist Paul Scarron (1610–1660), who was a member of the Chapter (see box on p. 178).

Maison de la Reine Bérengère, one of several old houses in the street of that name off place St. Michel, was not in fact the house of Queen Berengaria, who lived in the 13th century. It was built for a rich Alderman around 1490, and contains a museum of Maine folklore and local art, including glazed pottery from Malicorne (shut Mondays and Tuesdays). A timbered house with a death's head on the post is now the tourist information office. It is on a corner of a street cut into the old town in 1851 to link place des Jacobins with the river Sarthe and later called rue Wilbur Wright. Wright made the first aeroplane flight ever in France on 8th August 1908 from the racecourse now within the circuit of the Le Mans 24-hour sports car race, just to the south of the city (see box on p. 182). His statue by Landowsky is at the south end.

The town hall by place St. Pierre is the former palace of the Counts of Maine, built in 1760. To the east of the cathedral is Jardin d'Horticulture, a charming garden with rocks and cascading streams, and a terraced walk with views over the cathedral. It was designed in 1851 — just as that other

Paul Scarron

Paul Scarron (1610–1660) was an abbé, but a wit and man-about-town until he suffered an illness which led finally to paralysis. He obtained a prebend at Le Mans, but his illness worsened and he went to Paris to write for a living. His satires are said to have influenced Le Sage, Defoe, Fielding and Smollett. He made enough from writing to live well and to run a Bohemian household, receiving other writers and leaders of fashion and politics.

In 1652 he married a beautiful but penniless girl of 17, Françoise d'Aubigny. She was the granddaughter of the Protestant leader Théodore Agrippa d'Aubigny, but at 15 after her father and mother's death she was almost destitute. She brought some order and morality to his household and even his writings, for she was a severely upright lady by the standards of those days. His death in 1660 left her in poverty again, but her friend Madame de Montespan, mistress of Louis XIV, gave her the job of looking after her two children who were fathered by the king. She looked after them with such devotion that the king showered presents on her and she was able to buy the state of Maintenon and a marquisate. Though her morals were so severe, she managed to get such power over this autocratic king that she ousted Madame de Montespan from the Royal bed and became the Royal mistress. She had much political influence. When the queen died, she even persuaded the king to marry her in secret. When he died she retired to a home she had set up for poor girls of good families.

gardener Paxton was designing the Crystal Palace for London's Great Exhibition — by the great landscape gardener Alphand, who designed several Paris parks, including Boulogne. In a fine park off place des Jacobins in a last-century bishop's palace is the Tessé museum, which shows some good paintings and other works of art from the 14th to 19th centuries. The exhibition of old and modern photography is very interesting, and one room is devoted to paintings and engravings illustrating the comic scenes from Paul Scarron's *Comic Novel*.

By the river Huisne, 4km south-east of Le Mans by the Changé road D4, is **Epau Abbey**, founded by Queen Berengaria in 1230. The present buildings, much restored, date from the 14th century, except for the church, which is 15th century and has a large, almost dainty stained-glass window in the chancel and the recumbent figure of Berengaria on her tomb, returned from Le Mans Cathedral. The original abbey was burned down in 1365. Michelin says that the deed was done by 'brigands' but we were told that the locals did it to prevent the English fortifying it. Perhaps it was done by one of those marauding gangs of French mercenaries who went around in the Hundred Years' War fighting for whichever side would give them the most loot — and looting between battles.

Changé woods near the abbey is a leisure park of 253 hectares, with woodland, paths, sign-posted walks, picnic areas, playing grounds, and a jogging track.

The D304 north-west from Le Mans takes you to the little town of **Sillé-le-Guillaume**, where it is worth spending some time exploring the Sillé forest. This is part of the Parc Régional Normandie–Maine. There are pleasant walks and horse rides, with horses for hire, and you can walk or drive 4km into the woods to **Etang du Delais** where there are beaches, bathing, fishing, windsurf boards for hire, boat trips and pedalos. There is a sailing school with board and lodging provided.

Sillé town was named 'Guillaume' for William the Conqueror, who took the castle. It was replaced by a massive 15th-century pile which is now offices. Continuing on D35 you are on the granite slopes of the Coëvrons, passing through the Izé woods, and a little road to the left leads to the highest point of these hills at 375m, **Mont Rochard**, which has very good views. Rejoin D35 to Bais so that you can enjoy the delightful drive through the hills southward on D20 to Ste. Gemmes-le-Robert, then right on D517 to **Mézangers**, where there is a watersports centre, especially sailing and windsurfing, on **Etang du Gué de Selle**, a 10th-century church and the fine 14th–15th-century **Château du Rocher**.

This is almost no-man's land. Technically in the Mayenne, it is often lumped with Normandy northwards and sees few tourists. The D7 will take you to **Mayenne**, on the slope of two hills astride the Mayenne river. William the Conqueror took it in 1064 by having his troops throw burning brands over the walls, and during the Allied advance in 1944 it was almost totally destroyed in heavy fighting between Germans and Americans, because it was the last bridge intact over the Mayenne river. The heroism of a US sergeant, Mack Racken, enabled the Americans to take the bridge. It is not an exciting town, and most travellers would go from Mézangers to Evron and then across to Laval. **Evron** has one of the most beautiful churches in this part of France, the Basilica of Notre Dame. Legend says that it was founded because a 7th-century pilgrim brought back from Palestine a phial containing drops of milk reputed to be from the breast of the Virgin. While sleeping in the forest, he hung the relic on a thorn bush. When he awoke the thorn bush had grown so tall that he could no longer reach it. When he tried cutting it down, his axe stuck in the wood. So he called the Bishop of le Mans, who knelt before the tree, which promptly shrunk. It would for a Bishop, wouldn't it? The Bishop built a church there and founded a monastery so that the monks could guard the relic.

The 12th-century square-buttressed tower of the Basilica is joined to the 18th-century Benedictine abbey. Part of the nave is 12th-century Romanesque and the rest of the building is 14th century. There are remains of a 12th-century fresco showing the Virgin suckling the Child and the choir has 14th-century stained-glass illustrating the legend. Four 17th-century Aubusson tapestries, murals and a 13th-century statue of the Virgin in silvered wood are in one chapel.

Laval is an agreeable town astride the Mayenne at the north end of the deeply banked Mayenne valley down to Angers. The old town on the west bank surrounds the castle, which is in two parts. Vieux Château, from the 11th century, contains a mixed-bag museum, with tools of medieval craftsmen and naïve paintings, including a work by Henri Rousseau ('Le Dou-anier'), born here in 1844. Château Neuf, with a Renaissance façade, was restored and enlarged in the 19th century to serve as law courts. Grande Rue, down to the river, is lined with half-timbered houses with overhangs, and stone Renaissance houses with decoration. It reaches the river at Pont Vieux, a hump-backed bridge, once fortified. One of the old 'bateaux lavoirs' (laundry boats) the 'St. Julien', used until 1970, is a museum.

The unattractive Romanesque cathedral has been much altered but has some good artistic works, including fine 17th-century Aubusson tapestries. St Vénérand church over the bridge has fine Renaissance windows, but the most attractive church is the Gothic–Renaissance Notre-Dame d'Avénières, with huge wooden statues of Christ and St. Christopher, and modern windows by Max Ingrand.

Former Laval citizens include the Renaissance surgeon Ambroise Paré, who started ligature of arteries during amputations, Henri Rousseau and his friend the eccentric writer Alfred Jarry, innovator of the Theatre of the Absurd, and Alain Gerbault, tennis doubles partner to Jean Borotra and solo round-the-world sailor, lost in the Pacific in 1941.

Trappe du Port-du-Salut, 7km south, is the monastery where Port-Salut cheese was made until 1959. This is now produced in a factory at nearby Entrammes, although the monks still make their own cheese.

Take D1 south from Laval beside the river for pleasant valley views. Join D112 and soon D103 branches over the river to the Port-du-Salut Trappist monastery. There are splendid river views from a bridge if you turn off D112 at Houssay, crossing on D4, then take N162 to **Château-Gontier**, a fine old town of narrow winding streets founded by Foulques Nerra in the 11th century. He gave to the Benedictines the land for building the 11th-century Romanesque church of St. Jean in flint and red sandstone. The interior is pure Romanesque, but the stained-glass windows are modern, part of restoration after 1940 damage. The frescoes in the transept are 12th century. They include the story of Adam and Eve and of Noah's Ark. In the old Priory gardens, the Promenade-du-Bout-du-Monde has fine river views and a little zoo. The big quais with fine trees are a reminder of days when this was an important river port. Now the town has the biggest cattle market in France, especially for calves, with 4,000–5,000 head sold each Thursday. The noise can be fearsome.

The D22 leading to the hilltop village of Daon is an attractive road. A side road left at Daon, D213 takes you to a drive of plane and lime trees leading to the 15th–16th-century **Manoir de l'Escoublère**, a very big fortified farmhouse with four round towers and a well in its courtyard, all surrounded by a moat. By D22, D190 and D78 you reach the river again at Chenille-Changé. You can cross over the river shortly to Chambellay, from where a tiny road left leads to the fine-looking **Château du Bois-Mauboucher** (15th–17th century), standing almost on an island in a wood by a large lake. It is furnished and has a picture gallery.

The elegant house built in Le Mans in 1490 was named after Queen Berengaria, widow of Richard Coeur de Lion, King of England

Le Mans

Le Mans is the city of motor cars. Not only has it staged the great Le Mans 24-Hour Race for sports cars since 1923, but it was the pioneer city for French automobile design and construction.

The Bollée family started the industry there, and produced cars from 1873, when Amédée Bollée père brought out his first steam car, to 1924 when their last factory was taken over by the Englishman William Morris to produce his cars in France.

In 1878 Bollée père pioneered independent front suspension on his Mancelle car which was the first to have a front engine under a bonnet. From 1896 to 1913 his son Amédée produced advance design cars, such as the first shaft-driven car with spiral-bevel gearing and the then 'futuristic' streamlined torpedo racing cars in 1899 with a 20hp monobloc four engine with twin carburettors and a chassis independently sprung at the front, underslung at the rear. These cars approached 100 kph — incredible at the time. He concentrated on limited production expensive cars. His brother Léon started with a light three-wheeler in 1896 but graduated to large conventional cars.

You can see Bollée steam and petrol cars in the Automobile Museum of the Le Mans racing circuit, just across from the Automobile Club at the north end of the stands. It has bicycles, motorbikes and 150 vintage cars, showing the history of the car from the beginnings to 1949. Exhibits are shown on a rotating basis, so although you will not see all at once you can go several times and see something different! You can reach the museum and the Bugatti Circuit (see below) by driving under a tunnel from D139.

The 24-Hour race circuit is to the south of the city between D139 and D138, both of which form part of the two side legs, joined at the bottom by D140 and at the top by private roads. Pick it up at N138, drive down to the exciting Mulsanne corner, across on D140 to the other highspot, Arnage corner, up D139 to Porsche bend. There it joins private roads of the circuit past the karting track, a motorcycle track, to the famous S-bends or straight on past the stands to where the pits are located in the race. Just past the stands is the Bugatti Circuit, used as a school for racing drivers. Motorists can use it any day except Monday and motorcyclists any day except Monday mornings. The Bugatti Circuit is 4.24km round, the 24-Hour circuit 13.64km. The circuit for the first race in 1923, won by a Chenard Walcker at 57.2 mph, was much longer and went right into the streets of Le Mans, with hairy hairpin bends, but the circuit has since been altered several times for safety as speeds became higher, and to improve the view for spectators. First car to win at over 100 mph was a Jaguar in 1953, which averaged 105.8 mph. It was using disc-brakes, made by Dunlop — a new invention!

The great big Bentleys dominated in the early days, winning in 1924, then four times in a row, 1927–1930. Jaguars have won six times, too. Alfa Romeo won four times and, in recent years, when regulations have allowed cars which are virtually racing cars with sports bodies, Porsche have dominated.

Other notable winners have included Mercedes, Bugatti, Aston Martin, Ferrari, Lagonda and the old French Delahaye. Le Mans has produced some remarkable drives by non-winners, too. Tom Wisdom, dapper, be-monocled motoring correspondent of the old London *Daily Herald* and a brilliant road racing and rally driver, took a little Healey road sports car into third place behind two Mercedes by sheer consistent and faultless driving. Most successful driver ever at Le Mans has been Derek Bell, a Briton who tried Grand Prix Formula I but preferred long distance sports car races.

'Le Mans' is much more than a motor race. It is a carnival, with restaurants, bars, buffets, fairground. Tens of thousands of spectators picnic, hold all-night parties, dancing and generally enjoying themselves.

There is a racecourse for horses, Les Hunaudières, in the middle of the circuit, and here in 1908, at the invitation of the Bollées, Wilbur Wright made the first aeroplane flight in France.

Join N162 to Le Lion-d'Angers, on the banks of the Oudon just before it joins the Mayenne. This is stock-rearing country, specialising in horses, and a kilometre east on an accessible island is **Haras National de l'Isle-Briand** (National Stud) with about 80 stallions, including retired racehorses at stud, but the full number is there only between 15th July and 15th February. The stud was transferred here from Angers in 1974 and is ultra-modern. You can see the horses, barns, riding stables, harness room and forge.

Four kilometres down pop over the river on D291 to see the lovely flow-ered village of **Grez-Neuville**, where you can hire boats. The D191 beside the left bank is quite spectacular and even overhangs the river in places. But if you have not yet tired of old château, recross to the N162 to see **Le Plessis-Macé**.

'Plessis' meant a palisade — a defensive fence of stakes around a property and in the 11th century the building which stood here undoubt-edly would have had one. Macé was the name of the first owner, who

ended his days as a Benedictine monk in Angers but left behind a family to inherit. The property passed to the Beaumont family in the 14th century but it was in a bad state through the Hundred Years' War and rebuilding began in 1453. By 1483 Louis XI thought it good enough to stay there with his court. The 12th-century surrounding walls and towers and moat were kept, and the Flamboyant chapel of 1460 has an interesting wooden balcony.

After the du Bellay family took over in the 15th century, Francis I stayed (to hunt, of course) and later Henry IV stayed there. Then it became a farm and deteriorated into a near ruin when Countess Theobald Walsh saw it in the 1870s, took a liking to it and had it rebuilt. The Walsh family were origin-ally Irish Jacobites. There are various stories of how they arrived in the Nantes area, but most probably they were descended from the same Captain Francis Walsh who provided and captained the ship for James II's escape to France after the 1688 coup of William III of Orange, and deemed it

Chickens

Sarthe is the home of the famous Le Mans chickens, and Loué farm chickens which are free-range on grass and fed on wheat, maize and greenery. Both of these carry the 'Label Rouge', given only to certain products of high standards rigorously applied by law. The chicken label tells you how long they were raised, fed, last day for selling (one week maximum after killing), producer and place and production number.

Here is a popular local recipe for Loué farm chicken.

Marmite Sarthoise (for 4 people)

INGREDIENTS

200g of Loué farm chicken breast	nut oil, salt, pepper
120g of uncooked mushrooms	160g of rabbit back, boned
¼ litre of veal (or chicken) stock	¼ litre of white wine
80g of ham	½ litre of fresh cream
80g of carrots	200g of cabbage

METHOD

Cut chicken and rabbit into small pieces, ham and mushrooms into thin strips. Salt vegetables, steam for 10 minutes. Keep hot.

Dust chicken and rabbit pieces with flour, cook in oil for 3 minutes. Add mushrooms, mix, add ham. Cook for another 3 minutes. Take out of pan and keep warm. Glaze pan juices with white wine, reduce juices to ¼. Add stock and cream. Simmer for 1 minute, stirring. Add salt, pepper, nut oil, and meat and mushrooms. Mix and boil for 3 minutes, stirring. Serve with vegetables alongside.

wise to stay in Nantes, where he became a successful ship-owner. His son Antoine provided the ships for Charles Stuart ('Bonnie Prince Charlie') to cross to Scotland for his disastrous uprising of 1745. The Walsh family later bought the Château de Serrant (see page 188) and Theobald Walsh became Count Theobald de Walsh — not the only man in France to have snobbishly and without right added the aristocratic 'de' to his name.

The château (closed on Tuesdays and from 1st December–28th February) is worth seeing. Although it looks like a fortress from the outside, it looks like a country home from the courtyard. It must have made a fine farmhouse. In one courtyard corner is a delightful balcony reserved for ladies to watch jousting and other entertainments. The balcony opposite was for servants.

The N162 continues to Angers.

The Mayenne Valley and this part of the Loire Valley is attractive, with low hills, meadows and a multitude of little rivers — a quiet land where you can get away from other travellers even in mid-summer on the byways and in the little hamlets. it is a good place to hire a gîte if you seek peace.

Part Five:
Angers to the Atlantic

16

Angers to Nantes and the Coast

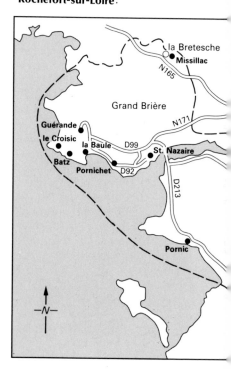

The Loire Valley west of Angers to Nantes and the sea is such a different world from the rest of Anjou and from Touraine that many French guide books on the Loire simply ignore it, lumping it with Brittany or with Vendée and Poitou-Charente to the south. Its history is different, too. Other than Nantes, it missed the industrial revolution almost completely, and it has missed the tourist revolution, too. Even its châteaux are mostly manor houses, important farmhouses which once controlled agricultural estates. For this is Muscadet country, producing that ever popular dry white wine from a grape called Muscadet, once the Melun grape of Burgundy, where it is no longer grown. And in fact much of the country north of the river was in Brittany, and Nantes was once the Breton capital. It is now the Loire–Atlantique, part of the Pays-de-la-Loire.

The A11 motorway from Angers to Nantes has done still more to isolate the valley villages from hurrying travellers, and the rebuilt N249 from Nantes to Vallet and Cholet passes under the local roads with no turn-offs, so we now find problems in reaching some of the great vineyards, like the Sauvion family's historic Château du Cléray.

There is one last château to see just west of Angers which rates with some

of the best in Touraine, and we would not miss it. It is Serrant, north of the river at St. Georges-sur-Loire. But don't go there direct from Angers, for the road on the south bank of the Loire, D751, is so much prettier. Turn off the N160 on to D751 just outside Angers, south of the Louet river at Rabaut. The road meets the Louet again at **Rochefort-sur-Loire**.

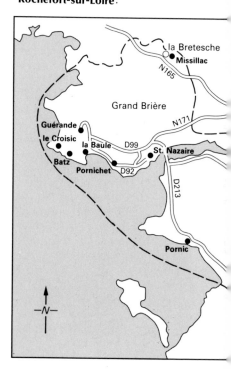

You will see several old houses with turrets or watchtowers lining the square, and the ruins of a castle on a spur of rock. The castle was part of a little fortified town, St. Symphorien, where river pirates lived. They were ex-League soldiers who had fought with the Duke of Guise and, finding the Religious Wars going against them, threw out the people from this little town and moved in with their families, preying on ships and villages. They were even feared in Angers. Their lair was attacked by troops under the Prince of Conti in 1592 and then by Marshal d'Aumont, but they had good and a very well organised defence.

Six years later Henry IV bought them out and demolished their stronghold. They moved down to the little river village of St. Croix, which

they renamed Rochefort. There they seem to have settled down and become worthy villagers. Now Rochefort is known for its white wines — Quarts de Chaume, best of the excellent Coteaux-du-Layon sweet wines. They are made with Chenin grapes but picked in October when over-ripe and attacked by the 'noble rot', *pourriture noble*, like Sauternes. The wine is luscious with a smell of honey and flowers. Alas, only about 100,000 bottles are made each year.

The road west along the Loire, the Corniche Angevine, is cut into a cliff face and has many tight bends for drivers and superb bird's eye views across the Loire valley for lucky passengers. At **La Haie-Longue** is a viewing table with a lovely panorama of the river and small side streams,

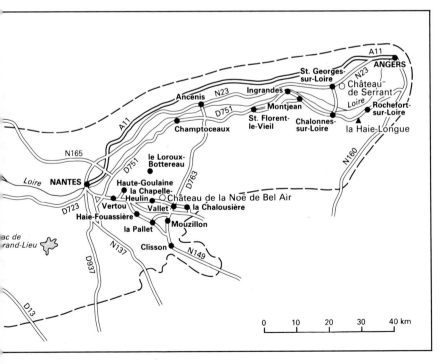

Château de Serrant: a splendid mansion with massive towers and cupolas, which once belonged to an Irish supporter of the Stuarts

meadows and hillside vineyards producing AOC Coteaux-du-Layon semi-sweet and sweet wines. The Corniche continues to **Chalonnes**, an old port with pleasant river views from the tree-lined quais where these days most of the boats tied up are for private pleasure: punts, launches, motor cruisers. Here you can cross the Loire for a sortie of 7km to St. Georges-sur-Loire, which isn't quite on the Loire these days, and the nearby **Château de Serrant**.

Architecturally, this is a remarkable château, for it has truly majestic symmetry and unity of Renaissance style, yet it was built over three centuries — 16th–18th. It was designed by the great Philibert Delorme for Charles

de Brie and begun in 1546. Delorme designed Fontainebleau and the Tuileries. The north tower, the main building and the right wing were completed — less than half the building — when the cost bankrupted de Brie. In 1636 it was bought by the genial Guillaume de Bautru, who made people laugh — even Richelieu, and became ambassador to England, Spain and the Netherlands. He added another storey and a matching tower at the other end. All these additions, and those later, followed the original blueprints of Delorme, which accounts for the unity of Renaissance design. Bautru's granddaughter, who married the Marquis de Vaubrun, Lieutenant General of the Royal Army, finished the château. And when her husband was killed on the Rhine, she added a chapel designed by the architect of Les Invalides (Jules Hardouin-Mansart) in the Marquis' memory and a white marble mausoleum by the sculptor Antoine Coysevox. The sculpture shows the Marquis and his wife with Victory flying towards them — a magnificent work. She is said to have set up her husband's heart on an altar lit by two candles.

With its massive round towers topped with cupolas and contrasting stone colouring of dark schist and white tufa, the château is certainly very striking and agreeable. The whole building is surrounded by moats. The only alterations were made by the Walsh family (see Le Plessis-Macé, page 183). They bought Serrant in 1730 and when Antoine de Walsh was made a count by Louis XV for helping Bonnie Prince Charlie to cross to Scotland in 1745 for his disastrous campaign to claim the Scottish crown, Walsh became Count of Serrant. Théobald de Walsh, Comte de Serrant, did create the lovely gardens and park with lakes reflecting gorgeous old trees. Do wander round it.

Over the fireplace in the library (which holds, we are told, 20,000 books) is a picture of Charlie talking to Antoine de Walsh.

The château is now owned by Jean-Charles de Ligne and is lived in. The furnishings are magnificent. So is the beautiful panelled staircase. There are excellent tapestries. One of several bedrooms in Empire style was specially decorated for a visit by Napoléon in 1808. It contains a fine bust of Empress Marie-Louise by Canova. And Napoléon really did sleep there. Despite the château being a private house, it is open for guided tours each

day from Palm Sunday to the last Sunday in October (closed Tuesdays except in July and August).

It is worth returning to the south side of the Loire for better scenery and less traffic. Montjean, on a rocky spur overlooking the river, was an important terminal until World War I for ships too big to get up to Angers. From here take D210 on a riverside embankment, with views to the north and to the vineyards south. It reaches a suspension bridge across to **Ingrandes**, a pretty place, once a very important river port and a link between Brittany, which started here, and Anjou on the south bank. There was smuggling across the river, too, for the Bretons stored salt on their side and it carried a tax in Anjou. On the deserted quais, with fine 17th- and 18th-century houses, is an 18th-century salt depot with arcades. The modern church (1956) is rather strange. It has an unusual belltower and very brightly coloured modern stained-glass by Bertrand.

Back on the south side, there are several more very attractive villages before you arrive at Champtoceaux. **St. Florent-le-Vieil** is the most striking. From the square at the top you can see the **Île Batailleuse**, dividing the Loire into two channels, and look down on boats.

On this island in 853 the Norseman Cidroc set up base for his fleet of 100 ships, even building storage for captured loot and a compound for prisoners. He was joined by 100 more ships under another commander and from here they pillaged, burned and murdered their way up the Loire, burning or destroying every town as far as Roanne. They occupied the base for 80 years until the Breton Alain Barbe-Torte returned from exile in Britain, raised an army, took Nantes from the Norsemen and cut them off from the sea.

St. Florent was one of the first places to revolt against the Revolution after Louis XVI was guillotined in March 1793, starting the tragic and vicious Vendéen War between the Republicans and the Royalist Catholics of the Vendée. The Vendéens were in revolt not only against the killing of the King and Queen but also against ill-treatment of priests and conscription into the Republican army. In October 1793, after a defeat at Cholet, the Royalists withdrew to St. Florent. Their leader Bonchamps, whose château La Baronnière was 4km south, was mortally wounded. The retreating Royalists locked 4,000 Republican prisoners in St. Florent church. About 80,000 Royalists — soldiers, old men, priests, women and children — crossed the Loire on a make-shift bridge of any wood they could lay their hands on, including doors, window frames and planks. Before crossing, they intended to kill their prisoners. It was that sort of war. But the dying Bonchamps ordered their release. Bonchamps is buried in St. Florent church. On his tomb in white marble is a fine sculpture by David of Angers. David's own father was one of the prisoners released by Beauchamps.

The D751 now follows meadows and gentle hills. Across another suspension bridge is **Ancenis**, a very attractive old port where sailcloth was made, now known for its pig market and wine. Its houses rise in tiers above the river. Near the railway bridge on the ring road is a big building of Les Vignerons de la Noëlle — a group of producers from all over the Loire Valley who make wines here by the most modern methods. They export around 400,000 bottles a year to Britain alone. You can taste and buy. A good chance to taste some of the lesser, cheaper wines.

Coteaux d'Ancenis wines (red, dry white and rosé) are little known. Labels tell you the name of the grape used — for red, Gamay or Cabernet Franc; for white, Pineau de la Loire, Pinot Beurot or Malvoisie (slightly sweeter). The whites are light, dry, fruity and refreshing. This north side of the river is on the edge of Muscadet-country, Coteaux de la Loire, stretching to Nantes. Better Muscadet comes from south-east of Nantes, Sèvre-et-Maine.

From Les Brevets, the D751 remains attractive all the way to Nantes. Just before Champtoceaux, on the borders of Anjou, Maine-et-Loire and Loire–Atlantique, the road swings up a rocky hill to follow a corniche through steep wooded hills on both sides of a gorge, with the Loire below. **Champtoceaux** is strung along a ridge, with good river views from a balcony behind the church, Promenade de Champlud. Down below the old port seems to be sleeping. The river runs through flatter land to Nantes.

Nantes (pop. 247,227) has something in common with Liverpool, for it grew on cotton, sugar, rum and the slave trade. But it has kept its importance to shipping to a greater degree than Liverpool. Rebuilding after World War II damage removed some of its historic character and, in a wave of modern industrialisation and aggressive technical 'progress', the city was almost torn apart to make way for high-rise buildings and wide, straight roads. Gone are the little trains which used to move goods from the quais and send

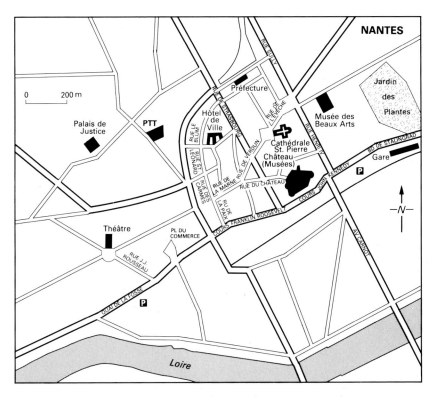

impatient drivers mad. Three Loire tributaries have gone underground and two islands have been swallowed by the city. Traffic flow has improved, but there are still horrific parking problems.

The port, at the mouth of the Loire, is navigable by large vessels and the shipyards, with those at St. Nazaire, make naval and commercial vessels, especially dredgers. There are sugar refineries, canneries, and factories producing refrigeration plants, oil-boring equipment, telephones, electronics, chemical products and ships' boilers. The first ship's engine using nuclear energy was produced here. The city also distributes Muscadet and Gros Plant wines.

A Gallic and then a Roman town, Nantes vied with Rennes through the Middle Ages for the title of capital of Brittany. The Dukes of Brittany and the French kings squabbled over it until the daughter of Duke François II, Anne of Brittany, married Charles VIII and subsequently Louis XII. Although just inside Brittany, Nantes was detached from it after the Revolution and made capital of the non-Breton Loire–Atlantique département. Today it is the capital also of the Pays-de-la-Loire region, entirely separate from Brittany, whose capital is Rennes. The two towns are bitter rivals.

François II began the Château des Ducs in 1466 and Anne continued it. A severe fortress, its most pleasant part is the Renaissance Tour de la Couronne d'Or, with fine Italian-inspired loggias. Henry IV signed the Edict of Nantes

There are peaceful backwaters in the busy industrial town of Nantes

here in 1598 giving religious and personal freedom to Protestants. When Louis XIV revoked the charter in 1685, the terrible massacre and persecution of Protestants started and many fled from France. In World War II Nantes was a persistent centre of the French Resistance.

There are two museums in the castle. Musée Salorges is devoted to ships and commerce, with models of 17th–18th-century slavers and sugar boats which made the town's fortune. Slaves were taken from the Guinea coast and sold in the French West Indies. Cane sugar was brought back to be refined at Nantes. The Musée d'Art Populaire has collections from Breton life and culture, including head-dresses, furniture and cooking equipment.

Nantes cathedral, St. Pierre, was begun in 1434, not actually completed until 1893, only to be badly damaged in 1944 and by a fire in 1972. It has an austere, dull façade but is more impressive inside, with vaulting 35m high. The

tomb of François II, by da Fiesola and Michel Colombe (1500–1507), with the Duke and Duchess lying on a white marble slab is a mature work of Renaissance art.

A museum devoted to the novelist Jules Verne, born here in 1828, is at 3 rue de l'Hermitage. The Musée de Beaux Arts has a miscellaneous collection of paintings with no outstanding works but enough to interest an amateur. Nantes has a lively carnival just before Easter.

St. Nazaire was built for ships too big to reach Nantes. The great Atlantic liners *France* and *Normandie* were built here and, despite the great slump in shipbuilding, it produces ships for the French navy, especially submarines, diesel engines and turbines for ships and railways. The residential and industrial areas are separated but it is not a very attractive place.

The submarine base was built by the Nazis during World War II occupation, mostly with slave labour, and had a covered lock to allow U-boats to come and go in secret. The base withstood an enormous tonnage of Allied bombs and is now used by industry.

In March 1942 the Royal Navy and British Commandos raided the docks of St. Nazaire, fighting in the streets for two days and causing enormous damage. The old destroyer *Campbeltown* filled with explosives was rammed into the huge gates of the Louis-Joubert dock, where transatlantic liners such as the *Normandie* docked in peacetime, and blown up, putting the port out of action for some time. Local people helped the raiders and

The inside of Nantes Cathedral is far more impressive than its austere façade

Duchess of Berry

Uphill from Nantes castle entrance, at No. 3 rue Mathelin-Rodier (Maison de Guigny), in 1832 the Duchess of Berry was found hiding in a secret recess behind a fireplace and was arrested. This resourceful and attractive young widow was daughter-in-law of the deposed Bourbon King Charles X and her infant son the Duke of Chambord was heir to the French throne, which had been stolen by Louis-Philippe ('the Citizen King'), who had been appointed Regent for the infant.

The Duchess, in exile at Holyrood in Scotland, landed at Marseilles to rouse a rebellion. She went to Nantes hoping to obtain support from Royalist Vendée. She hid in this house belonging to two sisters du Guigny and for six months, with a small printing press and a staff of two, she ran an opposition 'government' from an attic room, sending out proclamations and despatches to Governments around Europe.

Nantes was thick with police and troops looking for her, and a million francs reward was offered for information leading to her arrest. A clerk Deutz, working secretly for her, betrayed her. One evening her secretary saw the streets filling with soldiers. The Duchess, her maid and the two men just had time to hide in the secret place behind the attic fireplace. Unable to find the Duchess, the police left a heavy guard in the house for the night. Two policemen in the attic got cold and lit the fire. The four behind the chimney got warmer until the women's dresses caught alight. The Duchess wrote afterwards of how the gentlemen put out the flames — 'dispensing with ceremony'. The policemen slept, the fire died. But the policemen woke cold and relit the fire. This time the gentlemen failed in their duty. The Duchess put out the fire with her hands, but they were becoming asphyxiated and had to give themselves up. The Duchess was sent to prison but then admitted that she had made a second marriage with a Neapolitan marquis, so they released her as being politically finished. Anyway, Louis-Philippe was married to her sister, so she had some infuence. Her son when he grew up showed little desire to take the throne as Henry V, though he had three chances. It was said of him that 'he passed 40 years of blameless inertia' before dying in 1883 at the age of 63.

the Germans took terrible reprisals against the town.

The estuary at St. Nazaire was the scene of one of the greatest British Royal Navy tragedies on 17th June, 1940. When the German army had broken right through in France, 6,000 British troops were embarked at St. Nazaire aboard the troopship *Lancastria*. The ship was dive-bombed to bits, with the loss of 3,000 British lives.

In 1915 Canadian forces disembarked at St. Nazaire. On 26th June, 1917, the first American forces arrived.

North of the port as far as la Chapelle-des-Marais is la Grande Brière national park of 6,605 hectares, a third of which is marshland with 'islands' between. It was originally a forest flooded by the sea, which receded to leave peat bog as vegetation decomposed over centuries;

5,000-year-old fossilised tree trunks have been found. Over the five centuries water was pumped, drainage was improved and it became the common property of local people who caught fish and eels, shot wildfowl, cut peat, gathered rushes for thatching and wickerwork, propelling their flat-bottomed boats, '*blins*', for transport-ing cows and sheep top pasture. Locks and roads have now been built, and marsh turned into pasture.

This is the hinterland of the very attractive holiday area around la Baule (see box). On the north-east edge of Grande Brière on the Brittany border at Missillac is a very beautiful little 14th-century castle, **La Breteshe**, with an

Seaside Resorts

La Baule has been a seaside resort since the 1880s and remains fashionable and elegant even in this age of longhaul jet travel, thanks largely to the beauty of its bay, its 8km of clean sands, protected by 400 hectares of maritime pines planted in the 19th century to settle the dunes, and to the skilfully organised programme of international sporting events. There are big tennis championships, golf championships, show jumping with great international riders, and racing. La Baule keeps something of its snob appeal and yet is a family favourite. It is lively but never brash or vulgar. The casino thrives and the pleasure boat harbour between sea and salt marshes was there long before the European marina boom.

The interesting, photogenic fishing ports nearby are an added attraction. **La Baule-les-Pins**, also planted with pines, was added in 1930 and has a fine flower park. **Le Pouliguen**, to the west, is an old fishing port with narrow streets which became a resort back in 1854. The beach is sheltered by woods. Fishing boats still land white fish, crab and lobsters on the noisy quai.

Batz-sur-Mer comes next, between sea and salt marshes, a very Breton town of granite houses with a tall 17th-century church belfry as landmark. Three sandy beaches break the rocky coast.

Le Croisic, its neighbour, is a photogenic, busy little white fishing port and resort, with 17th-century houses lining the quay, boats landing shellfish, coastal traffic and pleasure yachts. The town was once entirely surrounded by water.

Pornichet, east of La Baule, was a salt-marsh workers' village which became a resort in 1860, the haunt of Paris journalists. It is at the end of the bay's long sand beach, and has a well-known racecourse.

Inland from Batz in the salt marshes is **Guérande**, a fortified medieval town built by the de Montfort family, with its ramparts from the Middle Ages still intact, flanked by eight towers and pierced by four fortified gateways. The old moats are now a circular promenade.

The **Marais Salents**, the marshes between Guérande and Batz, was a sea-covered bay when Julius Caesar's galleys under Brutus defeated the becalmed sailing boats of the Veneti by hooking them and landing men aboard. Caesar then wiped out the whole Veneti tribe.

hotel and golf-course attached. Built by the de Montfort family, the castle, with fairy-tale turrets and ramparts shielding its lawn, stands beside a lake, with a beautiful background of water, woods, and the greens, fairways and bunkers of the golf course (visits except Mondays). Hôtel Golf de la Breteche has been comfortably converted from the castle farm and stables.

South-east from Nantes the vine-yards begin almost immediately, producing the best Muscadet, with grapiness and a lasting flavour, and the lesser VDQS wine Gros Plant, made from a grape of the same name — very dry, acidic, sometimes fruity and always refreshing. Most of the best wines are produced around Vallet, Clisson, le Pallet and Loroux-Botter-eau. The old style Muscadet which was so splendid as an apéritif or with fish or white meat was fruity but slightly sharp and acidic. Now some producers offer a fuller, blander wine with less flavour or tang, to be drunk at any time. Muscadet-sur-lie means that it has been bottled straight off the lees (pips, skin, etc.) after fermentation, and not racked. This gives it more flavour. Sixty-five million bottles of Muscadet are produced each year, and only Beaujolais can beat that. There are hundreds of growers, so you need to know your producer.

For the vineyards, take N149 (*not* N249) from Nantes, then on to D756 towards **La Chapelle-Heulin**. Dozens of little growers offer Dégustations et Vente Directe (Tastings and Direct Sales) shown on boards outside. Along this stretch of D756 try Chevalliers Frères on the left, or turn left at La Chapelle-Heulin to Domaine des Gautronnières where Fleurance et Fils, a family of vignerons since the 17th

century, produce old-style Muscadets in the wood, concentrated and fresh on the palate. You can taste and buy. Just past Chapelle-Heulin is a drive left leading to **Château de la Nöe de Bel Air**, marked on the yellow Michelin map. Here le Comte de Malestroit's family have lived and made good wine since 1741. Their château was burned down in the Revolution and replaced by the elegant Palladian-style house you see now. In 1960 the present count put his wines on the market and they became known around the world. To taste and buy, you must telephone on 40.33.92.72.

From Vallet you can reach one of the very best producers, Sauvion et Fils, at **Château de Cléray** to the east by taking D756 as far as la Chalousière, then a little road D106 flying over the N249; at first cross-roads go left back over the N249. You will soon see the sign of the château. Grandpa Sauvion bought this historic château in 1935. Now son Ernest, helped by three of his sons, runs it with exuberance and flair. Locally, the firm is called '4S'. They produce a lovely 'sur-lie' wine, vital, lively, flowery and reliable. The château was burned in the Vendéen religious wars when it belonged to the same family as La Noë. The old caves are perfect for keeping wine. You can taste and buy, and English is spoken.

D763 leads to **Clisson**, another important old wine town, at the meeting of the Moine and Sèvre rivers, both crossed by old bridges. The town was burned down in 1794 in the Vendéen wars but rebuilt with the help of a great architect, Lemot of Lyon. The castle is ruined.

You can return to Nantes by N149, a splendid wine road with lots of boards offering tastings. Several are around **Haie-Fouassière**, 9km past le Pallet and just off to the left. Here too is the official Maison des Vins du Pays Nantais. **Le Pallet** was the birthplace of Peter Abélard (1079–1142), the theologian who got himself into a lot of trouble by falling in love with his young pupil Héloïse and presenting her with a son, and by teaching views on the Trinity which were regarded as heretical. Now it is very much a Muscadet town, and here you can taste one of the wines best loved in Britain, la Galissonnière, made in a property of that name by Pierre Lusseaud, using very modern methods, with three or four weeks' fermentation.

South of Nantes is the huge reedy **Lac de Grand-Lieu**, 7,000 hectares, rich in waterfowl and fish. On the coast, reached from Nantes by D751 west, is one of the treasures of this coast, the little port of **Pornic**.

This delightful fishing port forms an amphitheatre around an inlet south of St. Nazaire. The natural harbour is crowded with fishing boats and there is a new yacht marina under a corniche.

The small beach lies below a 13th-century castle which belonged to Gilles de Rais. Hero of the siege of Orléans with Joan of Arc, marshal of France at 25, he became rich by marriage, ran through his fortune and was accused of terrorising much of Brittany, kidnap-

Porte de Guerande: there is still no breach in the 15th-century walls of the old town

ping women and boys for his orgies and killing them. He was hanged at Nantes, but modern lawyers, studying the evidence at his trial, believe he was almost certainly 'framed'. It is a charming little place for boating, lazing, eating splendid seafood in little restaurants, and even when it is rather crowded in mid-summer the language you will hear is almost entirely French. It may not be very near the Loire river, but it is in the Loire–Atlantique and is a fine place to spend a few days at the end of a delightful but sometimes exhausting Loire journey.

Part Six:
Practical Information

Tourist Offices (Offices de Tourisme and Syndicats d'Initiative)

ANJOU — pl Kennedy, 49000 Angers (41.88.69.93).

CHER — 21 rue Victor Hugo, BP 145, 18003 Bourges (48.24.75.33).

EURE-et-LOIR — pl de la Cathédrale, BP 289, 28005 Chartres (37.21.54.03).

INDRE — pl de la Gare, 36000 Châteauroux (54.34.10.74).

INDRE-et-LOIRE — pl du Mar-Leclerc, 37042 Tours (47.05.58.08).

LOIRE-ATLANTIQUE — pl du Commerce, 44000 Nantes (40.47.04.51).

LOIR-et-CHER — Pavillon d'Anne de Bretagne, 3 av du Dr.-Jean-Laigret, 41000 Blois (54.74.06.49).

LOIRET — pl Albert Ier, 45000 Orléans (38.53.05.95).

MAYENNE — 84 av Robert Buron, 53000 Laval (43.53.18.18).

SARTHE — 38 pl République, 72000 Le Mans (43.28.17.22).

Recommended Hotels and Restaurants

A = Very Expensive, B = Expensive, C = Moderately Expensive, D = Moderate, E = Inexpensive

AMBOISE: 37400 Indre-et-Loire **Château de Pray**, 2.5 km north-east on D751 (47.57.23.67). Charming 13th-century château; lovely gardens. Traditional cooking. Rooms vary. Meals B–D. Rooms C–D.
Bonne Etape (restaurant), north-east on D751 (47.57.08.09). Rustic-modern, pretty garden. Cheaper menu good. Meals C–E.
Manoir St. Thomas (restaurant), pl Richelieu (47.57.22.52). Excellent young chef François le Coz moved to Renaissance manor in beautiful garden. Superb Touraine wines. Meals A–B.

198

La Brèche, rue Jules-Ferry (47.57.00.79). Near station; locals use it. Bourgeois cooking. Meals D–E. Rooms D–E.

ANCENIS: 44150 Loire-Atl **Val de Loire**, le Jarier, 2km east on N23 (40.96.00.03). Meals D–E. Rooms D.

ANGERS: 49000 Maine-et-Loire **France, Restaurant Plantagenets**, pl de la Gare (41.88.49.42). 'Grand' hotel modernised, pub snacks added. Meals D–E. Rooms D.
Le Quéré (restaurant), 9 pl Ralliement (41.87.64.94). Paul le Quéré is one of Loire's best modern chefs, his wife a famous sommelier. A–C.

AUBIGNY-SUR-NÈRE: 18700 Cher **Charmilles Restaurant**, Central Hôtel, 6 rue du Château (48.58.17.18). Good regional cooking. Meals D–E. Rooms D–E.

AZAY-LE-RIDEAU: 37190 Indre-et-Loire **Grand Monarque**, pl République (47.45.40.08). Restaurant shut 15th November–1st March. Old, cosy; good value meals. Run by Jacquet family since 1900. Meals C–E. Rooms D.
Aigle d'Or (restaurant), av A. Riché (47.45.24.58). Chef came from Château d'Artigny. Meals C–E.

BAUGÉ: 49150 Maine-et-Loire **Boule d'Or**, 4 rue Cygne (41.89.82.12). Logis. Meals C–E. Rooms D–E.

BEAUGENCY: 45190 Loiret **Ecu de Bretagne**, pl Martroi (38.44.67.60). Fine inn; traditional and regional cooking. Meals C–E. Rooms D–E.

BEAUMONT-SUR-SARTHE: 72170 Sarthe **Chemin de Fer**, Gare (43.97.00.05). Meals D–E. Rooms D–E.

BLOIS: 41000 Loir-et-Cher **Grand Cerf**, 40 av Wilson (54.78.02.16). Wide choice; regional dishes. Meals B–E. Rooms D–E.
Hostellerie de la Loire, 8bd Maréchal Lattre de Tassigny (54.74.26.60). Old style hostelry overlooking Loire. Old-style dishes. Meals C–D. Rooms D–E.

BRACIEUX: 41250 Loir-et-Cher **Bernard Robin** (restaurant), 1 av Chambord (54.46.41.22). Great modern chef. Old coaching Relais. Meals A–C.

CANDÉ-SUR-BEUVRON: 41120 Les Montils, Loir-et-Cher **Lion d'Or** (54.44.04.66). Pleasant rustic inn; traditional cooking. Meals D–E. Rooms D–E.

CHAMBORD: 41250 Bracieux, Loir-et-Cher **St. Michel** (54.20.31.31). Superb position facing castle. Excellent cooking. Meals B–D. Rooms D.

CHAMPTOCEAUX: 49270 Maine-et-Loire **La Forge** (restaurant), place des Piliers (40.83.56.23). Michelin star. Meals C–D.

LA CHARITÉ-SUR-LOIRE: 58400 Nièvre **Bonne Foi**, 91 rue Camille-Barrère (86.70.15.77). Imaginative young chef. Meals A–E.

LA CHARTRE-SUR-LE-LOIR: 72340 Sarthe **France, pl République** (43.44.40.16). Old-style inn. Excellent value. Meals C–E. Rooms D–E.

CHÂTEAU-GONTIER: 53200 Mayenne **Parc Hôtel**, Restaurant la Brasserie, av Joffre (43.07.28.41). Manor house, sound-proofed bedrooms. Meals B–E. Rooms C–E.

CHÂTEAUNEUF-SUR-LOIRE: 45110 Loiret **Capitainerie**, Grande-Rue (38.58.42.16). Pleasant inn alongside park. Meals C. Rooms D.

CHAUMONT-SUR-LOIRE: 41150 Onzain, Loir-et-Cher **Hostellerie du Château** (54.20.98.04). Shut 1st Dec–1st Mar. Very attractive. Fine garden. Pool. Meals B–E. Rooms B–D.

CHÊNEHUTTE-LES-TUFFEAUX: 49350 Gennes, Maine-et-Loire **Prieuré** (41.67.90.14). Lovely site overlooking Loire. Old priory. Very pricey. Meals A–B. Rooms A.

CHENONCEAUX: 37150 Bléré, Indre-et-Loire **Bon Laboureur** (47.23.90.02). Shut 1st Dec–1st Mar. Book — the world goes there. Regional cooking of local products. Meals A–C. Rooms C–D.
Renaudière (47.23.90.04). Shut 15th Nov–1st Mar. Cheaper. Excellent value. Meals D–E. Rooms D–E.
Gâteau Breton (restaurant) shut 15th Nov–15th Feb (47.23.90.14). Remarkable value, very cheap. Meals E.

CHINON: 37500 Indre-et-Loire **Boule d'or**, 66 quai Jeanne d'Arc (47.93.03.13). Logis. Good regional cooking. Convenient. Meals C–E. Rooms D–E.
Océanic (restaurant), 13 rue Rabelais (47.93.44.55). Bistro; outstanding fish. Meals E.
Rigollet 'Plaisir Gourmand' (restaurant), 2 rue Parmentier (47.93.20.48). Best chef in area. Regional cooking. Book. Meals B–D.
7km south — **Château de Marçay** (47.93.03.47). 15th-century château. Luxurious, fine grounds, expensive. Straightforward cooking. Meals A–B. Rooms A–B.

EVRON: 53600 Mayenne. At **Mézanger**, 7km north-west on route Mayenne — **Relais Gué de Selle**. (43.90.64.05). Old farmhouse. Meals C–E. Rooms D.

LA FERTÉ ST. AUBIN: 45240 Loiret **Ferme la Lande** (restaurant), route Marcilly-en-Villette (2½km north-east) (38.76.64.37). Old Sologne house. Distinguished chef. Meals E. Weekends C.

LA FERTÉ-ST.CYR: 41220 Loir-et-Cher **St. Cyr** (54.87.90.51). Modern, homely atmosphere. Meals C–E. Rooms C–D.
Commerce (54.87.90.14). Rustic Logis. Meals D–E. Rooms D–E.

LA FLÈCHE: 72200 Sarthe **Vert Galant**, Grande Rue (43.94.00.51). Simple auberge. 'Old France'. Good cooking. Meals C–E. Rooms D.

FONTEVRAUD L'ABBAYE: 49590 Maine-et-Loire **Croix-Blanche**, 7 pl Plantagenets (41.51.71.11). Welcoming. Regional cooking. Meals D–E. Rooms D–E.
Licorne (restaurant), allée Ste. Catherine (41.51.72.49). Outstanding, pricey. Book. Meals A–B.

GENNES: 49350 Maine-et-Loire **Hostellerie de Loire** (41.51.81.03). Attractive, flowered terrace over river. Traditional cooking. Meals C–E. Rooms D–E.

GIEN: 45500 Loiret **Beau Site Hôtel**, Poularde Restaurant, 13 quai Nice (38.67.36.05). River front. Good range of menus. Meals B–E. Rooms D.

LAMOTTE-BEUVRON: 41600 Loir-et-Cher **Tatin**, 5 av Vierzon (54.88.00.03). Simple Logis where sisters Tatin invented upside-down apple tart. Meals D–E. Rooms D–E.

LANGEAIS: 37130 Indre-et-Loire **Hosten**, 2 rue Gambetta (47.96.82.12). Good but no set menus. Meals–A. Rooms–D.
Duchesse-Anne, 10 rue Tours (47.96.82.03). Sombre-looking Logis but value Bourgeois meals D–E. Rooms D–E.

LAVAL: 53000 Mayenne **Bonne Auberge**, 168 rue Bretagne (43.69.07.81). Pretty creeper-clad inn on edge of town. Meals C–E. Rooms D–E.

LE MANS: 72000 Sarthe **Moderne**, 14 rue Bourg-Bélé (43.24.79.20.). Excellent cooking. Meals C–D. Rooms D.
Grenier à Sel (restaurant), 26 pl Eperon (43.23.26.30). Good modernish cooking. Meals B–E.

MISSILLAC: 44160 Loire-Atlantique **Golf de la Bretesche** (40.88.30.05). Converted from castle buildings. Own golf course. Meals B–E. Rooms C–D.
Parc de la Brière (40.88.30.12). Country Logis. Meals D–E. Rooms D–E.

MONTBAZON: 37250 Indre-et-Loire **Domaine de la Tortinière** (47.26.00.19). Shut 15th Nov–15th Mar). Delightful château in lovely park. Fine cooking. Meals A–B. Rooms B–C.

MONTOIRE-SUR-LE-LOIR: 41800 Loir-et-Cher **Cheval Rouge**, pl Foch (54.85.07.05). Renowned chef. Meals B–E. Rooms E.

MONTRICHARD: 41400 Loir-et-Cher **Bellevue**, quai du Cher (54.32.06.17). River views; modernised. Old-style cooking. Meals C–E. Rooms D.
At **Chissay**, 4km west on N76 — **Château de Chissay** (54.32.32.01). Savry family hotel. 13th–16th-century castle. Expensive luxury. Meals B–C. Rooms A.

MONTSOREAU: 49730 Maine-et-Loire **Bussy et Diane de Méridor** (41.51.70.18). Rustic inn; dining room overlooking Loire. Bedrooms 500m away in fine old house. Meals C–D. Rooms D.

NANTES: 44000 Loire-Atlantique **Colvert** (restaurant), 14 rue Armand-Brossard (40.48.20.02). Little bistro in old Nantes. Modern inventive chef. Meals D.
At **Les Sorinières** (12km on D178) — **Abbaye de Villeneuve** (40.04.40.25). Superb 18th-century abbey. Peaceful park. Relais et Châteaux Hotel. Meals A–D. Rooms A–C.
At **Haute-Goulaine** (11km east on N149) — **Lande-St. Martin** (40.06.20.06). Reliable, comfortable in pleasant gardens. Meals E(weekdays)–C. Rooms B–E.

NEVERS: 58000 Nièvre **Auberge Porte-du-Croux** (86.57.12.71). Pretty, terrace overlooks gardens. Very good value. Meals B–D. Rooms D–E.
Château Rocherie at Varennes Vauzelles (4km north on D7) (86.38.07.21). Charming hideout in big park. Good experienced chef. Meals B–E. Rooms D–E.

OLIVET: 45160 Loiret **Rivage**, 635 rue Reine-Blanche (38.66.02.93). Alongside Loiret river. Excellent traditional cooking. Meals C–D. Rooms D.

ONZAIN: 1150 Loir-et-Cher **Domaine des Hauts de Loire** (54.20.72.57). Hunting lodge in park with lake. Michelin star. Very expensive meals and rooms.

ORLÉANS: 45000 Loiret **Jean** (restaurant), 64 rue Porte-St. Jean, near Joan's statue in place du Martroi (38.53.63.32). Good value. Meals D–E.
Antiquaires (restaurant), 2 rue au Lin (38.53.52.35). Outstanding 'modern–traditional' cooking, good value. Meals C–E.
Crémaillère, 34 rue N. D. de Recouvrance (38.53.49.17). Superb simple cooking. Very expensive.

OUCQUES: (29km north-east from Vendôme, 15km north-west Talcy) — 41290 Loir-et-Cher **Commerce**, rue Beaugency (54.23.20.41). Small hotel. Outstanding cooking. Meals D–E. Rooms E.

PORNIC: 44210 Loire-Atlantique **Ourida**, 43 rue Verdun (40.82.00.83). Cosy. Good value meals. Superb fish. Meals D–E. Rooms D.

POUILLY-SUR-LOIRE: 58150 Nièvre **Relais Fleuri** (86.39.12.99). Old-style inn: nice garden; river views. Excellent cooking. Meals C–E. Rooms D.
L'Espérance, 17 rue René Couard (86.39.10.68). Regional dishes; expensive; good. Meals A–C. Rooms (4 only) D.

RICHELIEU: 37120 Indre-et-Loire **Puits Doré**, pl Marché (47.58.10.59). 17th-century historic monument. Good value. Meals D–E. Rooms D.

RILLY-SUR-LOIRE: (4km west of Chaumont) 41150 Onzain **Voyageurs** (54.20.98.85). Pleasant auberge. Traditional meals. Meals D–E. Rooms D–E.

ROCHECORBON: (3km from Tours) 37210 Vouvray, Indre-et-Loire **Fontaines**, 6 quai de Loire (47.52.52.86). Manor in park. No restaurant. Rooms D.
Lanterne, on N152, 48 quai de Loire (47.52.50.02). **Relais du Poste**. Superb value. No rooms. Meals D–E. Same owners — **Rosny**, 19 rue Blaise Pascal, Tours (47.05.23.54) (bed and breakfast) Rooms D.

LES ROSIERS: 49350 Gennes, Maine-et-Loire **Val de Loire** (41.51.80.30). Rustic; informal. Meals, rooms D–E.
Jeanne de Laval (41.51.80.17). Brilliant classical cooking by Michel Augereau. Pricey. Meals A. Rooms A–C.

SACHÉ: 37190 Azay-le-Rideau, Indre-et-Loire **Auberge du XIIe siècle** (47.26.86.58). Base of Saché château. Excellent chef keeps balance between classical and modern dishes. Meals B.

ST. AIGNAN: 41110 Loir-et-Cher **Grand Hôtel St. Aignan** (54.75.18.04). Overlooking river. Handsome arcaded hotel. Meals C–D. Rooms D–E.

ST. HILAIRE-ST. MESMIN: (7km south-west Orléans) 45580 Loiret **Escale du Port Arthur** (38.76.30.36). Charming quiet inn on banks of Loiret. Fine traditional cooking. Meals C–D. Rooms D–E.

SANCERRE: 18300 Cher **La Tour** (restaurant), 31 pl Halle (48.54.00.81). Classical cooking. B–D.
At **St. Thibault-St. Satur — Étoile**, quai de Loire (48.54.12.15). Lovely position overlooking Loire. Bourgeoise cooking. Meals C–D. Rooms (simple) D–E.

SAUMUR: 49400 Maine-et-Loire **Gambetta** (restaurant), 12 rue Gambetta (41.67.66.66). Chef-patron ex-Park Lane Hotel; Maxim's (Paris). Creative light cooking. Business lunch, regional and gastronomic menus. B–D.
Gare, facing station (41.67.34.24). Same family since 1919. Good value. Shut Nov–Apr. Meals C–E. Rooms D–E.

SULLY-SUR-LOIRE: 45600 Loiret **Grand Sully**, 10 bd Champ-de-Foire (38.36.27.56). Restored country hotel. Regional dishes. Meals B–D. Rooms D–E.
Pont de Sologne, rue Porte de Sologne (38.36.26.34). Traditional menus, good value. Meals D–E. Rooms D–E.

TOURS: 37000 Indre-et-Loire At **Joué-lès-Tours** (5km south-west on D86) — **Château de Beaulieu** (47.53.20.26). Lovely 18th-century manor in park, Classic cooking. Meals B–D. Rooms B–D.
Renaissance (restaurant), 64 rue Colbert (47.66.63.25). Classic favourites like coq-au-vin, steak-au-poivre. Chef-owner here since 1963. Meals D–E.
Barrier (restaurant), 101 av Tranchée (47.54.20.39). Truly great chef of classic cooking. Expensive — worth every franc. Meals A–B.
Univers Hôtel, Restaurant Touraine, 5 bd Heurteloup (47.05.37.12). Churchill, Napoléon, Hemingway slept here. Plumbing modernised. Chef from 'Barrier'. Meals C–D. Rooms B–D.
Central, 2 rue Berthelot (47.05.46.44). Hideout with garden in city centre. Delightful. No restaurant. Rooms D–E.

VENDÔME: 41100 Loir-et-Cher **Vendôme**, 15 fg Chartrain (54.77.02.88). Modernised rooms. Traditional cooking. Meals C–E. Rooms D.
Daumier (restaurant), 17 pl République (54.77.70.15). Very good value. Good fish. Meals B, D–E.

VERNOU-SUR-BRENNE: 37210 Vouvray, Indre-et-Loire **Perce Neige**, 13 rue Anatole-France (47.52.10.04). Family house in lovely gardens. Cooking good, rooms vary. Meals C–E. Rooms D.

VILLANDRY: 37510 Joué-lès-Tours, Indre-et-Loire **Cheval Rouge** (47.50.02.07). Shut mid Nov-Feb. Exit of château gardens. Meals B–D. Rooms D.

VOUVRAY: 37210 Indre-et-Loire **Grand Vatel**, av Brûlé (47.52.70.32). Pleasant. Good value. Meals C–D. Rooms D–E.

Events

AMBOISE (Indre-et-Loire): June, July — Summer Festival, includes drama in Château.

ANGERS (Maine-et-Loire): end June–mid July — Anjou Festival (concerts, ballet, plays, exhibitions).

BLOIS (Loir-et-Cher): mid-June — Floréal Blésois — carnival, river regatta.

BOURGES (Cher): May Carnival. End July–end August — Music concerts (classical, jazz, variety).

BOURGEUIL (Indre-et-Loire): first Saturday February — Wine Fair.

BUÉ-EN-SANCERRE (Cher): early August — Witch Fair, Folklore Festival.

CHAMBORD (Loir-et-Cher): end May–mid June — Festival (theatre, music, dance).

CHÂTEAUNEUF-SUR-LOIRE (Loiret): Whit-Sunday — Rhododendron Festival.

CHINON (Indre-et-Loire): first weekend in August — Medieval market in costume. Late August — Market 1900 (Fin de Siècle).

DOUÉ-LA-FONTAINE (Maine-et-Loire): mid-July — Floralies de la Rose (Rose Festival).

FONTEVRAUD — SAUMUR (Maine-et-Loire): September — Festival (theatre, music, dance).

JARGEAU (Loiret): mid-October — Foire aux Chats — *not* cats — Chestnut Fair (Châtaignes).

LOCHES (Indre-et-Loire): mid-July — peasant market; also Music Festival.

LE MANS (Sarthe): April (early) 24-hour motor-cycle race. Mid-June — 24-hour Car Race. Early July — Medieval Festival 'Les Cénomanies'. Late Sept: Formula 3000 car race.

MENETOU-SALON (Cher): Frairie des Brangers — festival recalling past history of village.

MONTOIRE-SUR-LE-LOIR (Loir-et-Cher): mid-August — World Folklore Festival each evening. Processions, dancing, concerts.

NANTES (Loire-Atlantique): early-July — Nantes Fête (International — arts, shows, carnival, boat trips, etc.).

OLIVET (Loiret): 2nd week in June — Watersports Festival.

ORLÉANS (Loiret): May–Oct — flower displays in Parc Floral de la Source. 2nd weekend in May — Festival of Joan of Arc.

ROMORANTIN (Loir-et-Cher): late-Oct — Sologne Gastronomic Days.

STE. MAURE-DE-TOURAINE (Indre-et-Loire): June Gastronomic Fair.

ST. SATUR (Cher): mid-Aug — Festival of Loire bargemen (old costumes, water jousting on river, etc.).

SAUMUR (Maine-et-Loire): end July — Cavalry School and Tank Tattoo.

SULLY-SUR-LOIRE (Loiret): Orléans and Loiret International Festival (music and drama at Château and other locations).

TOURS (Indre-et-Loire): late June–early July — International Touraine Music Festival at Grange de Meslay. May Flower Pageant.

Châteaux and Museums

Open 'daily' means morning and afternoon. Most open at 10am, shut for lunch (usually 12–2pm), afternoon closing times vary according to season (usually 5 or 6pm). Most museums in France shut on Tuesdays.

Châteaux

AMBOISE (Indre-et-Loire): Château d'Amboise (47.57.00.98). Daily all year, exc 1st Jan, 25th Dec.

ANGERS (Maine-et-Loire): Château d'Angers (41.87.43.47). Includes cathedral treasury, Musée des Tapisseries. Daily all year, exc public holidays.

AUBIGNY-SUR-NÈRE (Cher): Château de la Verrerie, 10km south-east (48.58.06.91). Daily, 1st Mar–1st Nov.

AZAY-LE-RIDEAU (Indre-et-Loire): Château d'Azay (47.45.42.04). Daily all year, exc 1st Jan.

BAUGÉ (Maine-et-Loire): Château du Roi René (41.89.18.07). Daily, mid June–mid Sept.

BEAUGENCY (Loiret): Château Dunois (38.44.55.23). Daily all year, exc. Tue Oct–Mar.

BEAUREGARD (Loir-et-Cher): Château de Beauregard, 9km north-west of Cheverny (54.70.40.05). Daily, Apr–end Sep, exc Wed, Oct–end Dec; closed 5th Feb–end Mar.

BÉTHUNE (Cher): Chapelle d'Angillon (48.73.41.10). Guided visits (audio-visual show). Daily, Palm Sunday–Oct, exc Sun am.

BLOIS (Loir-et-Cher): Château (54.74.16.06). Daily all year, exc 1st Jan, 25th Dec.

BOURGES (Cher): Palais Jacques Coeur, rue Jacques Coeur (48.24.06.87). Daily, all year exc public holidays.

BRISSAC (Maine-et-Loire): Château de Brissac (41.91.23.43). Daily Apr–3 Nov, exc Tue April–end Jun, mid Sept–3rd Nov.

CHAMBORD (Loir-et-Cher): Château de Chambord (54.20.32.20). Daily, exc public holidays.

CHÂTEAUNEUF-SUR-LOIRE (Loiret): Château (38.58.41.18). Gardens only: daily all year.

CHAUMONT-SUR-LOIRE (Loir-et-Cher): Château de Chaumont (54.78.19.47). Includes stables and park. Daily all year, exc 1st Jan, 1st May, 1st & 11th Nov, 25th Dec.

CHENONCEAU (Indre-et-Loire): Château de Chenonceau (47.23.90.07). Includes waxwork museum. Daily all year.

CHEVERNY (Loir-et-Cher): Château de Cheverny (54.79.96.29). Daily all year. **Château de Troussay**. Easter–11th Nov, Suns and school hols only.

CHINON (Indre-et-Loire): Château (47.93.13.45). Includes Fort St. Georges, Château du Milieu, Fort du Coudray; guided visits to Logis Royaux. Daily all year, exc Wed 1st Feb–mid Mar, 1st Oct–30th Nov.

GIEN (Loiret): Château (38.67.00.01). Includes Musée International de la Chasse. Daily all year.

GUÉ-PÈAN (Loir-et-Cher): Château du Gué-Péan, 1km east of Monthou-sur-Cher (54.71.43.01). Daily all year.

LANGEAIS (Indre-et-Loire): Château de Langeais (47.96.72.60). Audio commentaries. Daily, mid Mar–2nd Nov.

LOCHES (Indre-et-Loire): Château Logis Royal (47.59.01.32), Donjon (47.59.07.86). Daily all year, exc Wed Oct–mid Mar.

LE LUDE (Sarthe): Château (43.94.62.20). Gardens daily all year, château pm Apr–Sep. See also Son et Lumière (page 215).

MEUNG-SUR-LOIRE (Loiret): Château (38.44.36.47). Includes underground oubliettes. Daily mid Mar–mid Nov; Sat, Sun and holidays mid Nov–mid Mar.

MONTGEOFFROY (Maine-et-Loire): Château de Montgeoffroy (41.80.60.02). Daily late Mar–end Oct.

MONTOIRE-SUR-LE-LOIR (Loir-et-Cher): Chapelle St. Gilles (54.85.38.63). Daily all year, closed Wed from 1st Sep–mid Apr.

MONTRÉSOR (Indre-et-Loire): Château (47.92.60.04). Daily, 1st Apr–end Oct.

MONTREUIL-BELLAY (Maine-et-Loire): Château (41.52.33.06). Daily all year, exc Tues from Apr–1st Nov.

MONTRICHARD (Loir-et-Cher): Donjon (54.32.05.10). Daily mid Jun–mid Sep; Sat, Sun and public holidays mid–end Sep and 26th Mar–5th Jun.

MONTSOREAU (Maine-et-Loire): Château (41.51.70.25). Daily all year, exc Tue.

NANTES (Loire-Atlantique): Château (40.47.18.15). Daily all year, exc Tue.

ORLÉANS (Loiret): Hôtel Groslot, pl de l'Etape (38.42.22.30). Daily all year, exc Sat am.

LE PLESSIS BOURRÉ (Maine-et-Loire): Château du Plessis Bourré (41.91.66.25). Daily all year, exc Wed and Thur am, closed 15th Nov–20th Dec.

LE PLESSIS-MACÉ (Maine-et-Loire): Château du Plessis-Macé (41.91.64.08). Daily Jul–Sep, exc Tues; pm only Mar–Jun, Oct, Nov.

PLESSIS-LES-TOURS (Indre-et-Loire): Château (47.61.51.87) 1.5km south-east of Tours. Daily Feb–Nov exc Wed Feb–mid Mar, oct–Nov.

PONCÉ-SUR-LE-LOIR (Sarthe): Château (43.44.45.31). Includes gardens, dovecot. Daily all year, exc Sun am.

SACHÉ (Indre-et-Loire): Manoir (47.26.86.50). Daily all year, exc Wed Oct–Nov, Feb–mid Mar.

SAUMUR (Maine-et-Loire): Château (41.51.30.46). Includes Musée du Cheval, Musée d'Arts Décoratifs. Daily all year, exc Tue Nov–Mar.

SERRANT (Maine-et-Loire): Château de Serrant (41.41.13.01). Daily Apr–Oct, exc Tue Apr–Jun, Sep–Oct.

SULLY-SUR-LOIRE (Loiret): Château (38.36.25.60). Daily, Mar–Nov.

TALCY (Loir-et-Cher): Château de Talcy (54.78.19.47). Daily all year, exc Tue and public holidays.

USSÉ (Indre-et-Loire): Château d'Ussé (47.95.54.05). Daily, mid Mar–1st Nov.

VALENÇAY (Indre): Château (54.00.10.66). Includes Automobile Museum. Guided tours daily, 12th Mar–13th Nov.

VENDÔME (Loir-et-Cher): Château (54.77.01.33). Daily, 1st Apr–30th Nov exc Tue 1st Apr–end June, 1st Oct–1st Nov.

VILLANDRY (Indre-et-Loire): Château de Villandry (47.50.02.09). Gardens daily all year; château daily, mid Mar–mid Nov.

VILLESAVIN (Loir-et-Cher): Château de Villesavin, 3km west of Bracieux (54.46.42.88). Daily Mar–Sep; pm only Oct–20th Dec.

Museums

AMBOISE (Indre-et-Loire): Musée de l'Hôtel de Ville, rue François I (47.57.02.21). Daily all year, exc Sat, Sun, public holidays.
Musée de la Poste, 6 rue de Joyeuse (47.57.02.21). Daily Feb–Dec, exc Mon.
Manoir de Clos-Lucé, rue du Clos-Lucé (47.57.62.88). Daily Feb–Dec.
Pagode de Chanteloup, 2.5km south-east (47.30.08.30). Daily Apr–Sep, exc Mon.

ANGERS (Maine-et-Loire): Musée Jean Lurçat, 4bd Arago (41.87.41.06). Daily all year, exc Mon and public holidays.
Musée des Beaux-Arts, Logis Barrault, Galérie David d'Angers, rue du Musée (41.88.64.65). Daily all year, exc Mon and public holidays.
Logis Pincé, rue de la Roë (41.88.94.27). Daily, exc Mon and public holidays.

AVOINE (Indre-et-Loire): Central Nucléaire de Chinon (47.98.97.07). Daily all year, by prior arrangement.

BAUGÉ (Maine-et-Loire): Hôpital St. Joseph (Enquire at reception office). Daily all year, exc Thu am.
Chapelle des Filles du Coeur de Marie. Ring doorbell at 8 rue de la Girouardière. Daily, exc Sun am.

BEAUGENCY (Loiret): Tour of vieux quartier from Château Dunois (38.44.55.23).
Hôtel de Ville (38.44.50.01). Daily May–Sep, exc Sat pm, Sun; Tue–Fri pm, Sat am, Jan–Apr, Oct–Dec.

BEAULIEU-SUR-LAYON (Maine-et-Loire): Caveau du Vin. Daily all year.

BEAUMONT-PIED-DE-BOEUF (Sartre): Musée Sentinelle (Costume Museum) (43.44.29.83). Daily mid Jul–end Aug; Sun pm, May–Sep.

BLOIS (Loir-et-Cher): Musée Lapidaire, rue Mûnier (54.74.16.06). Apr–Sep, Wed–Sun.
Hôtel d'Alluye, just off Rue de Bourg Neuf can be visited during office hours.
Chocolaterie Poulain, Ave. Gambetta. To arrange a visit to the factory, telephone 54.78.39.21, ext. 339.

BOURGES (Cher): Cathédrale. Daily all year, exc Sun am. Audio-visual daily May–Sep, exc Tue, Sun am.
Guided tours of vieux quartier start at Office de Tourisme, 14 pl E. Dolet (48.24.75.33).

BOURGUEIL (Indre-et-Loire): Abbaye Benédictine (47.97.72.04). Fri–Mon, Jul, Aug; Sun pm and public holidays Easter–Jun, Sep.

BRIARE (Loiret): Musée de l'Automobile (1895–1960), rue Mal de Lattre de Tassigny (38.31.20.34). Daily May–Oct; pm only rest of year.

CHÂTEAUNEUF-SUR-LOIRE (Loiret): Musée de la Marine de Loire et du Vieux Châteauneuf (38.58.41.18). Daily Jul–Aug, exc Tue; Sat & Sun Apr–May; Mon, Wed, Fri pm, Sat & Sun, Jun, Jul, Sep–Nov.

CHINON (Indre-et-Loire): Tour of old town from Office de Tourism, pl Gén. de Gaulle (47.93.17.85). Daily May–Sep.
Musée de Vieux-Chinon, 44 rue Haute-St. Maurice (47.93.17.85). Daily Mar–Dec, exc Tue.
Musée des Arts et Traditions Populaires, Chapelle St. Radegonde (47.93.17.85). Daily, Jun–mid Aug.
Musée des Voitures Hippomobiles, route d'Avoine (47.61.08.94). Apr–Sep, Sat, Sun.
La Devinière, 7km south-west (47.93.13.45). Daily Mar–Dec, exc Wed.

CLÉRY-ST. ANDRÉ (Loiret): Basilique (38.45.70.05). Daily all year.

DOUÉ-LA-FONTAINE (Maine-et-Loire): Quartier des Douces, Arènes. Daily all year, exc Tue.

LA FLÈCHE (Sarthe): Le Prytanée National Militaire, Rue du parc (no public calls). Daily in school holidays.

FONTEVRAUD-L'ABBAYE (Maine-et-Loire): Abbaye (41.51.73.52). Daily all year, exc Tue and public holidays.

GIEN (Loiret): Musée de la Faïencerie, pl de la Victoire (38.67.00.05). Daily all year, exc public holidays.
Musée International de la Chasse (see page 114).

JARGEAU (Loiret): Musée 'Le Médailleur Oscar Roty et son temps', 3 pl du Petit Cloître (Paris (1)222.24.96). Sat pm, all Sun Jun–Sep.

LOCHES (Indre-et-Loire): Nocturnal tour of old town, Pavillon de Tourisme, pl Marne (47.59.07.98). Daily at 9.30pm, Jul–mid Sep.
Musée Lansyer et Musée du Terroir, rue Lansyer (47.59.05.45). Daily all year, exc Fri.

MONTRÉSOR (Indre-et-Loire): Chartreuse du Liget, 7km east in Fôret de Loche (47.94.20.02). Exterior daily.

LE MANS (Sarthe): Automobile Club de l'Ouest, Circuit de 24 Heures — entrance off D139 by Parc des Expositions (43.72.50.25). Daily all year, exc Tue.
Musée de Tessé, Jardin de Tessé (43.84.97.97). Daily all year.
Abbaye de l'Epau, 4km east (43.84.22.29). Daily 15th Sep–15th Apr, exc Thu.

NANTES (Loire-Atlantique): Musée d'Art Populaire Régional and Musée des Salorges (Naval Museum), in Château (40.74.53.24). Daily all year, exc Tue.

ORLÉANS (Loiret): Tour of vieux quartier from Maison de Tourisme, pl Albert I (38.53.05.95). Daily at 3pm, mid Jul–mid Sep.
Musée Historique et Archéologie de l'Orléanais, pl Abbé Desnoyers. Daily all year, exc Tue.
Musée de Jeanne d'Arc, pl Gén. de Gaulle (38.42.25.45). Daily May–Oct, exc Mon; rest of year pm, exc Mon.

Musée des Beaux Arts, 1 rue Fernand Rabier (38.53.39.22). Daily all year, exc Tue. **Cathédrale Ste. Croix** (38.53.47.23). Daily all year, pm.

RICHELIEU (Indre-et-Loire): Musée de l'Hôtel de Ville (47.58.10.13). Daily Jul–Aug, exc Tue; daily Jan–Jun, Sep–Dec, exc Tue, Sun.

ROMORANTIN-LANTHENAY (Loir-et-Cher): Musée de Sologne, Hôtel de Ville (54.76.07.06). Daily all year, exc Tues and Sun am.
Musée Municipal de la Course Automobile, faubourg d'Orléans (54.76.07.06). Daily mid Mar–end Oct, exc Tue and Sun am.

ST. BENOÎT-SUR-LOIRE (Loiret): Abbaye de Fleury (30.35.72.43). Daily all year, outside times of services, exc am and all Sun.

ST. LAURENT-NOUAN (Loir-et-Cher): Centrale Nucléaire (54.78.52.52). Daily all year, by prior arrangement in writing — 2 months notice.

SAUMUR (Maine-et-Loire): Musée d'Arts Décoratifs and Musee du Cheval, in Château (41.51.30.46). Daily all year, exc Tue.
Musée de la Cavalerie, av Maréchal Foch (41.51.30.46). Mid Apr–mid Oct, pm, exc Mon and Fri, all day Sun and public holidays; shut Easter.
Musée des Blindés (Tank Museum), pl du Chardonnet (no public calls). Daily all year.
École Nationale d'Equitation, St. Hilaire-St. Florent. Tours arranged at Office de Tourisme, 25 rue Beaurepaire (41.51.03.06).
Musée du Champignon, St. Hilaire-St. Florent (41.50.31.55). Daily mid Mar–mid Nov.

SAVONNIÈRES (Indre-et-Loire): Caves Pétrifiantes (47.50.00.09). Daily Apr–mid Sep; daily Jan–Mar, mid Sep–30th Dec, exc Wed, Thu.

SOLESMES (Sarthe): Abbaye St. Pierre (43.95.03.08). Abbey church daily all year.

TOURS (Indre-et-Loire): Daily audio-guided tours around the vieux quartier from Office de Tourisme, pl Maréchal Leclerc (47.05.58.08).
Musée des Equipages Militaires et du Train, rue du Plat d'Etain (47.61.44.46). Daily all year, exc Sat, Sun.
Musée des Vins de Touraine, 16 rue Nationale (47.61.07.93). Daily all year, exc public holidays.
Musée du Gemmail, et chapelle souterraine, 7 rue du Mûrier (47.61.01.19). Daily end Mar–mid Oct, exc Mon.
Musée des Beaux Arts, 18 pl François Sicard (47.05.68.73). Daily all year, exc Tue and public holidays.
Château Royal, quai d'Orléans (47.66.75.92). Daily mid Mar–mid Nov; pm only mid Nov–mid Mar.
Prieuré de St. Cosme, 3km west (47.20.99.29). Daily mid Mar–Sep; exc Wed Feb–mid Mar, Oct–Nov.

VENDÔME (Loir-et-Cher): Tour of vieux quartier from Office de Tourisme, rue Poterie (54.77.05.07). Daily all year.

Wine Tastings

Touraine

Château du Petit-Thouars, St. Germain-sur-Vienne, 37500 Chinon (47.95.96.40). Take D751 west from Chinon along south bank of Vienne river for 10km. Petit-Thouars is on the left (marked on yellow Michelin). Ask for Mme Boissinot, wife of the Maître du Chai. 10–12, 2–6. Red AOC Touraine.

Jacky Charbonnier, le Biard, Angé, 41400 Montrichard (54.32.10.06). Take N76 east from Chenonceaux, then little D17 on right just before Montrichard. Outside long modern chalet on left at Angé is a small notice 'Jacky Charbonnier — Vins'. 9–6. Red Cabernet and Gamay; white, rosé.

J.P. Monmousseau, Route de Vierzon, BP 25, 41401 Montrichard (54.32.07.04). Big plant on left going east out of Montrichard to St. Aignan. 9–11.30, 2–6.30. Half-hour tour of cellars possible. Big négociants owned by Tattinger.

Philippe Brossillon, Domaine de Lusqueneau, Mesland, 41150 Onzain (54.70.28.23). Mesland is just north of the Loire, across bridge from Chaumont, 4km north-west of Onzain. 8–12, 2–6. English spoken. Touraine–Mesland red; Gamay rosé.

J.-C. Poupault, 1 rue de la Loire, Chargé, 37530 Amboise (47.57.53.71). Cave in rock on D751 north-east of Amboise towards Chaumont.

Vouvray and Montlouis

Daniel Jarry, la Caillerie, route de la Vallée Coquette, 37210 Vouvray (47.52.78.75). After the N152 (going east) dips under the motorway at Tours, drive on for 6km watching for a tiny road on the left marked 'Vallée Coquette' (see yellow Michelin). The Jarry caves are 1,000m up this road on the right. 9–7. Superb dry, demi-sec and sweet Vouvray.

Cave Co-operative des Producteurs des Grands Vins de Vouvray, la Vallée Coquette, 37210 Vouvray (47.52.75.03). 250m before Jarry, on opposite side of road. Also has tasting and selling shop on corner of N152 and D47 to Vouvray. 8.30–12, 2–6 (including Saturday, Sunday). No English spoken, but tasting and ordering are easy because of cards and lists. You pay for tasting.

Gilles Champion, Valleé de Cousse, Vernou, 37210 Vouvray (47.52.02.38). Take D46 from Vouvray through Vernou-sur-Brenne. 3km along take D62 through Vallée des Vaux to Vallée de Cousse. Keep going, despite the road condition — it's a little place on the right. Open every day.

Marc Bredif, 87 quai de la Loire, Rochecorbon, 37210 Vouvray (47.52.50.07). Just outside Tours. Follow N152 under motorway. Rochecorbon is on the left 3km onwards. Bredif are towards Vouvray. Monday–Friday at 10.30, and 4. English spoken. Old wines, presses, bottles.

Cave Co-operative des Producteurs de Vin de Montlouis, 37270 Montlouis (47.50.80.98). On the corner of D751 and D40 road to Chenonceaux, just after passing Montlouis on way to Amboise. Every day 8–12, 2–6.

Chinon, Bourgueil and Saumur

Château de Ligré, Ligré, 37500 Chinon (47.93.16.70). Cross Vienne river at Chinon on D749, follow east for 9km towards Richelieu. Right on D26 for 2km, then left for Château (on left). Monday–Saturday 10–12, 3–5. Great Chinon wines.

Le Thélème, 7 pl Mirabeau, 37500 Chinon (47.93.49.39). In town. Tastings in wine bar 11–8. You pay for tasting. Restaurant attached.

Maison Audebert et Fils, av Jean Causeret, 37140 Bourgueil (47.97.70.06). In town. Preferable to phone, but not essential. 8–12, 2–6. English spoken. Excellent Bourgueil red, also Chinon, Saumur.

Ackerman-Laurance, St. Hilaire-St. Florent, 49210 Saumur (41.50.23.33). Suburb of Saumur on south bank of Loire, 3km along D751 towards Angers. Open 1 May–30th Sep, 9.30–11.30, 3–5 including weekends. Guided tour. Pioneers of Saumur sparkling wine.

Gratien et Meyer, Château de Beaulieu, route de Montsoreau, 49400 Saumur (41.51.01.54). On D947, south bank of Loire, 3km east of Saumur on Chinon road. Open every day 9–11.30, 2–5.30. Highly organised. English speaking guides. Sparkling Saumur.

Muscadet

Les Vignerons de la Noëlle, BP 102, 44150 Ancenis (40.98.92.72). Huge building plainly marked in Ancenis. It is on the ring-road marked '1' on yellow Michelin map. Coming from north (N923 or A11 motorway) turn left on this 'Poids Lourds' deviation road and it is on right near railway bridge. From south (D763) cross bridge and turn right immediately. Caves on left. 8–5. Wines from many growers throughout Loire.

Fleurance et Fils, Domaine des Gautronnières, 44330 La Chapelle Heulin (40.06.74.06). From Vallet on D756; at Chapelle Heulin turn left (or ask). 9–12, 2.30–7. Great Muscadet.

212

Château de la Noë de Bel Air, 44330 Vallet (40.33.92.72). On D756 Vallet to Chapelle Heulin road (marked on yellow Michelin). Phone first. See Chapter 16, page 196.

Pierre Lusseaud, la Galissonnière, le Pallet, 44330 Vallet (40.26.42.03). N149 north-west from Clisson (7km) or D116 from just south of Vallet (6km). 9–12, 2–6. English spoken. See chapter 16, page 196.

Sauvion et Fils, Château du Cléray, BP 3, 44330 Vallet (40.36.22.55). The new dual carriageway N249 east from Vallet has few turn-offs to villages, so you must make a deviation. Take D756 east from Vallet, then little 'white' road D106 right at la Chalousière over the N249; at first crossroads go left, back over N249. You will soon see the sign of Château du Cléray. 8.30–12, 2.30–6. English spoken. Superb Muscadet. See chapter 16, page 196.

Guilbaud Frères, Mouzillon, 44330 (40.36.30.55). On D763, 4km south of Vallet. 8–12, 2–5. World renowned Muscadet.

Pouilly-sur-Loire

Caves de Pouilly-sur-Loire, Le Moulin à Vent, BP No 9, av de la Tuilerie, 58150 Pouilly-sur-Loire, Nièvre, (86.39.10.99). Avoid the N7 deviation around Pouilly — take the old road. Open Monday–Saturday 8–12, 2–6. Pouilly Fumé, plus reds from Gien and Cosne.

Sancerre

Domaine Henri Bourgeois, Chavignol, 183000 Sancerre (48.54.21.67). 2km west of Sancerre. Every day 8–11, 3–7. English spoken. Best Sancerre white and red. Best caves to visit in this area.

Quincy

Raymond Pipet, Quincy, 18120 Lury-sur-Arnon, Cher (48.51.31.17). From N76 Bourges-Vierzon road turn west at Mehun on D20 for 4km. 9–12, 2–6. Fresh, light wine. Quincy white AOC.

Reuilly

Claude Lafond, Le Bois St. Denis, 36260 Reuilly, Indre (54.49.22.17). Every day 9–12, 2–7. Talented young grower. White Reuilly from Sauvignon grape; red Pinot Noir.

Markets

LOIRE-ATLANTIQUE: Nantes: Daily especially Saturday.
St. Nazaire: Daily except Monday; Onion Fair 15th September.
Vallet: Sunday; Wine Fair 3rd week March.

MAYENNE: Laval: Tuesday and Saturday morning.
Mayenne: Monday.

SARTHE: Beaumont-sur-Sarthe: Tuesday.
La Flèche: Wednesday, Sunday.
Fresnay-sur-Sarthe: Saturday.
Loué: Tuesday.
Le Mans: Daily except Monday; Friday most important.
Sablé-sur-Sarthe: Monday, Wednesday.

EURE-ET-LOIRE: Châteaudun: Tuesday, Thursday, Saturday.
Dreux: Sunday, Monday, Friday.
Maintenon: Thursday.

LOIRET: Beaugency: Saturday.
Gien: Saturday morning, Wednesday morning (poultry).
Orléans: Tuesday, Wednesday, Thursday, Saturday.
St. Hilaire-St. Mesmin: Monday, Wednesday, Friday (May–September); daily in cherry season.
Sully-sur-Loire: Monday.
Tigy: Asparagus Fair 3rd Sunday in May.

CHER: Aubigny-sur-Nère: Saturday.
Baugy: Friday.
Bourges: Daily.
Châteaumeillant: Friday.
Sancerre: Saturday; Tuesday (March to November).
Savigny-en-Sancerre: Thursday.
Vierzon: Tuesday morning, Wednesday, Saturday.

INDRE-ET-LOIRE: Amboise: Wednesday (glass), Friday, Saturday; Melon Fair 1st Wednesday in September.
Azay-le-Rideau: Wednesday; Wine Fair last weekend in February, Apple Fair last weekend in November.
Bourgueil: Tuesday; Wine Tasting 2nd Tuesday in September; Chestnut Fair 4th Tuesday in October.
Chinon: Thursday, Saturday, Sunday.
Joué-lès-Tours: Sunday, Wednesday, Thursday, Friday.
Langeais: Sunday morning.
Loches: Wednesday.
Montlouis-sur-Loire: Thursday; Wine Fair 3rd weekend February.
Vouvray: Wine Fair 2nd weekend August.

LOIR-ET-CHER: Blois: Daily, Sunday morning.
Droué: Tuesday.
Montoire-sur-le Loir: Wednesday.
Montrichard: Monday.
Selles-sur-Cher: Thursday.
Vendôme: Friday.

MAINE-ET-LOIRE:Angers: Daily.
Candé: Monday.
Chalonnes-sur-Loire: Tuesday, Friday.
Châteauneuf-sur-Sarthe: Friday.
Fontevraud l'Abbaye: Wednesday; Saturday morning.
Le Lion d'Angers: Friday.
Rochefort-sur-Loire: Wednesday.

Son et Lumière

Amboise: 'At the Court of Francis I' — 420 actors in costume, end Jun–mid Aug (Wed, Sat, some Fri). 10pm. 90 mins. (47.37.09.28)
Azay-le-Rideau: Easter; last weekend May–last weekend Sep. 10pm. 60 mins. (47.61.61.23).
Blois: Daily Jul, Aug; nightly except Thu, May, Jun; some days Apr, Sep. 10pm. 45 mins. (54.74.06.49).
Chambord: Jun 1–end Sep; also Easter; Fri, Sat, Sun; holidays Apr, May. 9.30pm or later. 35 mins. (54.20.31.32).
Chenonceau: 'Ladies of Chenonceau'. Easter; Whitsun; nightly mid Jun–mid Sep. 10pm or later. 90 mins. (47.29.90.07).
Cheverny: 'Hunting Party'. Late Jul — mid Aug (check days, usually Sat). 75 mins. (54.79.96.29).
Chinon: 'Charles VII — Accursed Child'. Mid Jun–mid Sep nightly. 9.45pm or later (47.93.17.85).
Le Lude: 'Sumptuous Nights on the Banks of the Loire'. 350 actors in costume; 300 lit fountains. Fri, Sat second weekend in Jun until first weekend Sep. 9.45pm or later. 105 mins. (43.94.62.20).
Valençay: Fri, Sat late June–mid Jul; most Sat, Sun in Aug. 9.30pm or later. 150 mins. (54.00.14.33).

Check times and days, which can change. Entrance fees vary from 20F–40F.

Index

216